G000294830

Safety in Numbers

*The Cassell Lesbian and Gay Studies list
offers a broad-based platform to lesbian, gay
and bisexual writers for the discussion of
contemporary issues and for the promotion
of new ideas and research.*

COMMISSIONING:
Steve Cook

CONSULTANTS:
Liz Gibbs
Christina Ruse
Peter Tatchell

Safety in Numbers

Safer Sex and Gay Men

Edward King

Foreword by
Cindy Patton

CASSELL

Cassell
Villiers House, 41/47 Strand
London WC2N 5JE

387 Park Avenue South
New York, NY 10016-8810

First published 1993

British Library Cataloguing-in-Publication Data
A catalogue entry for this book is available from the British Library.

ISBN 0–304–32699–2 (hardback)
    0–304–32701–8 (paperback)

Typeset by Fakenham Photosetting Limited, Fakenham, Norfolk
Printed and bound in Great Britain by Mackays of Chatham, plc
Designed by Peter Guy

Contents

Foreword

AIDS activists have been deeply aware of the ways in which the body is constituted through biomedical and social scientific discourse and policed through the public policy and health education programmes developed from academic research enterprises. But because of the peculiar modes of funding research and health care, we have been desperately dependent on precisely those scientific institutions and practices for any hope of medical care, anti-discrimination statutes or funded prevention programmes. For a decade now, AIDS activists and cultural critics have carved out a new kind of expertise in the territory once prized and protected by scientists and policy-makers: they have knitted together avant-garde social theory and practical work to develop exciting, volatile and surprisingly effective new ways to 'read' social science data and to develop programmes and policy from it. Public health professionals and governmental agencies who leapt into AIDS work late like to claim credit for any successes in managing the epidemic, but their major contributions have been to misdirect education and policy by 'de-gaying' the epidemic in a way that both ignores gay men's needs and expertise and fails to appropriately alert 'non-gay' people to their risks of contracting HIV through their own sexual and drug use behaviours.

Several varieties of cultural criticism – psychoanalytically inflected (Simon Watney), sociological (Dennis Altman), feminist (Paula Treichler and Jan Zita Grover), postmodern (Douglas Crimp) and my own odd combination of new journalism and Foucault – emerged in England, Australia and the USA, from the pens of people who traverse the border between the activist and academic worlds. Although deeply indebted to post-structuralist theory, this unprecedented wedge of politico-critical writing on a disease phenomenon now forms the basis for a new kind of critical theory and activism. It retains a strong gay liberationist/feminist framework that continues to prove useful in reinterpreting official science and policy and can be applied in health activisms which now extend beyond the HIV epidemic to breast cancer activism and other medical-political organizing.

Safety in Numbers marks a second wave of this unusual style of critical analysis. Like the earlier work of treatment activists who recognized the need to work with, but to some extent take over, the discourse and practices of clinical trials, King rejects the idea that social science is intrinsically unworkable, but he remains critical of its current use in government and even AIDS service organizations' policy and educational programming. King unites the best in contemporary health education theory with the deconstructionist advances in gay theory to produce a 'queer hermeneutic' of social science. Always privileging the local knowledge and variability of the gay men under study, he posits the usually mute objects summarized in statistics as active subjects whose safer sex strategies are evolving much faster than social scientists' research frames.

King's study has two major implications for future sociological work and the health policy based on it. First, the subjects of research now have the capacity not only to read their lives back into lifeless studies; our counter-interpretations may actually be 'better science'. But second, the belated government recognition that specificity or 'targeting' of prevention is urgent means that the veterans of HIV organizing *and our exciting new styles of 'doing the numbers'* are not just local guides to an unfamiliar gay world, but the policy and prevention experts who should be placed in charge in the next decade of the epidemic.

Cindy Patton
Philadelphia, 1993

Preface

BY the end of 1992 there had been a total of 19,065 reports of HIV-infected people in the United Kingdom. Of these, 60 per cent are believed to have become infected through sexual intercourse between men. During 1992 alone, 2487 cases were reported, of whom 62 per cent were gay or bisexual men. If heterosexuals who are believed to have become infected overseas are excluded, in order to get as clear a picture as possible of transmission patterns within the UK, the proportion of gay or bisexual men rises to over 70 per cent. Two-thirds of people with AIDS in the UK are still gay or bisexual men. In other words, there can be no doubt that the HIV epidemic in Britain continues disproportionately to affect gay men, and because up to one in five gay men in some parts of London is infected, it is clear that a gay man having unsafe sex is at much greater risk of getting or giving HIV infection than anybody else having unsafe sex in the UK.

It is upon straightforward statistics like these that one would expect the prioritization of AIDS education efforts to be based. Logic and reason would suggest that safer sex campaigns should be designed to reinforce and build upon the unprecedented successes of gay community safer sex activities in the early and mid-1980s, which in some cities resulted in new infections among gay men falling almost to zero. One would imagine that workers coming into professional HIV-prevention posts in National Health Service organizations and voluntary sector agencies would wish to learn from the ways in which gay men invented safer sex and established it as the norm of sexual behaviour in urban gay communities, and that they would use that accumulated knowledge to inform new initiatives designed both to sustain those behaviour changes and to begin the process in other sections of the community.

Instead, the opposite has happened. Since the second half of the 1980s, vastly more money has become available for HIV prevention, yet the level of safer sex activity targeting gay men has actually fallen, to the extent that by 1992, only 1.3 per cent of 226 agencies with a remit for AIDS education had *ever* undertaken – or funded others to undertake – *any kind* of work for gay or bisexual men. The grass-roots activism which had resulted in the precipitous decline in the transmission rate among gay men was allowed to wither and atrophy, as a professionalized model of health education took over, in which promoting safer sex was a job done by workers to 'clients', rather than a strategy of resistance to the epidemic that was shared between gay men and reinforced by peer pressure. Lesbian and gay groups tried not to involve themselves in the epidemic for fear of giving the impression that AIDS was a 'gay disease', and AIDS organizations which were originally set up by gay men to fight for gay men's interests went into a bureaucratic closet. While in the 1980s epidemiologists and clinicians wrote in the medical journals of decreasing HIV transmission among gay and bisexual men, by the 1990s their reports focused almost exclusively on signs of increasing unsafe sex and of new HIV transmissions.

This, in short, is what the de-gaying of AIDS entailed – and why this book has been written. Today, as the HIV epidemic among gay men shows no sign of abating and indeed is probably worse than ever, there is an urgent need to take advantage of the wisdom of hindsight. The strategies of the late 1980s, which were pursued generally in good faith and with good intentions, have resulted in disaster for gay men. No one could have predicted how hostility to the notion of high-risk groups – which was being misused to present members of high-risk groups as a threat to society and simultaneously to deny the very possibility of HIV transmission outside those groups – would result in the near total neglect of the ongoing needs of those most at risk. No one could have anticipated that AIDS educators, in attempting to prevent the outbreak among non-drug-using heterosexuals which was predicted by epidemiologists, clinicians and gay groups alike, would almost totally ignore the devastating epidemic taking place before their eyes among gay and bisexual men.

Safety in Numbers is intended to draw attention to the neglect of ongoing safer sex education for gay men and the reasons why that neglect must be remedied. It is not my purpose to seek to apportion blame for the de-gaying of AIDS, which in many instances has been the unpredicted outcome of actions taken with the best of intentions. However, with the benefit of hindsight, it is essential to acknowledge the mistakes of the past and take action to counter their harmful consequences for gay men's health. This will necessarily involve the 'unlearning' of many of the dogmas which have become established within both the statutory and the voluntary sectors in recent years, and which currently work to perpetuate the de-gaying process.

This process of 'unlearning' is something that I have gone through myself. I became involved in AIDS work in 1988, while a student in Oxford. I had quickly involved myself in the lesbian and gay political and social life of the city, being determined to take advantage of the opportunity to 'be myself' after the years of secretiveness and solitude while at school. I joined the Student Union standing committee on lesbian and gay rights and helped to organize speaker meetings and social events for the lesbian and gay society. Thus, when I volunteered with the local charity OXAIDS, I was coming from a perspective which recognized the epidemic as a key political issue for gay men.

At this time, the de-gaying of AIDS was still a more-or-less unchallenged phenomenon. The prevailing approach was to play down the involvement of gay men in the epidemic, whether as those most at risk or as those responsible for many of the most remarkable responses to the crisis. My earliest perspectives on AIDS were therefore informed by, and to some extent in sympathy with, the conventional view which concentrated on and emphasized the possibility of an explosion of HIV infection among heterosexuals. With hindsight, I am acutely aware that this required a suppression of my initial instinctive response to the epidemic as a gay political issue – in other words, almost a form of individual de-gaying.

The AIDS field has always relied heavily on the work of gay men, whose primary motivation is, inevitably, rooted in the epidemic's disproportionate impact upon gay and bisexual men. Yet since the second half of the 1980s, when the heterosexualized agenda came to dominate both the voluntary and statutory sectors, many gay men involved in AIDS work have in effect had not only to deny the significance of their own sexuality but also to forsake their commitment to the interests of other gay men. This has resulted in an uncomfortable sense of division between those of us committed to the re-gaying of AIDS and other gay AIDS workers. For example, the endless stream of media reports or television documentaries and dramas which focus exclusively on heterosexuals and HIV is seen as commendable from the de-gayed perspective, whereas for advocates of re-gaying it is just further evidence of the prevailing indifference to the ravaging epidemic among gay and bisexual men.

Safety in Numbers reflects the reassertion of an analytical approach which insists on the importance of acknowledging and responding to the impact of the epidemic upon gay and bisexual men in Britain. In addition to documenting the reasons why and the means by which de-gaying occurred, it is also an account of some of the most important lessons to be learnt from the early community-based safer sex activism. I have aimed to bring together scattered, inaccessible and in some instances hitherto undocumented material relating to gay men and safer sex, and to organize it into an accessible and coherent structure.

The book's focus is tightly upon men who identify as gay, rather than upon all homosexually active men, for two reasons. First, most of the experience in HIV prevention for gay and bisexual men comes from activities at the heart of the gay population, rather than at its fringes. It is from these precedents that there is most to be learned. Secondly, gay men on the commercial scene are relatively easy to contact, and safer sex campaigns which encourage them to act as informal peer educators in their everyday social and sexual lives are likely also to result in the wider dissemination of safer sex messages to the men whom they meet in public cruising areas such as parks and toilets.

Safety in Numbers describes the success of AIDS education strategies which aimed to establish safer sex as the expected norm of sexual behaviour among the diverse population of gay and bisexual men, with the ultimate goal of modifying gay identity so that it *means* safer sex. Moreover, it relates how those strategies were devised not by professional health educators, doctors, scientists or other 'experts', but primarily by gay men whose 'expertise' lay in their familiarity with the many ways in which gay men live and relate to one another. Nevertheless, the book also illustrates my conviction that the sciences of epidemiology and behavioural and social science research can be harnessed as powerful allies, rather than enemies, of community responses to AIDS. In describing evidence from the medical and social sciences literature, I have sought to demonstrate how those disciplines can help ordinary gay men concerned about HIV to explain the importance of grass-roots activities and argue for work targeting gay men to be given its due priority.

I make no pretence that this is an impartial book. At a time when those most at risk from AIDS have been failed so badly even by their own organizations, studied indifference has become the enemy against which advocates for the interests of gay men are pitted. What is more, I myself have been closely involved in many of the activities and debates outlined in these pages. Between 1990 and 1992 I was employed by the Terrence Higgins Trust as its first health education officer with designated responsibility for working with gay men, and worked with the Trust's Gay Men's Health Education Group volunteers to produce resources such as the *Tales of Gay Sex* materials. I represented the Trust on the British Standards Institution's technical committee on condom standards; co-ordinated the Trust's input into the ground-breaking video *The Gay Man's Guide to Safer Sex* and co-wrote the follow-up *Getting It Right*; collaborated in the survey which revealed the extent of the neglect of prevention work for gay men; was a member of the HEA advisory group which resigned in 1992; and became a director of Gay Men Fighting AIDS when it was founded by Peter Scott. Rather than distorting and biasing my views, I consider that the personal insights provided by this degree of involvement have enhanced my ability to pass informed comment in this field.

Pressures of space and of time as well as the need to maintain a clear focus have required that the scope of the book is tightly defined. It is important that it be seen as complementing other materials which provide more specific advice on, for example, the targeting of particular groups of gay and bisexual men such as black men or older men. It has also not been possible to discuss here the complex question of the relationships between alcohol and recreational drug use and sexual behaviour. Additional sources of advice for those involved in the planning and implementation of specific prevention activities are suggested in Chapter 3.

The ideas in this book have been deeply informed by the friends and colleagues with whom I have worked during the last few years. I should therefore like to acknowledge my debts to the other members of the Terrence Higgins Trust's health education team, especially Jamie Taylor; to Robin Gorna; to the volunteers in the Trust's Gay Men's Health Education Group; and to the directors of Gay Men Fighting AIDS. The staff at the Trust's library, especially Della Hirons, were particularly helpful during my research. Peter Scott and Keith Alcorn have provided immeasurable inspiration and insight, and made many helpful comments on early drafts of this material. I would like to thank my boyfriend Rob Kemp for his good humour and encouragement throughout the intensely antisocial six months when I was writing, and for his many useful comments and suggestions on the text. Finally, I am especially indebted to Simon Watney, whose writings played a key role in shaping my earliest interest and involvement in the AIDS field, and whose dedicated activism and reliable friendship continue to be a profound inspiration to me. In taking responsibility for the content of *Safety in Numbers*, I can only hope that it does justice to the intelligence, enthusiasm and commitment of them all.

List of Abbreviations

AJPH	*American Journal of Public Health*
Am.J.Epidem.	*American Journal of Epidemiology*
Ann.Int.Med.	*Annals of Internal Medicine*
BMJ	*British Medical Journal*
J.AIDS	*Journal of Acquired Immune Deficiency Syndromes*
JAMA	*Journal of the American Medical Association*
J.Inf.Dis.	*Journal of Infectious Diseases*
MMWR	*Morbidity and Mortality Weekly Reports*
NEJM	*New England Journal of Medicine*

For Rob

Chapter one

Tracking the Epidemic

THERE IS SOMETHING IN MY BLOOD
AND IT'S TRYING TO FUCKING KILL ME.

● *David Wojnarowicz*[1]

IN May 1981 Dr Michael Gottlieb and colleagues in Los
Angeles hospitals diagnosed the fifth case of unexplained *Pneumocystis carinii* pneumonia seen in young, previously healthy, gay men
since October 1980, and alerted the Centers for Disease Control
(CDC). On 5 June 1981 the CDC published a short report on the
cases in its bulletin *Morbidity and Mortality Weekly Reports*
(*MMWR*).[2] Soon after, reports from San Francisco and New York
described 26 cases of Kaposi's sarcoma (KS) in young gay men since
early 1979. AIDS had arrived.

But long before 1981, HIV had been silently infiltrating the
gay communities of America. Now alerted to the possible presence
of a sexually transmitted agent, gay groups and gay doctors began
the task of deducing strategies to prevent its spread. The behaviour
changes which resulted were rapid and substantial, but in the gay
capitals of the United States the virus had already had an enormous
impact. By 1981, when the first cases of AIDS were noticed, a high
proportion of gay men in cities such as San Francisco and New
York were already infected with HIV, and the virus continued to be
transmitted during the early 1980s as gay men struggled to understand and adapt to the epidemic.

This pattern might well have been duplicated elsewhere, and
indeed it was in countries such as France, where both gay insti-

tutions and the state were slow to respond. However, the rapid development of gay community-based safer sex campaigns in much of the industrialized world meant that behaviour changes occurred to a sufficient degree, at a sufficiently early stage, for HIV epidemics on the scale of that in America to be averted successfully.

This first chapter documents the emergence of HIV among the gay communities of the United States and Britain, and the rapid implementation of risk reduction strategies to prevent further transmission after the syndrome was recognized.

Before HIV

Before there were safer sex advertisements, the American gay press carried hepatitis B vaccine promotions. By the late 1970s, sexually transmitted diseases had come to be seen as a part of sexual life for the urban gay man. Dennis Altman has described how:

> the growth of both gay assertion and a commercial gay world meant an affirmation of sex outside relationships as a positive good, a means of expressing both sensuality and community. In some ways this was no more than adopting and pushing further general attitudes towards 'liberated' sexuality that developed during this period. In others it was taking one of the most characteristic features of homosexual life as it had existed before such assertion – promiscuity, often in fleeting and anonymous encounters due to fear of discovery – and making of it a virtue.[3]

The concept of 'gay community', envisaged in the 1960s and 1970s as a broad political, social and cultural ideal, evolved in practice through the development of the commercial gay scene, where sexuality was integrated into consumerism. Facilities such as gay bathhouses and backroom bars removed the barriers to immediate sex, whether as an anonymous short-term transaction or as part of the quest for partnership and love. They also allowed sexually transmitted diseases (STDs) to flourish.

Altman has argued that gay men and medical professionals failed to take these diseases seriously:

> The fear of echoing traditional moralistic condemnations of homosexuality, indeed of sexuality, meant that most doctors were unwilling to think through the implications of these diseases and that many gay men accepted frequent medication with strong antibiotics. Being responsible about one's health was equated with having frequent checks for syphilis and gonorrhea, and such doubtful practices as taking a couple of tetracycline capsules before going to the baths.[4]

So, for example, the epidemic levels of hepatitis B among gay men during the late 1970s did not result in the widespread adoption of preventive behaviours such as the use of condoms. Instead, such measures were only recommended to individuals who were 'supercarriers' of hepatitis B. However, from 1978 'cohorts' of gay men were recruited from STD clinics in cities with large gay populations, such as New York and San Francisco in the United States and Amsterdam and London in Europe. In these studies, thousands of men who presented to clinics for treatment of diseases or just for check-ups had blood samples taken and tested for hepatitis B serological markers; they also agreed to return to the clinic to provide ongoing information about their sexual behaviour and regular specimens of blood. In 1980, trials of the Merck hepatitis B virus vaccine ('Heptavax B' vaccine) were begun, comparing the efficacy of the vaccine with an inactive placebo. In order to be able to test for a protective effect of the vaccine, only the subset of men who initially tested negative for hepatitis B were enrolled in the trials.

In San Francisco, 6697 gay and bisexual men were screened for the various studies of the incidence, prevalence* and prevention

---

*   *Incidence* is defined as 'the number of new events (e.g. new cases of a disease) in a defined population, within a specified period of time'. In relation to HIV, it counts the number of new cases which occur during a given period, rather than the cumulative total. *Prevalence* is defined as 'the number of persons in a given population with a disease or an attribute at a specified point in time'. In relation to HIV, it counts already existing as well as new cases: in other words, all cases existing at the specified time.

of hepatitis B at the City Clinic between 1978 and 1980. Blood samples were taken from all of these men, and unused sera were frozen and stored. Between April 1980 and July 1981, 359 men who had not been exposed to hepatitis B were enrolled in the vaccine trial. Blood was drawn at the time of each trial injection and at 1-, 2-, 4-, 6-, 8- and 12-month intervals from the date of the first dose, and every six months thereafter; these samples were then frozen and stored. In October 1981 the trial was stopped when the vaccine's efficacy was proven, and trial participants who had been allocated to placebo were offered vaccination.[5]

In Amsterdam, 685 gay men seronegative for hepatitis B were enrolled in a vaccine trial between November 1980 and December 1981. They were followed in the trial until December 1982. In addition to detailed descriptions of their medical and sexual histories, participants gave blood samples during each of the first 5 months of the study and every 3 months thereafter.[6] In New York, blood samples were stored from 4398 men participating in studies of hepatitis B beginning in 1978.[7] And in Britain, blood specimens taken from gay men for routine diagnostic tests for hepatitis B were stored in a bank at the Public Health Laboratory Service Virus Reference Laboratory in London and in provincial centres from 1980 onwards.[8]

Tracking the epidemic

These blood samples were to be of huge importance – far greater than the donors could imagine at the time. When the ELISA test for antibodies to HIV became available in 1984, it was possible to unfreeze and test these stored blood samples for the presence of HIV (then known variously as human T-cell lymphotropic virus type III [HTLV-III], lymphadenopathy-associated virus [LAV] and AIDS-related virus [ARV]). The results showed the emergence and rapid spread of HIV within these gay communities, and provided invaluable data about the rate of progression from the time of HIV infection to the development of AIDS.

Gay men were recruited for other cohort studies from relatively early after the recognition of the epidemic. At the outset these studies' emphasis was on describing the natural history of AIDS, defining and quantifying factors believed to be causally involved in the disease such as psychoactive drugs, sexual practices and infections, and providing a repository of blood specimens linked to individual case histories for research purposes. When HIV was established as the necessary causal agent of the disease in 1983, the cohort studies could narrow their focus: participants who were seropositive on entry to the studies could be compared with those who remained seronegative and those who seroconverted during the course of follow-up, and the factors that correlated with infection could be assessed and quantified.[9] During the 1980s many cohort studies were established at centres throughout the western world; some conducted long-term follow-up of hepatitis B vaccine trial participants; others recruited men through gay bars, clubs or publications, or through STD clinics.

Other research methodologies can also be used. In many countries, reliable information on the number of individuals seeking consenting HIV antibody testing, the proportion testing HIV-positive and their breakdown in terms of epidemiological risk groups is centrally collected, usually in anonymized form. In addition, information on the incidence and prevalence of other sexually transmitted diseases such as gonorrhoea, syphilis and hepatitis B allows the monitoring of temporal trends in sexual behaviour which might also allow HIV transmission. It is from these various sources that we are able to piece together something of an epidemiological history of the early years of the epidemic.

Cautions and provisos[10]

This chapter presents a range of different kinds of information, which can be fitted together to produce a consistent picture of events in the early to mid-1980s. But it is nevertheless important to approach the data with some caution. There are a number of reasons why it is impossible to reconstruct the history into a form that is entirely free from doubt or alternative interpretations.

First, the figures and statistics that will be described reflect reported patterns of infection and behaviour change in particular groups of gay men, which cannot be assumed to reflect circumstances among all gay men. Part of the problem is the lack of 'baseline' data relating to the numerical size of the populations of gay men and bisexual men, or the frequency and nature of their sexual behaviour. The extent to which sexual identity and behaviour vary between different groups of homosexually active men across and between the boundaries of race, age, class, locale, relationship status and so on remains under-researched. The safest approach to any data, therefore, is to view them in isolation, judging each individual study on the merits of its methodology, and resisting the inclination to extrapolate from its findings to the wider populations of gay and bisexual men. However, during an epidemic, such data with all their limitations are often the only information upon which health educators can base their interventions and monitor their success. It thus seems appropriate to attempt to reach some generalized conclusions on the basis of the available studies, as a framework within which to analyse and understand past educational strategies, and plan future ones.

Particular kinds of data are subject to particular biases and provisos. Cohort studies often recruited their members from among regular attenders of sexually transmitted disease (STD) clinics, who were clearly among the most sexually active of gay men, and the least likely to have been practising sexual behaviours with little or no risk of the transmission of disease. As increasing numbers of gay men adopted safer sex, the incidence of other sexually transmitted diseases as well as HIV fell; presumably this also reduced the need for men practising safer sex to attend STD clinics, and rendered the population of clinic attenders increasingly likely to consist disproportionately of men who had not been reached or persuaded by safer sex messages.

Similar considerations apply to the data from the hepatitis B vaccine cohorts. The initial sample who were screened for hepatitis B antigen were STD clinic attenders; however, trial participants were those without prior exposure to hepatitis B, who therefore probably represent a subset of the sample who were younger or who had become sexually active more recently, or whose preferred sexual behaviour was likely also to place them at lower risk of HIV infection. In the few cases in which data are available which distinguish between the initial pool as a whole and those selected for a vaccine trial, HIV infection rates are indeed significantly lower among the trial participants.

Other cohorts have recruited from gay pubs, clubs and bathhouses or gay social and political groups, whose members are unlikely to be representative of the spectrum of homosexually active men. Those individuals who agree to participate in such studies may possess and be motivated by factors which set them apart from other gay men, and which might correlate with greater or less than average risk; for example, they may wish to help researchers because an ex-partner or lover has HIV or AIDS, or in an irrational attempt to ward off the virus through their involvement. Generally in sex surveys, participants have been found to have more liberal sexual attitudes and to be more sexually active than non-participants.[11]

Membership of a research study is likely in itself to produce changes in attitude and/or behaviour, which then differ from the attitude/behaviour of those not participating in a study. Most cohort studies have felt an ethical obligation to advise members on sexual risk reduction and to offer access to counselling and HIV antibody testing; to this extent, studies are likely themselves to serve as a form of educational intervention, rather than simply to reflect the effects of other such interventions.

Moreover, prospective cohort studies, which recruit participants and then monitor those participants over extended periods of time, inevitably become increasingly less representative of the wider population from which the participants were drawn. Unless the cohort is 'topped up' periodically, its members are 'ageing'. This may mean that after some years, a cohort of gay men may produce findings which do not necessarily reflect the realities for younger gay men or others who have recently come out, in terms of behaviour, lifestyle, attitudes and so on.

Researchers must also control for biases in information which is self-reported, particularly in reports relating to sexual behaviour:

> Privacy, embarrassment, and fear of reprisals are but a few of the reasons that may motivate people to conceal their true sexual behavior. In contrast, some people may find it rewarding to embellish their actual sexual performance and experience (bragging). These barriers to accurate reporting aside, even highly motivated and uninhibited respondents

may have trouble recalling how often and with how many people they have performed particular sexual behaviors.[12]

Thus, in questionnaires and interviews relating to sexual behaviour, subjects are likely to under-report activities which are stigmatized or which they themselves perceive, or believe the researchers to perceive, as 'wrong', such as unsafe sex. Conversely, reports of activities perceived as safer sex, such as reductions in numbers of partners or in unprotected intercourse, are likely to be exaggerated. This is described as 'self-presentation bias'. Furthermore, recollection of the details of sexual encounters may blur with time; then, '[t]he more distant the sexual events a person is asked to recall, the more important personal salience may become in shaping what is reported'.[13] The accuracy of recall of particular sexual acts may also be subject to specific biases, since people with a large number of partners and an extensive sexual repertoire may have greater difficulty recalling occurrences of individual parts of that repertoire than those with more limited sexual experience. These factors can have significant consequences: 'Measurement error will bias estimates of the prevalence of high-risk sexual behaviors, lead to misidentification of at-risk populations and, thereby, hamper prevention efforts.'[14]

All of these factors are very familiar to researchers, and study designs usually include methods of controlling for their effect. Questionnaires may include repeated or slightly varied questions designed to corroborate the responses; prospective studies may compare reported behaviour at a particular time with the same behaviour recollected at a later stage in the study; reported changes in sexual behaviour may be compared with changes in the rates of HIV seroconversion or other sexually transmitted diseases. These measures generally indicate that gay men are accurate reporters of their own sexual behaviour. The characteristics of clinic attenders who agree to participate in a study may be compared with those of individuals who are not requested or who decline to take part, and statistical methods used to adjust for any variances. Similar methodology may be used to attempt to cancel out predictable differences in sexual behaviour or seroprevalence on the basis of previous sexually transmitted diseases, use of specific sexual partner meeting-places, and so on.

9: Tracking the Epidemic

Some of the statistics reviewed in this chapter relate to sero-prevalence of HIV among those who either choose to take the antibody test or are tested anonymously in such a way that the test result cannot be linked back or communicated to the subject. These data are subject to a number of biases. First, men choosing to take the test when it became available in 1984 may not have been typical of other STD clinic attenders, let alone the gay population at large. Over the years, willingness to take the test is likely to have been influenced by shifting factors such as the disincentive of prejudice and discrimination, and the positive incentive of the improving treatment for asymptomatic people with HIV. Thus, as explained by Hilary Hillier of the Department of Health's Statistics and Research Division in the 1988 Cox Report:

> Most of the surveys [of seroprevalence among homosexual men] show an apparent decline in seroprevalence over time, with higher levels being found in 1985 than in 1987. This possibly reflects that fact that those at highest risk were tested first, or that those at highest risk are less likely to be tested now than previously.[15]

To complicate matters further, data from the Middlesex Hospital in late 1986 suggested that men who chose to take the test were less likely to be infected than those who did not: 11.4 per cent of gay men who requested the test were infected, compared with 25.3 per cent of gay men anonymously tested at that time.[16] A similar finding has been reported from the USA, in which gay STD clinic attenders who did not volunteer for HIV antibody testing were 7.3 times more likely to be infected than those who did.[17]

The Cox Report aimed to predict the course of the epidemic over the following two to five years. Its authors summarized other shortcomings in using reported antibody test results:

> (i) it is certain that only a proportion of those who are infected present for testing, and this proportion may well be different in the various risk groups and in different parts of the country;
>
> (ii) there is only limited information on those tested and found to be seronegative;
>
> (iii) some patients attend more than one clinic and use false

names (there is no requirement for patients attending GUM [genito-urinary medicine] clinics to give their real names). Laboratories do their best to detect duplicate results but they cannot always succeed.[18]

There are also shortcomings in using other sexually transmitted diseases as markers for sexual activity which might allow HIV transmission. Not only do STD data reflect at best the sexual behaviour of an inevitably unrepresentative sample of all gay or bisexual men; the reporting of the incidence of STDs to central health bodies may be voluntary and incomplete, and may not include information on important factors such as sexuality and age. Trends in the incidence of other STDs may have changed as a result of factors other than awareness of HIV: for example, Dutch researchers have reported that gonorrhoea incidence rates in the Netherlands began to decline in 1981, preceding the onset of significant awareness of AIDS or the first cases of AIDS in the Netherlands, and the decline was subsequently reinforced by the effects of sexual behaviour changes among gay and bisexual men.[19] There has also been some debate in the medical literature about the extent to which gonorrhoea incidence rates do correlate with unsafe sex.[20] There is little information on the possible confounding effects of any changes in the diagnostics or treatment of STDs. From early in the epidemic a history of hepatitis B infection was reported to be a reliable marker of increased risk of HIV infection; since the early 1980s, however, the welcome availability of the hepatitis B vaccine may have had the effect of disrupting any such correlation.

Moreover, the development of increasingly sophisticated safer sex strategies among gay men is also likely to distort this evidence. There are indications that some gay men may be choosing to have unprotected anal sex in particular circumstances in which it is less likely to result in a substantially increased risk of HIV infection: for example, some gay men in relationships have reported taking the HIV antibody test and, if both partners are negative, choosing to practise unprotected intercourse.[21] Men who know themselves to be HIV-positive may choose to have unsafe sex only with infected partners.[22] In both these instances sexual activities that carry a risk of HIV infection are being practised in an informed manner in circumstances where the likelihood of transmission to hitherto uninfected individuals is genuinely reduced or eliminated. Nevertheless, other sexually transmitted diseases may be transmitted, and may then be wrongly assumed to correlate with increasing opportunities for HIV transmission.

Seroprevalence in San Francisco

Information on the arrival of HIV in the gay centres of America comes from HIV antibody testing of the stored blood samples from members of hepatitis B serological studies in New York[23] and San Francisco[24] from 1978 onwards. Of these, the greatest number of published data comes from the San Francisco City Clinic cohort.

This study recruited 6875 gay men in 1978. Retrospective testing found that 4.5 per cent of the whole sample were infected with HIV at that time. In the space of one year seroprevalence almost tripled to 12 per cent, and doubled again in 1980 to 24 per cent. In other words, in the year that AIDS was first recognized as a new medical phenomenon of unknown cause, the ratio of seropositive persons to persons with AIDS was a colossal 825:1.

Seroprevalence continued to rise during the early 1980s. Figures for the years 1981–83 have not been published; however, researchers have estimated that infection continued at a steady rate of 11 per cent per year for this period. By 1984, 67.4 per cent of the cohort were infected with HIV, rising to 73.1 per cent in 1985.

Fuller data are available for the subgroup of hepatitis B seronegative men who were actually enrolled in the vaccine trial. As noted above, this group of men would be expected to have an incidence of HIV infection lower than the average for the whole of this cohort, by virtue of the same sexual behaviours which also prevented them from becoming infected with hepatitis B. Of 320 hepatitis B seronegative men, 0.3 per cent were already infected with HIV in 1978. Over the next four years the cumulative incidence of HIV infection increased sharply to 4.1 per cent, 13.8 per cent, 28.1 per cent and 42.4 per cent respectively. However, in 1983 only 7.4 per cent of those who were previously uninfected tested positive for HIV antibodies, indicating a dramatic decrease in the annual infection rate from the previous year's 19.8 per cent. By

1984, 48.4 per cent of the trial participants were seropositive, and thereafter this figure remained essentially stable, reaching 50.9 per cent in 1988. From 1985 onwards only a relatively low annual incidence of between 0.7 and 2.6 per cent was observed, including absolutely no seroconversions during the whole of 1987.

The San Francisco Men's Health Study has also provided information on seroprevalence and sexual behaviour modification among West Coast gay men.[25] This cohort has the added advantage that its members were recruited through a form of random population sampling, rather than from an STD clinic or a hepatitis B vaccine trial. Researchers identified the 19 census districts (or 'tracts') of San Francisco which had the highest cumulative incidence of AIDS up until December 1983, then selected from each a number of street blocks directly proportional to the size of the tract. Then a sample of households inversely proportionally to the size of each block was selected, and any single men aged between 25 and 54 living in those households were invited to join the study. This produced a cohort of 1034 unmarried men, 809 of whom were gay or bisexual. When compared with the city-wide data on single men gathered in the previous census, the cohort was under-representative in 25- to 29-year-olds, and over-representative in 35- to 44-year-olds, white-collar workers and those who had received college education.

On entry into the study between June 1984 and January 1985, 48.6 per cent of the gay men were already HIV-positive. (No heterosexual men were infected.) Participants were retested and reinterviewed every 6 months; the seroprevalence rose by a further 1 per cent to 49.6 per cent during the first half-year, but remained stable thereafter. However, as a number of cohort members died each year, but the proportion of surviving members who were HIV-positive remained more or less constant, a low level of continuing HIV transmission was still occurring. Among seronegatives, the annual rate of seroconversion remained between 3 and 6 per cent until the end of 1986, falling to less than 1 per cent during the second half of 1987.

The likelihood of a participant being HIV-positive on entry to the study was related to his previous sexual history. While little difference in seroprevalence was seen between those identifying as gay and those identifying as bisexual (49.2 per cent compared with

46.2 per cent respectively), over 70 per cent of men who had had more than 50 sexual partners during the preceding two years were infected, compared with only 17.6 per cent of those with no partners during that period. Nearly 23 per cent of men who reported no receptive anal intercourse for at least two years were nevertheless HIV-positive, indicating that at least that proportion – and the researchers suggest that this is the minimum figure[26] – was already infected by late 1982. Every single one of these infected men indicated that they had practised passive anal sex before June 1982.

Researchers at San Francisco General Hospital (SFGH) put together another cohort from three groups of gay men: a group randomly selected from the neighbourhood, a group of STD clinic attenders and a number of the sexual partners of people with AIDS (PWAs).[27] On entry to the study in late 1984, a total of 62 per cent were HIV-infected; seroprevalence varied predictably between the groups, from 39 per cent of the neighbourhood sample to 71 per cent and 74 per cent of the clinic attenders and the partners of PWAs respectively. During 1985, 8 per cent of previously seronegative men in this cohort became infected with HIV; by 1988, this annual seroconversion rate had fallen to less than 1 per cent.

Looked at together, these studies show that gay men in San Francisco were becoming infected with HIV as early as 1978, and that by the mid-1980s perhaps 50 per cent of all gay men in the city had become infected, with those who had the greatest number of sexual partners in the early years of the epidemic being at the highest risk. In all three cohorts, the annual rate of HIV transmission was greatest during the earlier years, but fell to between 0 and 3 per cent in 1987–88. There is also evidence that the decline in seroconversions occurred in parallel with dramatic changes in the cohort participants' reported sexual behaviour.

Behaviour changes in San Francisco

The most significant change in the sexual activity of men in San Francisco appears to have been a dramatic reduction in their number of sexual partners, in accordance with the most common AIDS prevention advice to gay men at this time. In the earliest years, the modes of transmission of the putative undiscovered causative agent of AIDS were a matter of conjecture, and details such as the efficacy of condoms in preventing transmission of this agent during anal sex were largely speculative. The relative merits of the various approaches to risk reduction are discussed in Chapter 2.

The SF Men's Health Study reported substantial changes in the sex lives of its participants over time. Comparing the 6 months between January and June 1984 with the same 6 months in 1986, there was a 60 per cent decrease in the number of men who had over ten or more sexual partners during this period.[28] Likewise, by late 1987 seronegative men had reduced the prevalence of receptive anal sex with two or more partners from 14 per cent on entry to about 3 per cent and seropositive men had reduced insertive anal sex with two or more partners from 39.6 per cent in 1985 to approximately 5 per cent by late 1987.[29] Data on condom use among these men were not reported.

In November 1983, the AIDS Behavioral Research Project based at the University of California surveyed 655 gay men in San Francisco regarding their sexual practices during the previous month and the same month one year earlier. Of these men, 454 were contacted again in May 1984, and others were also enrolled, reaching a total of 754 men in 1984. In each subsequent November, surviving study members were sent a questionnaire for self-completion, providing longitudinal data for 508 men who returned every questionnaire between 1984 and 1988.[30]

Study participants were recruited from four different gay milieux. Some were handed questionnaires as they left three popular San Francisco bathhouses; some were approached when they left a gay bar; others who chose not to go to gay bars or baths to meet sexual partners were recruited through the gay press and gay organizations; and men in committed (although not necessarily monogamous) relationships who had participated in a similar earlier study were also sent questionnaires. Overall, the researchers estimated that their sample was somewhat more sexually active than would be seen in a random sample of San Francisco gay men.

In each of these groups, significantly fewer men reported

meeting two or more sexual partners at the baths, bars, discos or other locations in 1983 compared with one year earlier. This is not to say, however, that these men stopped having sex; rather, they reduced their number of partners. Between November 1982 and May 1984 the proportion of men who had two or more sex partners per month fell from 60 per cent to 42 per cent; for men not in relationships from November 1983, the average number of sex partners per month fell from 6.3 to 3.9. The proportion of men in committed relationships decreased between 1982 to 1983; however, those who were in relationships in 1983 were more likely to be monogamous.

In terms of the type of sex practised, changes between 1982 and 1984 were described as 'selective'.[31] There was little reduction in unprotected receptive anal sex among men in monogamous relationships, 'possibly because they feel protected by their monogamy'. Single men and men in open relationships did have less unprotected anal sex; as there was no corresponding increase in condom use, it appears this represented a move away from all anal sex rather than a move towards condom use.

Between 1984 and 1988 condom use did become significantly more common; it was practised by 23.8 per cent of non-monogamous men in 1988, compared with only 15.2 per cent in 1984. The proportion having unprotected anal sex continued to fall, from nearly 50 per cent in 1984 to 12 per cent in 1988. There were similar trends among monogamous men, although these men were still the least likely to use condoms during anal sex.

In 1985 the Centers for Disease Control reported the results of a telephone survey which contacted a random sample of San Francisco gay men drawn from telephone numbers listed with only men's names, and weighted according to census information on the proportion of unmarried men in the specific city tracts. In August 1984, 500 men were interviewed, and 301 agreed to participate again in April 1985. The proportion of men who said they were monogamous, celibate or performed 'unsafe' sexual practices only with a steady partner increased from 69 per cent to 81 per cent over this period. (It should be noted that for the purposes of this survey the definition of 'unsafe' sex included oral sex with exchange of semen, which is now broadly accepted to carry at most a low risk of HIV transmission.) The proportion who had practised unprotected anal sex outside a regular relationship during the past 30 days fell from 18 per cent to 12 per cent.[32]

Cases of rectal gonorrhoea among gay men in San Francisco have plummeted since the early 1980s, and remain on a plateau: 1299 cases were reported to the San Francisco Health Department in 1984; in 1985, 708 cases; in 1986, 379 cases; in 1987, 197 cases; and by 1991, the last year for which full data were available, the rate had fallen still further to 134 cases, representing a ten-fold decrease over the 7-year period.[33]

Seroprevalence and behaviour change in New York

The New York hepatitis B studies enrolled 4394 gay men beginning in 1978; 378 of these were recruited for a prospective AIDS study early in 1984. Researchers studied HIV seroprevalence in samples taken from 212 of these men every 3 to 6 months from 1978 or 1979, and a further 166 men who had only one previous blood specimen taken in the late 1970s. Of this cohort, 6.6 per cent were already infected with HIV by 1978/79. By 1981 this had risen to 20 per cent, and had reached 43.7 per cent in 1984. The annual seroconversion rates among uninfected men ranged from 5.5 per cent to 10.6 per cent during these years, with the highest levels occurring in 1982 and 1983.[34]

Seroprevalence figures for gay men attending a private medical practice in central Manhattan during 1982–83 confirm that by then HIV was firmly established. Samples from 66 out of 85 men who visited the practice consecutively in June 1982 were tested, and 53 per cent were found to be HIV-positive. Samples from 29 of the uninfected men were taken in June 1983, and 4 of these (14 per cent) had seroconverted, giving an infection rate of 1.2 per cent each month. Infection with HIV was strongly correlated with both the number of sexual partners in the preceding year and the practice of unprotected receptive anal sex. None of the 8 men who had had fewer than 10 partners during the last 12 months was infected, compared with more than half of those men with between 10 and 50 partners, and more than 70 per cent of those with more than 50 partners. Of the men who had not had receptive anal sex during the last year, 29 per cent were HIV-positive, indicating that a significant number of men were infected by 1980 or earlier; however, 74 per cent of men who had experienced passive anal intercourse with more than 20 men during the previous year were seropositive.[35]

Between June and October 1985, researchers interviewed 745 New York gay men to assess the extent and type of sexual behaviour modifications. Of these men, 291 were recruited from gay organizations, events or clinics; the remaining 454 were recruited by personal referral from the 291 already interviewed. Respondents were asked to recall their sexual activity during the 12 months immediately before they first heard about AIDS, which on average was in July 1981. This was compared with their reported behaviour during the 12 months prior to interview in 1985, and analysed in terms of number of partners, type of sex and, rather curiously, whether the sex took place in a private home or elsewhere.

The participants reported a 34 per cent decline in the use of bathhouses during this period. The median frequency of both passive and active anal sex declined by over 75 per cent, and receptive anal sex to ejaculation decreased by 100 per cent. There were also changes in the use of condoms: in the year prior to hearing about AIDS, condoms were used in only 1 per cent and 2 per cent of episodes of active and passive anal sex respectively, but by 1985 they were being used in an average of 20 per cent and 19 per cent of occasions respectively. However, at least half of the men did not use a condom for anal sex either before or after they heard about AIDS.[36] In terms of the specific risk reduction strategies advocated in the early 1980s (some of which, of course, proved to be unnecessary or mistaken[37]), 15 per cent of those with multiple partners in the year before they heard about AIDS became celibate or monogamous, 31 per cent of those who had sex outside a private home pre-AIDS now restricted sex to the home or had become celibate, and 29 per cent of those practising receptive anal sex or rimming had stopped having these forms of sex or become celibate. In total, 40 per cent of the participants had changed at least one aspect of their sexual behaviour in line with contemporary advice.[38]

Of these men, 624 were contacted for follow-up interviews

in both 1986 and 1987.[39] These showed that the behaviour changes seen in 1985 were maintained and increased in subsequent years. Use of bathhouses continued to decline: 50 per cent had attended a bathhouse for sex at least once in 1981, compared with only 8 per cent in 1987. More men abstained from anal sex altogether, and by 1987 the proportion of men who always used condoms had risen to 58 per cent and 62 per cent of those practising active and passive anal sex respectively. As of 1987, 82.9 per cent of the participants had avoided unprotected passive anal sex for at least a year, whether through abstinence or the use of condoms.

These changes clearly resulted in reduced HIV transmission. Among the men who stopped unprotected passive anal sex in 1985, 22 per cent were HIV-positive, while of those who continued practising unsafe sex beyond 1985, 48 per cent were infected, representing a three-fold difference in risk. This effect was most pronounced among men who had an annual total of more than 15 partners in the year before they heard of AIDS: 26 per cent of those who avoided unsafe sex from 1985 were infected, compared with 64 per cent of those who continued unprotected passive anal sex. As of late 1986, it was estimated that in total 37 per cent of the sample were infected with HIV, a figure significantly lower than those described earlier. This probably reflects the fact that these men were recruited from a more diverse cross-section of the New York gay population, and should act as a reminder of the variance such factors can introduce. Among this cohort, the annual rate of new infections fell to 3 per cent in 1986, and less than 1 per cent in 1987.

The Multicenter AIDS Cohort Study

In mid-1983 the Centers for Disease Control issued a formal request for investigators to propose cohort studies in cities with both high and low incidences of AIDS, to evaluate approximately 1000 gay and bisexual men periodically for at least two to three years. Eventually, separately designed studies in Baltimore, Chicago, Los Angeles and Pittsburgh were blended into a collaborative multicentre study employing standardized procedures and measures to research the natural history of HIV disease, and risk factors for infection and disease progression. The combined project was called the Multicenter AIDS Cohort Study, or MACS.[40]

Participants were recruited between April 1984 and April 1985, from somewhat different sources at the four sites. In Baltimore, researchers appealed for volunteers in both gay and 'mainstream' newspapers, and through personal contact with gay community leaders. In Chicago, men were drawn from the attenders at a clinic founded by and for gay men, and from participants in an existing hepatitis B vaccine study. The Los Angeles site used a combination of a pre-existing AIDS cohort study, gay organizations, announcements in the gay press and referrals from other healthcare professionals, while in Pittsburgh, where the gay scene was less developed, researchers visited all known gay bars and baths to enrol men in a preliminary screening study, from which volunteers for MACS were recruited.

A total of 4955 men were recruited, of whom 1693 (34 per cent) were HIV-positive on entry. Seroprevalence varied from site to site, and correlated with lower levels of sexual activity and lower rates of other sexually transmitted diseases. The highest seroprevalence was in Los Angeles, where 51 per cent were infected; in Chicago, Baltimore and Pittsburgh seroprevalence was 43 per cent, 31 per cent and 21 per cent respectively.

Of the men who were uninfected at entry to MACS, 368 (11.3 per cent) seroconverted by the end of 1989. The incidence rate was highest in the earliest stages of follow-up; 42 per cent of these 368 men became infected during the year between July 1984 and June 1985. Thereafter there was a significant decline in seroconversion at all sites, and the rate stabilized at between 0.5 per cent and 1.7 per cent, although an increase was seen in Chicago during 1989. Racial differences were apparent at two sites: in Baltimore and Chicago black men were more likely to become infected than white men, and Hispanic men were also at greater risk than white men in Chicago. Men under 35 were also significantly more likely to seroconvert, particularly in Chicago.[41]

Substantial sexual behaviour changes occurred at all sites. Over two years of follow-up of 2915 initially uninfected men, the proportion who reported using condoms with all of their partners rose from 3 per cent to 28 per cent, while the proportion whose partners never used condoms fell from 54 per cent to 38 per cent. The study also produced evidence that men were choosing between two distinct risk reduction strategies: men who used condoms with some or all of their partners tended not to reduce their number of partners as well, whereas among men who never used condoms, the proportion reporting more than 8 partners during the previous 12 months fell from 69 per cent to 22 per cent.[42]

Researchers at the Baltimore site analysed their data on changes in sexual behaviour according to participants' HIV antibody status. Overall, after 6 months of follow-up, cohort members had reduced their number of partners to 81 per cent of the initial number, and after one year in the study to 66 per cent of the initial number. At this point, two-thirds of the men chose to learn their HIV antibody status. Over the following 6 months the number of partners fell again in all groups, but there were significant differences between those who knew they were positive, those who knew they were negative, and those who had chosen not to know: compared with the initial number of partners, the reductions were to 45 per cent, 55 per cent and 47 per cent respectively. A similar differentiation was observed in relation to the number of partners with whom participants practised unprotected receptive anal sex: compared with the initial number, the reductions were to 42 per cent, 62 per cent and 57 per cent respectively.[43]

Summary: the United States experience

HIV was clearly becoming established at least among the more sexually active members of the gay populations in New York and San Francisco during the late 1970s. By the time the first cases of AIDS were recognized in 1980, approximately a quarter of these men were already infected with HIV. That HIV was the cause of AIDS was not discovered until 1983, by which time over 40 per cent were HIV-positive. This discussion has focused heavily on studies of seroprevalence during the first five years or so; however, it is important to keep in mind that these data could only be produced retrospectively after the HIV antibody test became available in mid-1984, when about 50 per cent of these gay men were already infected. Among all exclusively homosexual men in the USA, the CDC estimated that between 20 per cent and 25 per cent were infected by 1986–87. For bisexuals and men who occasionally had sex with other men, the estimated seroprevalence was 5 per cent.[44]

Despite ignorance of the causative agent during those earliest years, studies quickly established two factors which were associated with the development of AIDS: a high number of sexual partners, and practising anal sex. As described in Chapter 2, it was these risks about which the earliest safer sex advice warned, and which behavioural studies consistently show to have declined since as early as 1982. At one clinic in New York with a clientele predominantly of gay men, the percentage of rectal cultures which were positive for gonorrhoea fell from 30.3 per cent in 1980 to 16.5 per cent in 1983.[45] The Lower West Side Health District contained the highest number of gay men, and gonorrhoea rates in this district had consistently been higher than those in other districts. In 1981 the rate of reported cases in males had been 3750 per 100,000, but by 1983 this had fallen to about 2200 per 100,000, a decrease of 45 per cent. Local epidemiologists considered that 'the most likely interpretation of these data is a shift in the lifestyle patterns of gay men'.[46] A review of the evidence by the Centers for Disease Control in 1987 suggested that the infection rate among gay men was greatest during 1980 to 1984, and fell from 1984 onwards.[47] By 1985 the incidence of rectal gonorrhoea among gay men in San Francisco had fallen to levels a quarter or less of those seen at the beginning of the decade. However, HIV was by now so common that any act of unprotected anal sex carried a significant risk of infection – and condom use was far from universal among men who still practised anal sex. There is also very little indication of any significant uptake of safer sex among men in monogamous relationships, despite the fact that many of those relationships only began after HIV had already become endemic. During the same period in which rectal gonorrhoea in San Francisco fell by 73 per cent, the prevalence of HIV infection in the City Clinic cohort increased by 280 per cent.[48]

Compared with the very high seroprevalence among gay men in New York, San Francisco and Los Angeles, most of the rest of the USA had relatively low incidences of HIV infection. It is important to stress that this comparison is in relation to the cities which have been hit by AIDS as badly as anywhere in the world; what is relatively low incidence among gay men in the USA, such as the 21 per cent seroprevalence at the Pittsburgh MACS site in the mid-1980s, nevertheless represents a very serious epidemic affecting tens of thousands of lives.

In general terms, similar behaviour changes to those observed in San Francisco and New York also occurred in these lower incidence areas. Speaking in late 1983, Daniel William of St Luke's-Roosevelt Hospital Center in New York was already able to point to evidence indicating:

> significant progress at achieving risk reduction. From 1982 to 1983 the prevalence of gonorrhea in the Denver gay male population has reduced 32% and the total number of diagnosed cases of gonorrhea in gay men has declined 39%. In Madison, Wisconsin, there has been a 50% decline in the numbers of different sexual partners encountered during a 6-month period.[49]

Gonorrhoea incidence rates in Madison decreased from 6.8 per cent of gay men who were screened to 2.2 per cent during the same period.[50] The number of cases of gonorrhoea seen in gay men in Denver continued its decline: by 1990 there had been a 95 per cent decrease from the peak of 1809 cases in 1982, to only 82.[51] Studies in Chicago in 1984–85 suggested that over three-quarters of gay men had reduced the number of their sexual partners, and 20 to 25 per cent of those having receptive anal sex were using condoms or the less reliable strategy of withdrawal before ejaculation.[52] During these years the annual seroconversion rate for members of the Chicago MACS cohort was a high 7 per cent.[53]

However, there was also evidence that men in low prevalence areas may have been less likely to adopt the recommended risk reduction measures, perhaps because of underestimating the local risk of infection. Of 107 gay men in New Mexico contacted through gay and AIDS organizations in 1985, only 4 had always used condoms when they had unprotected passive anal sex during the previous year, while 69 per cent had never used condoms. Over half of the 80 per cent of men who had changed their sex lives in response to AIDS had adopted the strategy of reducing partner numbers. Seroprevalence in the survey was 20 per cent.[54] Likewise, 45 per cent of gay men recruited at a gay social event in Ohio in 1985 reported that they were still practising unprotected anal sex, although 83 per cent reported reducing their numbers of sexual partners over the last two years.[55]

Seroprevalence in the United Kingdom

As in the United States, data on the introduction and early dissemination of HIV among gay men in Britain can be deduced from HIV antibody testing of stored blood samples. Sera collected for investigation of possible hepatitis B infection were preserved in the Public Health Laboratory Service (PHLS) Virus Reference Library in London and similar public health laboratories in provincial centres. Data from these samples along with some which were submitted specifically for HIV antibody testing were analysed in 1985.[56]

Of specimens from gay men in London, 5.2 per cent were already HIV-positive in 1980, rising to 34.1 per cent in 1984. The proportion of samples from 5 provincial centres which was positive for HIV antibodies in 1984 varied from 1.6 per cent to 11.2 per cent, and on average was 5.1 per cent.

A number of studies have reported on seroprevalence among attenders at particular STD clinics in London. As with the figures just cited, these are likely to be from men at higher than average risk of HIV infection. At the Middlesex Hospital in London, anonymous HIV antibody tests were performed on samples taken from all men attending the STD clinic for syphilis serology during 1 week in March 1982, 1 week in July 1984, 1 week in April/May 1985, 3 weeks in January 1986, 1½ weeks in November/December 1986 and 4 weeks during November/December 1987. Seroprevalence in British men (as opposed to, say, American visitors) increased from 3.7 per cent in 1982 to 21 per cent in 1984 and 18.1 per cent in

1985; during 1986–87 it was stable at approximately 25 per cent. This reflects a sharp increase in the incidence of HIV among British men of 7.4 per cent per year from 1982 to 1984, falling to less than 2 per cent thereafter. In 1982, 6 out of 10 infected men were non-British, 4 of whom were from North America, indicating that the epidemic was not necessarily yet firmly established among British gay men; by 1984, however, only 7 out of 33 seropositive men were not British.[57]

Doctors at St Mary's Hospital established a cohort of 170 gay men in 1982–83, some through an advert in the gay press, others from the hospital's Praed Street STD clinic. In 1983–84, 133 were re-evaluated, and 103 were seen for a third time in 1984–85. On entry, 33 men (19 per cent) were HIV-positive; they had had a significantly greater number of sexual partners compared with uninfected men. During the course of 1983, 5 more men seroconverted, a further 8 during 1984, and 2 in 1985.[58]

Between June 1983 and July 1984, blood samples were taken from 308 gay men who were screened for hepatitis B or syphilis at the Middlesex, St Mary's and St Stephen's Hospitals in London, or who had volunteered for studies of AIDS at 2 of these centres; 17 per cent were infected with HIV.[59]

A collaborative study by consultants in genitourinary medicine and the PHLS reported seroprevalence at STD clinics between 1985 and 1987, starting with 4 clinics and rising to 17 by 1987. At the two clinics in south-east England – Dulwich in London and Brighton – seroprevalence among gay and bisexual men was 12.9 per cent in 1985, 15.2 per cent in 1986 and 14.6 per cent in 1987. Corresponding findings at the other sites were 5 per cent, 6.3 per cent and 3.1 per cent respectively. In all centres and during each year, infection rates among bisexual men were significantly lower than those among gay men.[60]

The PHLS also reported on the prevalence of HIV among people who requested the antibody test between October 1986 and December 1987.[61] Outside London, 3607 gay or bisexual men were tested, of whom 4 per cent were HIV-positive. Seroprevalence among 1412 gay or bisexual men in London was 15.1 per cent, which is significantly lower than that seen in anonymized surveys of STD clinic attenders such as that at the Middlesex Hospital, reported above. This would appear to confirm the suggestion that prevalence in those who come forward for testing may underestimate the infection rate in the given population.[62] This means that although gay men who attend STD clinics may be more likely to be HIV-infected than those who do not, prevalence among those men who request testing at the clinic may nevertheless be lower than that among all gay men who attend clinics.

One of the most influential British studies is the ongoing Project SIGMA (Socio-sexual Investigations of Gay Men and AIDS) cohort study, established in 1987 'to estimate the prevalence of HIV antibody in homosexually active men, to assess the uptake and spread of safer sexual practices and to estimate, over a three year period, the rate of seroconversion in that group'. During 1987/88, 508 gay men were recruited from London and 270 from Cardiff, South Wales, through advertisements in the gay press, gay clubs and pubs, talks to gay groups and 'snowball' sampling through the social networks of respondents. Only 40 per cent reported that they were regular attenders at STD clinics, indicating that this is a different study population from that in the studies described above. Of the Londoners, 42 per cent had previously had an HIV antibody test; on entering the study, approximately two-thirds of the men in each city agreed to provide blood for antibody testing. Of this subsample, 9.2 per cent of men in London were HIV-positive, and 3.4 per cent of those in South Wales; if the results of men who took the test independently prior to July 1988 are included, prevalence was 13.8 per cent in London and 4.4 per cent in Cardiff. Clinic attenders were indeed more likely to be infected than non-attenders; for Londoners, the respective figures were 15.6 per cent versus 3.8 per cent. In addition, younger men were more likely to be HIV-positive than older men; 15 per cent of men under 21 were found to be infected.[63]

In 1988 the Department of Health and Welsh Office Working Group published a report (known as the Cox Report after its principal author) that estimated, among other factors, the incidence and prevalence of HIV in England and Wales. It included an estimate of the prevalence of HIV among gay men based on published and unpublished surveys, which concluded that between 15 per cent and 25 per cent of London clinic attenders were infected, and 2 per cent to 5 per cent of clinic attenders outside London; for non-clinic attenders, estimates were 5 per cent and 0.5–2 per cent within and outside London respectively. Of all homosexuals in the UK, of whom there were estimated to be the unusually low total of 650,000, between 2 per cent and 5 per cent were thought to be infected with HIV.[64]

In 1993, the Communicable Disease Surveillance Centre reported results from its programme of 'unlinked anonymous HIV antibody testing'. Part of this entailed the testing of specimens of blood taken from attenders at 2 STD clinics in London and 4 elsewhere in England and Wales. In London, 3926 samples from gay or bisexual men were tested during 1990 and 1991, of which 21 per cent tested HIV-positive. This figure obscures substantial variance between the 2 London clinics: in 1991, prevalence was 14 per cent at one and 28 per cent at the other. Outside London, 50 out of 924 specimens collected during 1990–91 were positive, giving a prevalence of 5 per cent. The overall prevalence among gay and bisexual men aged over 25 was 20 per cent, and 12 per cent among those aged under 25. Thirty samples from men aged under 19 were tested in London during 1991, of which 4, or 13 per cent, were HIV-infected.[65]

Behaviour changes in the United Kingdom

As in the USA, the major elements in the changes gay men made in their sex lives in response to the threat of AIDS appear to have been reductions in the number of sexual partners and in the practice of anal sex.

Researchers at London's Middlesex Hospital reported on sexual behaviour modifications in 100 gay men considered to be at 'increased risk of AIDS' who completed questionnaires in 1984–85 and 1986. The monthly number of sexual partners fell from 3 to 1, and the proportion of men who had 'one night stands' declined from 97 per cent to 64 per cent. There were also significant reductions in the number who practised anal sex with more than 2 partners during a typical month. However, there was no statistically significant increase in the use of condoms for either active or passive anal sex.[66]

In 1986 gay journalists undertook a survey of 326 men in central London gay pubs and clubs in order to assess the effects of safer sex campaigns on sexual behaviour. Of these gay men, 48 per cent reported that they had reduced the number of their sexual partners, and of the 53 per cent who were still practising anal sex, nearly half were now using condoms. Condom use was most common among men with multiple sexual partners. Overall, 95 per cent reported that they had received safer sex information, and 75 per cent said that they welcomed and followed that advice.[67]

Project SIGMA has also produced considerable numbers of data about changes in the sexual activity of cohort members. In both 1987/88 and 1988/89, 690 men were interviewed. At the second interview, participants reported an increase in the number of partners, which rose by 47 per cent over the year, but a smaller rise in the number of partners with whom anal sex took place. Overall, this meant that the proportion of men having anal sex declined. The increase in anal sex could largely be explained by a 7 per cent increase in the proportion of men who had regular partners, with whom anal sex is more likely to occur.[68] Comparing 1987 interviews with those in 1991, overall patterns of sexual activity with regular partners remained very similar, with about 70 per cent not practising anal sex, and 10 per cent always using condoms for anal sex, and 19 per cent using condoms inconsistently or not at all. With casual partners, overall levels of condom use for anal sex increased: in 1987, 8 per cent always used condoms, rising to 12 per cent in 1991, although about 85 per cent of men did not practise anal sex with casual partners. However, these collated statistics obscure substantial variations in given individuals' sexual behaviour over time, as some men who had been practising unsafe sex adopted safer behaviours, and vice versa.[69]

SIGMA collaborated with London gay newspaper *Capital Gay* in an informal survey of changes in readers' reported sexual behaviour between 1985 and 1988. Questionnaires were published in the paper, eliciting 1292 responses in 1985 and 1483 in 1988. The proportion of respondents who had receptive anal sex fell from 44 per cent to 32 per cent, while the proportion taking the active role in anal intercourse decreased from 45 per cent to 31 per cent. More men had adopted safer sex practices such as mutual masturbation: 81 per cent in 1988, compared with 60 per cent in 1985.

Use of condoms during anal sex with casual partners was 36 per cent.[70]

Another postal survey of gay groups, clinics and AIDS organizations in 1988 produced 269 replies. Of those who were sexually active, 51 per cent reported insertive anal sex, which for nearly all included ejaculation. Of these men, 69 per cent used condoms, and of those who did not, three-quarters reported that anal sex only took place within a stable relationship. Indeed, the commonest reason given by men who explained why they did not use condoms was that they were in a relationship, and many of them had chosen to have unprotected sex with their regular partner after both had taken the HIV antibody test. Of the sample, 46 per cent had practised receptive anal sex during the last year.[71]

Another British cohort study recruited 502 gay men during 1988 and the first half of 1989. Over half were contacted through gay pubs, clubs and organizations, and a further quarter through STD clinics; most of the others were referrals from those already interviewed. Most of the men lived in London, Oxford, Manchester or Northampton. Of these men, 383 reported having had anal sex during the preceding year. During receptive anal sex, 60 per cent always used condoms with non-regular partners, 22 per cent inconsistently used condoms and only 18 per cent never used them. With regular partners, these figures were much lower: only 43 per cent always used condoms, 25 per cent were inconsistent and 33 per cent never used condoms.[72]

Declining levels of STDs

Changes in the incidence of other sexually transmitted diseases provide supporting evidence for considerable changes in gay men's sexual behaviour in the 1980s. Doctors at the Royal Infirmary in Edinburgh reported a steady fall in the incidence of gonorrhoea among gay men since 1982, and a decline in syphilis since 1984. By 1987 rates of rectal gonorrhoea had fallen to about one-tenth of their 1982 level.[73] At the Middlesex Hospital in London, gonorrhoea rates among gay and bisexual men remained at a fairly constant level of between 14 per cent and 17 per cent of men seen at the clinic between January 1982 and March 1983. During the next 6 months, however, prevalence fell to approximately 10 per cent, coinciding with the first substantial media coverage of the epidemic in both the gay and the general circulation press.[74] The rate continued to decline by an average amount of nearly 3 per cent per year, reaching only 5.1 per cent in 1986, and by 1987 there was no significant difference between gonorrhoea rates in homosexuals and in heterosexuals − the first time this had occurred at the clinic.[75]

At St Mary's Hospital in London, the first noticeable decline in gonorrhoea rates was seen in 1985. Among gay men, the incidence of rectal gonorrhoea was reduced by 53 per cent between 1983 and 1986, and that of urethral gonorrhoea fell by 70 per cent.[76] In 1985, doctors from the Westminster and St Stephen's Hospitals in London wrote to the gay press to congratulate gay men on 37 per cent and 43 per cent reductions, respectively, in the incidence of rectal gonorrhea compared with the rates one year earlier.[77] At St Stephen's, the number of cases of gonorrhoea among gay men who were new attenders was halved from 14 per cent to 7 per cent between 1985 and 1986, and a similar trend was seen in the incidence of homosexually acquired early infectious syphilis. A small but increasing proportion of cases of gonorrhoea were seen in men who knew they were HIV antibody positive; while this suggests that a proportion of infected men may have been continuing to place other men at risk of HIV infection, it may also indicate that the practice of unsafe sex was increasingly becoming concentrated among a 'core' of men who were resisting behaviour change.[78]

Syphilis rates in Britain had been declining slowly between 1976 and 1984: most cases were in homosexually active men. In 1985 and 1986 this decline was 'markedly accelerated in the age-groups 20–24, 25–34 and 35–44 years'.[79] Similarly, the annual total of laboratory reports of hepatitis B among gay men in England and Wales, which was increasing steadily between 1980 and 1984, fell from 150 reports in 1984 to about one-third of this total in 1987.[80] The Cox Report concluded that 'although increasing use of Hepatitis B vaccine may have contributed to this fall it is likely that a substantial proportion was the result of behavioural change'.[81]

Summary: the United Kingdom experience

Compared with the United States, HIV did not have such a headstart in Britain. By the time that AIDS was recognized as a new medical phenomenon in 1980, prevalence among gay men attending STD clinics in London was only a quarter of that among gay men in San Francisco or New York. As in the American cities, annual infection rates were highest during the first three to five years of the epidemic; however, the introduction of sexual behaviour changes while the level of infection was still relatively low meant that seroprevalence was prevented from rising to the levels seen in New York and San Francisco.

In the UK, the HIV epidemic among gay men disproportionately affects London. Even the non-clinic based Project SIGMA found that approaching 15 per cent of gay Londoners were infected, while STD clinic surveys have suggested that by 1992 perhaps a quarter of attenders were HIV-positive. These figures compare with prevalence estimates which rarely rise above 10 per cent even for STD attenders outside London.

The first evidence for changes in sexual behaviour dates from 1983, when a decline in gonorrhoea rates was seen at the Middlesex Hospital; at other clinics this decline was not observed until 1985. By 1986 there was evidence that men were reducing the number of their sexual partners and cutting down on anal sex; use of condoms seems to have taken somewhat longer to become firmly established. In practice, instances of sex which carries a risk of HIV transmission have continued to be relatively commonplace: recent data from Project SIGMA suggest that in 1990, 'condoms were always used by just under two-thirds and never by a seventh' of participants during anal sex with casual partners, and much less frequently during anal sex within relationships.[82]

Conclusion

In San Francisco and New York, a high proportion of sexually active gay men had already become infected with HIV even before the first cases of AIDS were diagnosed. Although many gay men responded quickly by acting on contemporary risk reduction advice, the relatively high likelihood that a sexual partner would be infected meant that even the reduced level of unsafe sex in the earliest years still resulted in many more new infections taking place.

In Britain, however, gay men became aware of the existence of the epidemic at a time when HIV was not yet so firmly established in the urban gay population. Here, and in other countries such as Canada, Australia and the Netherlands, the widespread but still far from complete adoption of safer sex in the first half of the 1980s prevented the development of an epidemic of comparable size to that in the USA.

The relative effectiveness of the various risk reduction strategies recommended at this time, and the ways in which safer sex became established as the expected norm of gay men's sexual behaviour in the 1980s, have not been well documented. They are the subject of the next chapter.

Notes

1. David Wojnarowicz, 'Spiral', in *Memories That Smell Like Gasoline*. Artspace Books, San Francisco, 1992.
2. CDC, *MMWR*, 5 June 1981.
3. Dennis Altman, *AIDS and the New Puritanism*, p. 142. Pluto Press, London, 1986.
4. *Ibid.*, p. 143.
5. Nancy A. Hessol *et al.*, 'Prevalence, incidence and progression of human immunodeficiency virus infection in homosexual and bisexual men in hepatitis B vaccine trials, 1978–1988', *Am. J. Epidem.*, 130(6): 1167–75 (1989).
6. Godfried J. P. van Griensven *et al.*, 'Changes in sexual behaviour and the fall in incidence of HIV infection among homosexual men', *BMJ*, 298: 218–21 (1989); Godfried J. P. van Griensven *et al.*, 'Surrogate markers for HIV incidence among homosexual men', *J. Inf. Dis.*, 159(6): 1157f (1989).
7. Cladd E. Stevens *et al.*, 'Human T-cell lymphotropic virus type III infection in a cohort of homosexual men in New York City', *JAMA*, 255(16): 2167–72 (1986).
8. P. P. Mortimer *et al.*, 'Prevalence of antibody to human T lymphotropic virus type III by risk group and area, United Kingdom 1978–84', *BMJ*, 290: 1176–8 (1985).

9. The objectives of the collaborative Multicenter AIDS Cohort Study (MACS) established between April 1984 and April 1985 typify such studies: see Richard A. Kaslow *et al.*, 'The Multicenter AIDS Cohort Study: rationale, organization, and selected characteristics of the participants', *Am. J. Epidem.*, 126(2): 310–18 (1987).

10. For a thorough review of these issues, see Joseph A. Catania *et al.*, 'Methodological problems in AIDS behavioral research: influences on measurement error and participation bias in studies of sexual behavior', *Psychological Bulletin*, 108(3): 339–62 (1990). A brief discussion of the comparison of survey data relating specifically to gay men's sexual behaviour changes is contained in Ron D. Stall *et al.*, 'Behavioral risk reduction for HIV infection among gay and bisexual men', *American Psychologist*, 43: 878–85 (1988).

11. Catania, *op. cit.*, pp. 344, 358.

12. *Ibid.*, p. 340.

13. *Ibid.*, p. 345.

14. *Ibid.*, p. 341.

15. Hilary Hillier, 'Appendix 3 Estimation of HIV prevalence in England and Wales – the direct approach', in Department of Health and Welsh Office, *Short-term Prediction of HIV Infection and AIDS in England and Wales: Report of a Working Group*, pp. 48–52. HMSO, London, 1988.

16. C. A. Carne *et al.*, 'Heterosexual transmission of HIV infection' (letter), *The Lancet*, ii: 41 (1987).

17. Harry F. Hull *et al.*, 'Comparison of HIV-antibody prevalence in patients consenting to and declining HIV-antibody testing in an STD clinic', *JAMA*, 260(7): 935–8 (1988).

18. Department of Health and Welsh Office, *op. cit.*, p. 13.

19. M. J. W. van de Laar *et al.*, 'Declining gonorrhoea rates in the Netherlands, 1976–88: consequences for the AIDS epidemic', *Genitourinary Medicine*, 66: 148–55 (1990).

20. See, for example, D. R. Tomlinson *et al.*, 'Does rectal gonorrhoea reflect unsafe sex?' (letter), *The Lancet*, 337: 501–2 (1991); P. D. French *et al.*, 'Preventing the spread of HIV infection' (letter), *BMJ*, 302: 962–3 (1991).

21. Such strategies are discussed in detail in Chapter 4.

22. However, people with HIV are usually advised to practise safer sex in order to avoid infection with other STDs or reinfection with HIV. It is hypothesized that either of these may accelerate HIV disease progression.

23. Data on this cohort are taken from Stevens, *op. cit.*

24. Data on this cohort are taken from James W. Curran *et al.*, 'The epidemiology of AIDS: current status and future prospects', *Science*, 229: 1352–7 (1985); Harold W. Jaffe *et al.*, 'The acquired immune deficiency syndrome in a cohort of homosexual men: a six year follow-up study', *Ann. Int. Med.*, 103: 210–14 (1985); CDC,

'Update: acquired immunodeficiency syndrome in the San Francisco cohort study, 1978–1985', *MMWR*, **34**: 573–5 (1985); Francis J. Bowden *et al.*, 'AIDS prediction and intervention' (letter), *The Lancet*, i: 852–3 (1986); Hessol, *op. cit.* Studies of the natural history of AIDS and of gay men's behaviour changes, based on this cohort, took place from 1983 onwards.

25. Data on this cohort are taken from Warren Winkelstein Jr. *et al.*, 'Sexual practices and risk of infection by the human immunodeficiency virus', *JAMA*, **257**(3): 321–5 (1987); Warren Winkelstein Jr. *et al.*, 'Selected sexual practices of San Francisco heterosexual men and risk of infection by the human immunodeficiency virus' (letter), *JAMA*, **257**(11): 1470–1 (1987); Warren Winkelstein Jr. *et al.*, 'The San Francisco Men's Health Study: III. Reduction in human immunodeficiency virus transmission among homosexual/bisexual men, 1982–86', *AJPH*, **76**(9): 685–9 (1987); Warren Winkelstein Jr. *et al.*, 'The San Francisco Men's Health Study: continued decline in HIV seroconversion rates among homosexual/bisexual men', *AJPH*, **78**(11): 1472–4 (1988); Maria L. Ekstrand *et al.*, 'Maintenance of safer sexual behaviors and predictors of risky sex: the San Francisco Men's Health Study', *AJPH*, **80**(9): 973–7 (1990).

26. Winkelstein, 'The San Francisco Men's Health Study: III'.

27. Andrew R. Moss *et al.*, 'Seropositivity for HIV and the development of AIDS or AIDS related condition: three year follow up of the San Francisco General Hospital cohort', *BMJ*, **296**(6624): 745–50 (1988).

28. Winkelstein, 'Selected sexual practices'.

29. Winkelstein, 'The San Francisco Men's Health Study: continued decline in HIV seroconversion rates'.

30. Leon McKusick *et al.*, 'AIDS and sexual behavior reported by gay men in San Francisco', *AJPH*, **75**(5): 493–6 (1985); Leon McKusick *et al.*, 'Reported changes in the sexual behavior of men at risk for AIDS, San Francisco, 1982–4 – the AIDS Behavioral Research Project', *Public Health Reports*, **100**(6): 622–9 (1985); Leon McKusick *et al.*, 'Longitudinal predictors of reductions in unprotected anal intercourse among gay men in San Francisco: the AIDS Behavioral Research Project', *AJPH*, **80**(8): 978–83 (1990).

31. McKusick, 'AIDS and sexual behavior'.

32. CDC, 'Self-reported behavioral changes among homosexual and bisexual men – San Francisco', *JAMA*, **254**(18): 2537–8 (1985).

33. Michael Callen, 'Your country needs you!', *QW* magazine, New York, 14 June 1992.

34. Stevens, *op. cit.*

35. James J. Goedert *et al.*, 'Determinants of retrovirus (HTLV-III) antibody and immunodeficiency conditions in homosexual men', *The Lancet*, ii: 711–16 (1984).

36. John L. Martin, 'The impact of AIDS on gay male sexual behavior patterns in New York City', *AJPH*, 77(5): 578–81 (1987).

37. See Chapter 2.

38. John L. Martin, 'AIDS risk reduction recommendations and sexual behavior patterns among gay men: a multifactorial categorical approach to assessing change', *Health Education Quarterly*, 13(4): 347–58 (1986).

39. John L. Martin *et al.*, 'The impact of AIDS on a gay community: changes in sexual behavior, substance use, and mental health', *American Journal of Community Psychology*, 17(3): 269–93 (1989).

40. See Kaslow, *op. cit.*

41. Lawrence A. Kingsley *et al.*, 'Temporal trends in human immunodeficiency virus type 1 seroconversion 1984–1989', *Am. J. Epidem.*, 134(4): 331–9 (1991).

42. Roger Detels *et al.*, 'Seroconversion, sexual activity, and condom use among 2915 HIV seronegative men followed for up to 2 years', *J. AIDS*, 2(1): 77–83 (1989).

43. Robin Fox *et al.*, 'Effect of HIV antibody disclosure on subsequent sexual activity in homosexual men', *AIDS*, 1(4): 241–6 (1987).

44. William Booth, 'CDC paints a picture of HIV infection in U.S.', *Science*, 15 January 1988, p. 253.

45. CDC, 'Declining rates of rectal and pharyngeal gonorrhoea among males – New York City', *JAMA*, 252: 327 and 331 (1984).

46. Reported in Dan Alan Hirsch and Roger W. Enlow, 'The effects of the acquired immune deficiency syndrome on gay lifestyle and the gay individual' (paper delivered at conference in November 1983), *Annals of the New York Academy of Sciences*, 437: 273–82 (1984).

47. CDC, 'Human immunodeficiency virus infection in the United States: a review of current knowledge', *MMWR*, 36, Supplement p. S-6 (1987).

48. James W. Curran *et al.*, 'The epidemiology of AIDS: current status and future prospects', *Science*, 229: 1352–7 (1985).

49. Daniel C. William, 'The prevention of AIDS by modifying sexual behavior' (paper delivered at conference in November 1983), *Annals of the New York Academy of Sciences*, 437: 283–5 (1984). The Denver gonorrhoea statistics are given in Franklyn N. Judson, 'Fear of AIDS and gonorrhoea rates in homosexual men' (letter), *The Lancet*, ii: 159–60 (1983). The Madison figures are in R. Golubjatnikov *et al.*, 'Homosexual promiscuity and the fear of AIDS' (letter), *The Lancet*, ii: 681 (1983).

50. Reported in Hirsch and Enlow, *op. cit.*

51. Franklyn N. Judson, 'Fear of AIDS and incidences of gonorrhea, syphilis, and hepatitis B, 1982–1990', *VII International Conference on AIDS*, Florence, abstract W.C.3030 (1991).

52. C. A. Emmons *et al.*, 'Psychosocial predictors of reported behavior patterns among gay men: a multifactorial approach to assessing change', *Health Education Quarterly*, **13**: 347–58 (1986); J. G. Joseph *et al.*, 'Magnitude and determinants of behavioral risk reduction: longitudinal analysis of a cohort at risk for AIDS', *Psychology and Health*, **1**: 73–96 (1987).

53. J. Phair, unpublished data cited in Clifton C. Jones *et al.*, 'Persistence of high-risk sexual activity among homosexual men in an area of low incidence of the acquired immunodeficiency syndrome', *Sexually Transmitted Diseases*, **14**(2): 79–82 (1987).

54. Jones, *op. cit.*

55. Leonard H. Calabrese *et al.*, 'Persistence of high risk sexual activity among homosexual men in an area of low incidence for acquired immunodeficiency syndrome', *AIDS Research*, **2**(4): 357–61 (1986).

56. Mortimer, *op. cit.*

57. C. A. Carne *et al.*, 'Rising prevalence of human T-lymphotropic virus type III (HTLV-III) infection in homosexual men in London', *The Lancet*, i: 1261–2 (1985); C. A. Carne *et al.*, 'Prevalence of antibodies to human immunodeficiency virus, gonorrhoea rates, and changed sexual behaviour in homosexual men in London', *The Lancet*, i: 656–8 (1987); C. Loveday *et al.*, 'Human immunodeficiency viruses in patients attending a sexually transmitted disease clinic in London, 1982–7', *BMJ*, **298**: 419–22 (1989).

58. J. N. Weber *et al.*, 'Three-year prospective study of HTLV-III/LAV infection in homosexual men', *The Lancet*, i: 1179–82 (1986).

59. R. Cheinseng-Popov *et al.*, 'Prevalence of antibody to human T-lymphotropic virus type III in AIDS and AIDS-risk patients in Britain', *The Lancet*, ii: 477–80 (1984).

60. Collaborative Study Group, 'HIV infection in patients attending clinics for sexually transmitted diseases in England and Wales', *BMJ*, **298**: 415–18 (1989).

61. PHLS, 'Prevalence of HIV antibody in high and low risk groups in England', *BMJ*, **298**: 422–3 (1989).

62. Carne, 'Heterosexual transmission'.

63. Andrew J. Hunt *et al.*, 'Seroprevalence of HIV-1 infection in a cohort of homosexually active men', *Genitourinary Medicine*, **66**: 423–7 (1990).

64. Department of Health and Welsh Office, *op. cit.*

65. Public Health Laboratory Service AIDS Centre *et al.*, 'Unlinked anonymous monitoring of HIV prevalence in England and Wales: 1990–92', *Communicable Disease Report*, **3**(1): R1–R11 (1993).

66. Carne, 'Prevalence of antibodies'.

67. S. W. Burton *et al.*, 'AIDS information' (letter), *The Lancet*, ii: 1040–1 (1986).

68. Peter M. Davies *et al.*, *Longitudinal Study of the Sexual Behaviour*

of Homosexual Males under the Impact of AIDS. Final Report Submitted to the Department of Health. Project SIGMA, London, 1990.

69.   Peter Weatherburn *et al., The Sexual Lifestyles of Gay and Bisexual Men in England and Wales.* HMSO, London, 1992.

70.   Peter Davies, 'Safer sex – still a long way to go', *Capital Gay*, 28 April 1989.

71.   S. Golombok *et al.,* 'Condom use among homosexual men', *AIDS Care*, 1(1): 27–33 (1989).

72.   Ray Fitzpatrick *et al.,* 'Factors influencing condom use in a sample of homosexually active men', *Genitourinary Medicine*, 66: 346–50 (1990).

73.   C. Thompson *et al.,* 'Trends in sexual behaviour and HIV incidence in homosexual men' (letter), *BMJ*, 298: 673 (1989).

74.   I. V. D. Weller *et al.,* 'Gonorrhoea in homosexual men and media coverage of the acquired immune deficiency syndrome in London 1982–3', *BMJ*, 289: 1041 (1984).

75.   Carne, 'Prevalence of antibodies'; Loveday, *op. cit.*

76.   M. C. A. Gellan *et al.,* 'Declining incidence of gonorrhoea in London: a response to the fear of AIDS?' (letter), *The Lancet*, ii(8512): 920 (1986).

77.   J. K. Oates *et al.,* 'Well done, gay men!' (letter), *Capital Gay*, 29 November 1985.

78.   A. G. Lawrence *et al.,* 'Changes in sexual behaviour and incidence of gonorrhoea', *The Lancet*, i: 982–3 (1987).

79.   Chief Medical Officer, *On the State of the Public Health. The Annual Report of the Chief Medical Officer of the Department of Health and Social Security.* HMSO, London, 1987, cited in A. M. Johnson *et al.,* 'Appendix 5. Evidence for recent changes in sexual behaviour in homosexual men in England and Wales', in Department of Health and Welsh Office, *op. cit.*, pp. 56–7.

80.   S. Polakoff, 'Acute viral hepatitis B: laboratory reports 1980–1984', *BMJ*, 293: 37–8 (1986); S. Polakoff, 'Decrease in acute hepatitis B incidence continued in 1987', *The Lancet*, i: 540 (1988).

81.   Johnson, *op. cit.*

82.   Project SIGMA, *Update*, p. 6, March 1992.

Chapter two

Changing Behaviour

One headline you won't see in the mass media:
'Safer sex works; gay men prove it.'
● *Canadian AIDS Society*[1]

IT is clear that during the 1980s, gay men modified their
sexual behaviour in response to the emergence of AIDS, and that
these modifications had a dramatic effect on rates of transmission
of HIV. Although in the gay centres of America seroprevalence had
already reached high levels before the existence of HIV was even
suspected, in subsequent years new infections were markedly
reduced, and in countries where HIV had not yet established itself
to the same extent, the worst-case scenarios were successfully
averted. The key element in this successful response is evident: gay
men reduced their practice of unprotected anal sex, the practice
which epidemiological studies quickly showed to be implicated in
nearly all cases of HIV transmission between gay men.

The cause or causes of this reduction in unsafe sex have
never been fully analysed; indeed, so many factors appear to have
been at work that it is impossible to single out just one. However,
there has also been a lamentable failure to research and attempt to
understand what have been described as 'the most profound behavior changes ever observed in the literature on health behavior
change'.[2] British AIDS educator Simon Watney has noted that:

> one of the oddest and most tragic aspects of this epidemic is
> the feeling that nothing can be learned from the gay com-
> munity ... I think this is madness. If you have a demon-

strably effective model for cutting down on transmission, why isn't it imitated? Why are we the last people ever to be consulted in any government-run safer sex campaigns?[3]

It might be the case that the strategies that worked for gay men in the 1980s may be inappropriate for other social constituencies, and may no longer be effective even for gay men in the second decade of the epidemic. However, in the absence of any other strategy for producing sexual behaviour change which has an even remotely comparable record of success, it is folly to ignore these lessons from the past.

This chapter first reviews the three specific behavioural changes most commonly advocated by HIV prevention campaigns for gay men – reducing the number of sexual partners, reducing the practice of anal sex and using condoms for anal sex – and concludes that their relative impact on transmission rates varied significantly. It then examines how risk reduction advice was defined, and discusses both accurate and mistaken views about how the behaviour modifications were achieved in practice.

Reduction in numbers of partners

In late 1981, the US Centers for Disease Control began a case-control study in an attempt to identify the behaviours involved in the epidemic. Of the living people with AIDS, 75 per cent were interviewed, and their answers to 62 questions covering all aspects of their lives were compared with those of heterosexuals and other gay men who did not have AIDS. Only one substantial difference was found: the men with AIDS tended to have had twice as many sexual partners as the controls, and their partners were also more likely to have been highly sexually active.[4] In addition to establishing that AIDS was probably caused by a sexually transmitted agent, this study initiated one of the most significant phenomena in the early years of the epidemic – the focus on the number of sexual partners.

The importance of promiscuity in the spread of sexually transmitted diseases is well established: in low prevalence situations, the number of sexual partners is the most significant determinant of the risk of infection. The kind of sex which is practised is, of course, also significant; the effect of having many partners is to increase the risk of exposure to an infected person, but not to increase the risk of transmission during that individual sexual contact. Most gay men in cohort studies have reported that they practised unprotected anal sex during the late 1970s and early 1980s, simply because there was no obvious reason why they should not.[5] When HIV first entered the gay communities of San Francisco and Los Angeles, the more sexually active men were at greater risk than those with fewer partners, because the virus was still relatively uncommon.

However, the significance of the number of one's sexual partners rapidly diminished. By 1984, a number of surveys of apparently healthy gay men found no clear-cut association between HIV seropositivity and the total reported number of sexual partners.[6] Once HIV prevalence has reached a certain level in a population, anyone having unsafe sex faces a significant risk of becoming infected with HIV, regardless of their number of partners. One statistician illustrated this phenomenon thus:

> Consider, for example, an early stage of the epidemic, when the prevalence of infectious carriers is 2% of a given population. If one person selects two partners from that population and another selects 30, the first would be less than one-tenth as likely to encounter the virus: his probability is 4%, compared with 44%. But if, at a later time, the prevalence has increased to 40%, the first individual has a risk almost two-thirds that of the second: 64% compared with nearly 100%. In such a setting, reducing one's number of new sexual partners to any number greater than zero may be insufficient to substantially reduce the risk of infection in the long run. This appears to be the situation currently facing the homosexual population.[7]

In practice, this means that 'to isolate "promiscuity" as the most important risk factor would be an inadequate approach ... Once prevalence is relatively high, even a 10-fold reduction in the cumulative number of partners, everything else being equal, would not clearly reduce the cumulative risk of infection.'[8] For example, in 1987 researchers on the Multicenter AIDS Cohort Study estimated that urban gay men who had unprotected receptive anal sex with only 1 partner in the course of a year were 300 per cent more likely to become infected with HIV than those who consistently practised safer sex; engaging in unsafe sex with only 5 partners a year resulted in an 18-fold increase in the likelihood of seroconversion.[9] Thus, adopting consistent safer sex practices is the most important preventive measure once the epidemic is firmly established.

Unfortunately, this important distinction between the number of sexual partners and the kind of sex practised with those partners was rarely made in early epidemiological studies. This can make them very hard to interpret. For example, many studies observed that, as described in a review of HIV infection among a cohort of gay men in the Netherlands, 'seropositive men had more sexual partners than did seronegative men, during their entire life, the previous five years, and the previous six months'. But relatively few looked any deeper, when they might have discovered that, as in this instance:

> a positive relation was found between the number of partners with whom anal receptive sexual techniques were performed and the presence of anti-HIV, whereas the number with whom masturbation was performed was shown to be related to the *absence* of anti-HIV ... This leads to the conclusion that it is not the number of partners in general which is a risk factor for HIV infection, but that it is essential to distinguish between the performed sexual techniques.[10]

In terms of its impact on HIV transmission rates among gay men, the importance of reductions in the number of partners must therefore depend on the prevalence of HIV among gay men at the time. In other words, this strategy when viewed alone may have made a significant contribution to preventing HIV transmission among gay men *in areas of low prevalence*, but is likely to have had little effect in areas of rapidly increasing or already high seroprevalence.

In the United States, partner reductions appear to have been the most widespread and the most substantial behaviour change among American gay men during the early years, yet it seems unlikely that it had much effect on the course of the epidemic there. Reporting the results of a study of behaviour changes between November 1982 and May 1984, a group of San Francisco researchers reported that:

> Overall reductions in the frequency of sexual activity, including the number of times gay couples have sex, suggest that gay men are inhibiting their sexual activity in all contacts rather than simply shifting from specific unsafe acts to 'safe sex' acts.[11]

In a sample of New York gay men, 64 per cent reported that they had had more than 20 partners per 6 months in the years before AIDS; by 1984 less than 20 per cent still had as many partners, but 46 per cent were still having anal sex, and condom use was reported to be 'infrequent'.[12] Gay men in Denver were found to have had a 40 per cent to 50 per cent decrease in their number of partners for each of the three years between 1983 and 1985, while only a relatively low 41 per cent said that they had 'changed their type of sex'.[13] Among 305 gay men interviewed in Ohio, 'an area of relatively low incidence for AIDS and low seroprevalence for [HIV]', in autumn 1985, 83 per cent said that they had intentionally limited their number of sexual partners over the preceding two years, yet 45 per cent were still practising passive anal sex without a condom, and only 26 per cent had stopped having unsafe sex because of AIDS.[14] In all these cases, but particularly in the high incidence cities of New York and San Francisco, it is most unlikely that partner reductions, in the absence of the adoption of safer sex practices, made a significant contribution to slowing the spread of HIV.

In Britain, the behaviour changes of the early 1980s also consisted predominantly of reductions in the number of sexual partners, including the selective avoidance of sex with people considered particularly likely to be infected. In early 1985 there was a vigorous debate in the letters page of the *Capital Gay* newspaper over the Terrence Higgins Trust's allegedly 'racist' advice that gay men should avoid sex with men who had been sexually active in North America during the previous three years. A similar distinction was made within the UK, with the Oxford Gay Group warning its members to avoid sex with Londoners.[15]

A survey of 326 men in central London gay pubs and clubs in 1986 found that 48 per cent reported that they had reduced their number of partners, although about a quarter of the sample was still practising unsafe anal sex. However, condom use was most common among men with multiple sexual partners, suggesting that many of the men continuing to have unprotected sex may have been in relationships.[16] In another study, 100 men were reported to have reduced their monthly average number of partners from 3 to 1 between 1984/85 and 1986. Anal sex also became less common, but increases in condom use were not statistically significant, with no more than 25 per cent always using condoms during active or passive anal sex. The researchers suggested that these findings, viewed alongside the low annual rate of increase in HIV prevalence between 1984 and 1986, 'support the view that behaviour change has occurred at an earlier stage of the epidemic than in the USA and may thus have prevented the continued rapid rise in HIV prevalence seen there'.[17]

In summary, then, the risk reduction strategy of limiting the number of one's sexual partners was, in isolation, unlikely to have had a substantial impact on the development of the epidemic in the United States. So many gay men were infected with HIV before the existence of the virus was even suspected that a gay man who continued to have unprotected anal sex with even a relatively small number of partners still faced a high probability of encountering an infected partner. However, in areas of lower prevalence such as Britain in the mid-1980s, having had unprotected anal sex with fewer sexual partners is likely to have had a genuinely significant impact on the risk of infection.

Reduction in anal sex and uptake of condoms

By March 1983 it was established that 'the distribution of AIDS cases parallels that of hepatitis B infection, which is transmitted sexually and parenterally';[18] in practical terms, this meant that contact with body fluids presented a risk of infection.[19] Stopping anal sex or using condoms could reasonably be assumed to reduce that risk substantially.[20]

As mentioned above, it appears to have been more usual for men to stop anal sex altogether, rather than to continue fucking but start to use condoms. It is notable that a number of the earliest papers in the medical literature describing gay men's behaviour modifications in response to AIDS observe that use of condoms was too infrequent among study members to allow an assessment of their effectiveness as a barrier against HIV.[21] In some instances, this may have been a response to safer sex campaigns which presented condoms only as a last resort for those who were determined to carry on practising anal sex.[22]

This is not to say that condom use did not become more frequent. A sample of gay men in New York were asked retrospectively about changes in their sexual behaviour during the year after they first heard about AIDS, which on average was in July 1981. When the median number of episodes of anal sex involving condoms was calculated, the figure was zero, as over 50 per cent of the group did not use a condom. However:

> a different picture emerges by calculating the per cent of anal intercourse episodes during which condoms were used. In the pre-AIDS year, condoms were used an average of 1 per cent of the time respondents engaged in insertive anal intercourse and 2 per cent of the time they engaged in receptive anal intercourse. In contrast, during the post-AIDS year condoms were used an average of 20 per cent of the time respondents engaged in insertive anal intercourse and 19 per cent of the time they engaged in receptive anal intercourse.[23]

While this still means that condom use was so low, and HIV prevalence already so high, that it may not have had a significant impact on the course of the epidemic, this example is a useful reminder of the ways in which different methodological approaches may lead to significantly different conclusions.

When assessing condom use, the important factor is the proportion of occasions of anal sex in which they were used. Other measures, such as the total number of men who used condoms, will be less revealing unless they take account of considerations such as changes in the overall number of men practising anal sex, whether with condoms or not. Thus, among 361 gay men in a Vancouver cohort study, condom use increased markedly in 1986/87 compared with 1984/85. Men were defined as 'usually' using condoms if they utilized protection in more than 60 per cent of the occasions in which they had receptive anal sex. In 1984/85 only 4 men usually used condoms, but by two years later nearly 40 per cent usually used condoms if they had passive anal sex with a regular partner, and over two-thirds did so with casual partners. At the same time, the proportion of the sample who had any anal sex fell somewhat, from 75 per cent in 1984/85 to 63 per cent in 1986/87.[24] (This study showed significant differences in sexual behaviour modification between seropositive and seronegative men, and in sex with regular partners as compared with casual partners. These factors are discussed in detail later in this chapter.)

Very similar data were reported from the Multicenter AIDS Cohort Study in a paper analysing safer sex practices among 2915 uninfected men over an 18-month period from 1985. The number using condoms with all their partners rose from 72 (3 per cent) to 427 (28 per cent) of those who practised anal sex. At the same time, the number of men who had anal sex fell from 2338 to 1547. During the study period, 232 men – 8 per cent of the sample – became infected with HIV, indicating that this incomplete adoption of safer sex had reduced, but by no means stopped, transmission of the virus. Of those who seroconverted, 97 per cent did not use condoms with all their partners in anal sex; however, 7 men who reported consistent use of condoms also became infected, perhaps 'due to condom failure, improper usage, occasional nonuse, errors in recall, or other types of sexual activity'.[25]

In the UK, Project SIGMA has provided substantial and important data on penetrative sex and condom use. The average annual number of sexual partners since each cohort member became sexually active was compared with the average annual number during the previous five years alone, and the reported number during the last year; the hypothesis being that the effects of safer sex education since 1983 would be apparent in a decline in the reported total number of partners during the last year, as well as during the whole of the previous five years. This did indeed appear to be the case: the number of partners per year fell from a lifetime mean of 14.1 to 10.5 during the past five years. A similar reduction occurred in the number of partners with whom anal sex took place, from a lifetime mean of 3.7 per year to 2.4 during the last five years. The decline in numbers of partners was most pronounced among men from London.

The data also suggested that the proportion of men engaging in anal sex had increased slightly during the previous year, and this trend was confirmed by follow-up in 1989,[26] 1990 and 1991.[27] Unfortunately in the 1989 report the researchers defined unsafe sex as 'anal intercourse with or without condom', and it is therefore not reported whether there was an increase in condom use in line with that in anal sex. Data from the 1990 interviews revealed that:

> only half always use condoms for fucking or being fucked. There is a clear difference in condom use depending on what sort of relationship is had with the other partner. With the regular partner more never used a condom than always did … With casual partners condoms were always used by just under two-thirds and never by a seventh.[28]

Of the cohort members, 661, or 71.1 per cent, had used a condom during sexual activity at least once by 1988. While a tiny proportion had first used condoms during the 1970s, 'condom use took off rapidly from 1984, with the peak year for new first time users being in 1986'.[29] In the month preceding their initial interview by researchers in 1987/88, 29 per cent of the whole sample had practised active anal sex, of whom nearly 40 per cent always used a condom and nearly 50 per cent never used one. During the previous month, 27 per cent had practised receptive anal sex, of whom 42.5 per cent always used a condom and over 45 per cent never used one.

Again, the type of relationship between the partners was very important: for insertive anal sex condoms were always used with regular partners by nearly 35 per cent of respondents, compared with 78 per cent who always used a condom with casual partners. For receptive anal sex, the proportions were 36 per cent and 70.5 per cent respectively. This has very significant implications; the researchers pointed out that:

> If receptive anal intercourse without a condom is regarded as a gross measure of the magnitude of unsafe sexual behaviour then, in this cohort, 14.4% (134) of the whole sample risked HIV infection in the month prior to interview. Conversely, if receptive anal intercourse with a casual sexual partner, without a condom, is considered an adequate measure of unsafe sexual behaviour then only 1.8% (17) of the whole sample risked HIV infection in the preceding month.[30]

Project SIGMA reiterated that '[t]he most significant factor associated with testing positive is the number of partners fucked with', rather than the number of sexual partners regardless of the type of sex practised.[31] Given that condom use for anal sex remained 'far from universal', this correlation is unsurprising, and reducing the number of penetrative sexual partners is likely to have had a significant protective effect.

The Netherlands provides a case-study of a country in which gay men were actively discouraged from using condoms for anal sex, in favour of giving up fucking altogether. Researchers on two Amsterdam cohort studies calculated that the mean number of partners with whom uninfected men had passive anal sex and with whom HIV-positive men had active anal sex fell drastically from 1984/85; however, the number of partners with whom condoms were used 'remained more or less stable'. HIV transmission rates fell from 1984, and reached zero in 1987, coinciding with these behaviour changes.[32] It seems clear that in Holland, use of condoms played at most a small role in stopping the spread of HIV among gay men.

This discussion has examined individual strategies such as reducing the number of partners, reducing or avoiding anal sex, or using condoms for anal sex. In practice, however, many gay men used combinations of these approaches, some adopting monogamy but having unprotected anal sex with their partner, others having many partners but little anal sex, others reducing their number of partners and using condoms inconsistently, and so on. The relative value of such complex strategies is virtually impossible to assess; however, it has been suggested that combinations of these different approaches can result in a greater overall reduction in the risk of HIV transmission than would be predicted from their individual effects.[33]

Defining safer sex

The earliest safer sex advice for gay men was published in 1982. In this year, Bay Area Physicians for Human Rights, a group of lesbian and gay doctors, published a leaflet on *Kaposi's Sarcoma in Gay Men*,[34] Houston's Citizens for Human Equality produced *Towards a Healthier Gay Lifestyle: Kaposi's Sarcoma, Opportunistic Infections and the Urban Gay Lifestyle, What You Need to Know to Ensure Your Good Health*,[35] and the fledgling Gay Men's Health Crisis (GMHC) in New York published their first *Newsletter*, discussed below, and distributed a quarter of a million copies of their *Health Recommendation Brochure* to local gay bars in November and December 1982.[36] In 1983 these were joined by further publications from GMHC, a booklet by the Harvey Milk Gay Democratic Club of San Francisco entitled *Can We Talk?*,[37] and Richard Berkowitz and Michael Callen's 40-page booklet, *How to Have Sex in an Epidemic: One Approach*.[38]

With the notable exception of the last publication, these materials did not speculate on the relative safety of specific sex acts, but instead recommended three main types of behaviour modification: reducing the number of different sexual partners; eliminating the exchange of body fluids during sex; and 'knowing your partners' by avoiding places characterized by sexual anonymity, such as bathhouses.[39] These engendered some controversy, which even spilled over into the materials themselves. For example, the first GMHC newsletter, published in July 1982, reported a range of opinions on risk reduction, the most directive of which said 'A number of physicians, many of them gay as well, have advised their gay patients to moderate their sexual activity, to have fewer partners, and to have partners who are in good health. It is the *number* of sexual partners, not sex itself, that increases risk'; however, other 'contributions to the same newsletter questioned the seriousness of the epidemic, which at that time had affected only 278 men, thus effectively undermining even that advice.[40] The first Public Health Service guidelines for gay men, issued in March 1983, amounted to two sentences advising that 'Sexual contact should be avoided with persons known or suspected to have AIDS. Members of high-risk groups should be aware that multiple sexual partners increase the probability of developing AIDS.' These recommendations were published in *Morbidity and Mortality Weekly Reports*, and were thus unlikely to come to the attention of all but a handful of gay men anyway.[41]

It was *How to Have Sex in an Epidemic: One Approach* which pioneered the approach to safer sex which we recognize today. It was virtually the only safer sex publication which proposed a specific theory of what caused AIDS, on which its advice about specific sex acts was based. Berkovitz and Callen were patients of Dr Joseph Sonnabend, a New York physician with a general practice consisting largely of gay men, and their booklet reflected his judgement that AIDS was caused by repeated exposure to semen containing CMV, a herpes virus which is relatively common among gay men. Sonnabend's multifactorial theory also posited that 'foreign' sperm itself was immunosuppressive. The authors recognized that 'if a new, as-yet-unidentified virus is responsible for AIDS, the measures proposed to prevent CMV transmission are likely to be effective in preventing the spread of any such virus', and indeed, the behaviour changes suggested in *How to Have Sex in an Epidemic: One Approach*, such as the use of condoms for anal sex, would also have prevented HIV transmission.[42] Other gay men and doctors also came to the conclusion that it should be possible to deduce strategies to prevent disease transmission; a doctor at London's Middlesex Hospital who was trying to offer helpful advice to gay men in 1983–84 has described how:

> One had to do something. There was no evidence that a sheath would help prevent the transmission of the virus but sheaths had had a significant effect on other infections and the abandonment of barrier methods of contraception had played a part in the increases in, for example, *Chlamydia trachomatis*, papillomavirus and herpes simplex virus infection. It was reasonable to assume, therefore, that, whilst a sheath might not always work, it would impede the spread of AIDS.[43]

By deducing a means by which gay men could continue to 'have sex in an epidemic' but take rational precautions to make that sex safer, *How to Have Sex in an Epidemic* provided the model for safer sex campaigns for gay men ever since. As it made clear, '[t]he key to this approach is modifying what you do – not how often you do it nor with how many partners'.[44] Gradually, the unhelpful advice to reduce the number of one's partners or to limit sex to people one knew all but died out, to be replaced by increasingly sex-positive prevention campaigns focused on specific sex acts. In a 1986 review of gay safer sex materials, in which 22 different publications from around the USA (probably representing the vast majority of such publications) were collected, no fewer than 19 explained the specific unsafe practices to avoid, as opposed to merely making vague statements about avoiding the exchange of body fluids.[45]

Berkowitz and Callen's booklet was absolutely explicit in distinguishing between the risk of disease transmission through gay sex, and the act of sex itself: 'Sex doesn't make you sick – diseases do'.[46] In this, it was among the first responses to AIDS which acknowledged the importance of maintaining and building gay esteem, not for purely 'gay-political' reasons, but as a fundamental part of successful safer sex education. As the developers of GMHC's safer sex workshops argue:

People who devalue themselves on the basis of being homosexual are more likely to devalue their homosexual sexual
partners as well. The premise of any safer-sex act is a wish
that [HIV] not be transmitted. Should a person be filled with
self-hate, he would be less likely to be concerned about his
own safety. Indeed, such self-loathing may be the motivation
for self-destructive behaviour. Additionally, if this self-
hatred is directed at his homosexuality, he might wilfully act
out this feeling in sexual recklessness, which could both
expose himself to the virus and also transmit the virus to his
partner, the other person involved in this hated homosexual
act.[47]

At least to this extent, promoting gay self-esteem is itself a form of
safer sex education.

In Britain, the evolution of safer sex advice was a somewhat
haphazard affair. In 1981–82, AIDS was still a predominantly
American disease, and British activists seemed unclear what they
could do other than to increase awareness of the existence of a new
health problem. As discussed earlier, crude strategies such as avoiding sex with Americans or Londoners and reducing the overall
number of sexual partners were common in the early 1980s. The
development of specific safer sex guidelines in the United States was
also highly influential. While care services came to be based on the
model of community care services most notably pioneered in San
Francisco on the West Coast, British safer sex activists in groups
such as London Gay Switchboard and the Terrence Higgins Trust
had stronger links with GMHC and East Coast activities. The
Trust's first major educational initiative was the reprinting and
distribution of a GMHC leaflet in late 1983,[48] and the subsequent
home-grown materials and interventions were very much based on
American risk-reduction models. By the late 1980s HIV prevention
advice had largely rejected messages about numbers of partners,
not least because there was little reliable epidemiological data on
seroprevalence, and because of the danger that reducing one's sexual contacts could be seen as an *alternative* to using condoms
consistently for anal sex.

The impact of factual information

Many of the earliest leaflets, posters and advertisements targeting AIDS education messages to gay men concentrated on communicating the latest medical knowledge about the specific ways in which the disease (or, more precisely, HIV) was transmitted during gay sex. For example, the 1986 review of American safer sex materials mentioned above found that 'the large majority of pamphlets provide very specific information concerning what practices should be avoided'; indeed, this review concluded that most leaflets contained only factual information, rather than more sophisticated reasoning in favour of adopting safer sex, with the result that the sole aim of the materials appeared to be to 'enhance knowledge about risk factors for AIDS and modes of transmission of the viral agent'.[49] By 1986, 95 per cent of a sample of over 300 men in London's gay pubs and clubs reported that they had received such safer sex information.[50] What is less clear is the importance of written factual information in bringing about behaviour change.

One of the several possible explanations of the mechanisms by which individuals change to safer sex suggests that they first become *aware* of information about HIV/AIDS, then develop *beliefs* about the accuracy of the information and, accordingly, positive or negative *attitudes* towards safer sex.[51] However, the data from research studies are contradictory. Cohen reported that:

> Some empirical studies begun in the peak or declining stages of the epidemic found a relationship between amount of information and change to safer sex. Many others, particularly those done later in the epidemic, found no relationships between the amount of information and safer sex.[52]

But this does not necessarily mean that such a link does not exist:

> One plausible reason for finding few relationships between information and AIDS is that by the time empirical studies

were fielded, basic information about AIDS had saturated the middle-class highly educated gay communities in which most of these studies were being conducted.[53]

In other words, straightforward factual information about both safer sex and unsafe sex is likely to have had the greatest impact during the earlier years of the epidemic. It is also likely to be particularly important for those just beginning their sexual careers and developing their sexual identities. Accurate information is clearly the prerequisite for well-informed decisions about sexual practice. However, its impact on an individual who is hostile to or distrustful of the information will inevitably be minimal. In this respect it was surely of critical importance that the providers of safer sex information in the earliest years were gay groups, AIDS organizations that were perceived as being genuinely a part of the gay community, institutions such as gay publications and other gay men encountered socially.

Accurate and specific information may be the prerequisite for behaviour change, but further elements may be needed both to help those who practise risky behaviours to change those behaviours, and to help those who practise only safe behaviours to continue behaving that way.[54] In other words, individuals must be motivated to adopt and sustain safer sex. Research suggests that a critical factor which can provide that motivation is the individual's perception of attitudinal and behavioural norms within his own social circle, or, to put it more generally, community values.

The importance of peer norms

As Simon Watney has observed: 'Since the earliest years of the epidemic, safer sex education among gay men has been most successful when rooted in the recognition that HIV is a community issue, requiring a community-based response.'[55] This does not mean simply that the individuals and groups best placed to undertake safer sex education for gay men were themselves gay. It also reflects that fact that some aspect of *gay* identity, as opposed to homosexual desire *per se*, leads gay men to feel that on varying levels they share interests, beliefs and values with other gay men.

This concept of group norms appears to have functioned as an important mechanism by which safer sex came to be perceived as an integral part of what it meant to be gay in the 1980s.

A number of studies have shown that there is a clear link between gay men's opinions of how their partners and peers view safer sex, and their own sexual behaviour. This is not particularly surprising: many people derive their sense of what is appropriate or inappropriate behaviour from the words and actions of their partners and friends, and take their lead from influential individuals.[56] Research on other health issues, such as stopping smoking or undertaking physical training after a heart attack, has shown that 'individuals with strong social ties are more likely to alter health-threatening behaviors than those with weaker social connections to others', and that 'it is not only the presence of a social network, but behavior and values within the network, which influence health behaviors'.[57]

In 1984 the San Francisco AIDS Foundation, funded by the San Francisco Department of Public Health, commissioned a market research firm to conduct a telephone survey of 500 gay or bisexual men to inform the planning of an educational campaign. Among its conclusions, this initial survey recommended that the campaign 'should emphasize the social acceptability of safe sex' rather than highlighting 'only the risks of unsafe practices'.[58] The result was a message disseminated through public forums, advertisements in the gay press and an AIDS helpline which stressed the efficacy of safer sex and the view that 'safer sex has become a legitimate social norm', claiming that most gay men in San Francisco had changed their sexual behaviour in response to HIV.[59] In follow-up interviews with 301 of the initial sample of men, a decline in unsafe sex with casual partners correlated with acceptance of the concepts of 'safe sex efficacy' and 'safe sex legitimacy', suggesting that this early attempt to manipulate community norms may have been effective.[60]

Relatively little research investigating the effect of gay social networks and gay social norms on sexual behaviour has been published. Some of the most revealing information on the importance of community identification in the adoption of safer sex has come from the Australian Social Aspects of the Prevention of AIDS (SAPA) project, a joint research initiative between the community-based AIDS Council of New South Wales (ACON) and social scientists at Macquarie University.[61] Individuals' degree of 'attachment to gay community' and engagement in and identification with gay life was assessed using a number of measures. These distinguished between cultural/political involvement (such as reading the gay press, using gay stores and businesses, joining gay organizations), social involvement (such as having many gay male friends and spending much of one's social life with other gay men and/or in gay pubs and clubs), sexual involvement (based on the number of casual partners and use of sex venues such as saunas) and public commitment to one's gay identity (measured by the degree to which men had disclosed their sexual identity to others). The results showed that:

> In general, men in contact with others, via attachment to gay community – sexual, social or cultural/political – are most likely to have changed their sexual practice. They have the informed social support necessary to modify their behaviour. Men who are isolated from others like themselves and are unattached to gay community in any form are those least likely to change.[62]

Other researchers have failed to find any significant correlation between involvement on the gay scene or in gay organizations and safer sex, suggesting that sexual behaviour is not influenced by such participation *per se*. Rather, any effect on behaviour is dependent on the prevailing norms within that community network, and perceptions of how others behave and how one is expected to behave oneself.[63] While in most studies those social norms have grown to be supportive of safer sex, some have identified subcultures in which the practice of unsafe sex appears to be the norm. Under such circumstances, individuals who were involved in these gay networks were *more* likely to have unsafe sex than those who were not.[64]

Investigators on the Chicago arm of the Multicenter AIDS Cohort Study analysed the importance of a range of factors on the adoption of safer sex between 1984 and 1986, by comparing the results of two questionnaire surveys completed by 637 men. The variables examined included knowledge of AIDS, perceptions of one's personal risk of infection and the effectiveness of behaviour change in preventing it, ability to control sexual impulses, belief that science would find a vaccine or cure in the near future, involvement in gay networks and beliefs regarding the sexual behaviour of others in those networks (i.e. social norms). During the 6-month period between the two questionnaires, all three of the risk-reducing behaviours recommended at that time – namely, avoiding anonymous partners, avoiding passive anal sex, or using condoms or withdrawal to avoid exchange of semen – increased in frequency. While no effect of gay network participation *per se* could be detected, '[t]he belief that one's peers were adopting recommended behavioral changes was positively and consistently related to subsequent behavioral risk reduction'.[65] The investigators also observed that:

> These analyses do not provide support for enthusiastic and wide-spread HIV-antibody testing of at-risk populations, in the belief that this will create a sense of increased risk, and therefore motivate behavioral changes. On the contrary, they suggest that factors other than perceptions of risk generally lead to behavioral risk reduction and that those who feel themselves to be at increased risk may even be *less* likely to develop appropriate changes.[66]

These findings have been duplicated by several other studies. Research in gay bars in San Francisco in August 1987 also showed that 'lower social support for safe sex was associated with being at high risk'.[67] Analysis of two longitudinal surveys of San Francisco gay men indicated that '[h]igh levels of positive support for changing sexual risk behaviors from informal sources (e.g., friends, siblings, lovers) were related to reports of always using condoms in 1988'.[68] Likewise, among gay men in Florida, Washington and Alabama in late 1988, those who avoided unprotected anal sex were 'more likely to consider safer behavior an accepted norm within their social network', and 'condom use was predicted by perceived norms favoring safer sex'. This suggests that 'primary prevention campaigns that convey risk precautionary behavior as an accepted peer norm or interventions that directly modify social norms to encourage health promotion and discourage continued high-risk practices may now be especially important'.[69] In 1989, researchers evaluated the effectiveness of a small group lecture on HIV and safer sex with or without an accompanying skills training session intended to promote the legitimacy and social acceptability of safer sex, and to discuss and rehearse the negotiation of safer sex in sexual encounters. After one year, gay men who received both the lecture and the skills training had increased the proportion of episodes of anal sex in which they used condoms to a far greater extent than men who received the lecture alone; however, it is impossible to assess which parts of the skills training may have been the most important in achieving this change.[70]

In part, the promotion of safer sex as the new gay 'community norm' was achieved by community-based groups through the distribution of appropriate information and advice, and through the gay press's coverage of the epidemic. However, Michael Rooney and Peter Scott point out that:

> A number of commentators have also described an elusive but important phenomenon of spontaneous activism against AIDS by gay men not only in existing gay organisations but also through informal friendship networks. This was reflected in events such as workshops, informal discussions and practical outreach which individual gay men or small groups of gay men undertook independently. A grass-roots community ferment was created in which gay men were intensively talking to each other about AIDS and safer sex as peer-educators, friends, lovers and sexual partners.[71]

Through this range of interventions, gay men were continually persuaded and repersuaded about the importance of safer sex, and supported by the knowledge that their partners and peers were also experiencing the same transition from a culture of unsafe sex to one of safer sex.[72]

Thus, research consistently demonstrates that 'efforts undertaken by community-based organizations to develop new norms for safer sexual behavior may be of special importance'.[73] Hence Simon Watney's comment that 'community development is effective AIDS education, in so far as worldwide evidence strongly suggests that gay pride has played a major role in preventing HIV transmission by establishing safer sex not just as a set of techniques, but as a fundamental aspect of gay cultural practices'.[74]

● *The role of the gay press*

Paul van Reyk has described the central role played by the Australian gay press in the early 1980s in raising awareness both of the significance of the emerging epidemic and of safer sex practices:

> The gay press was central to this response. It was this press that first began conscientiously and objectively to record the course of our emerging understanding of the illness and its transmission. It was in this press that safe sex was first defined and which continued to re-define it as more became known. It was this press that began seriously talking about lifestyle issues. And it did it all in the language which the community knew and accepted. An arse was an arse and a fuck was a fuck.[75]

Before the epidemic, lesbian and gay publications in much of the industrialized world had established a key role in formulating and disseminating community norms. They defined the shared concerns of lesbians and gay men, reported on social and cultural events, and provided news and information about both progress towards and threats to the civil rights claims of lesbians and gay men. At a time when the visible gay community was much smaller than it is today, and fewer such publications existed, the gay press had a highly influential position.

Gay newspapers and magazines in Britain and the USA as well as in Australia rapidly recognized the important implications of early reports about AIDS. During the first half of the decade, the *New York Native* and its sister magazine *Christopher Street* printed many of the most influential pieces of journalism in the history of the epidemic. Larry Kramer's speculation that 'one of the many things we've done or taken over the past few years may be all it takes for a cancer to grow from a tiny something-or-other that got in there who knows when from doing who knows what'[76] and Richard Berkowitz and Michael Callen's article 'We know who we are: two gay men declare war on promiscuity' provoked a massive debate about the role of 'lifestyle' factors in the aetiology of the epidemic.[77] Callen and Berkowitz's piece also prefigured their ground-breaking guide to safer sex *How to have Sex in an Epidemic: One Approach*. Dr Larry Mass, one of the co-founders of GMHC, wrote regular medical updates for the *Native*, to the extent that it became known as 'the AIDS newspaper'.[78]

In London, the free weekly newspaper *Capital Gay* ran regular small news stories from 1981 onwards, and from July 1984 through until the end of the 1980s published a weekly column dedicated to AIDS. For the first two years this was called 'Meldrum on AIDS', after its writer Julian Meldrum, who was also closely involved with the Terrence Higgins Trust. It was subsequently renamed 'Body Matters' and written by Tony Whitehead, chair of the Trust's Steering Committee and Directors between 1983 and 1988. Peter Weatherburn and Andrew Hunt have described how '[b]y late 1984 *Capital Gay* had become the centre for much of the AIDS-related debate in London'.[79] 'Meldrum on AIDS' and 'Body Matters' provided reliable and varied information on AIDS, reporting the latest findings published in the medical journals, discussing the social and psychological impact of the epidemic, and, most of all, explaining and debating the evolving safer sex recommendations. Given the connections between its writers and the Terrence Higgins Trust, it is not surprising that *Capital Gay* vigorously supported the organization, publicizing its views as a counterpoint to the hysterical homophobia which characterized most mainstream press reporting at this time, and advising its readers of the availability of new Trust leaflets.

It is impossible to know with certainty how important the gay press was in influencing gay men's perceptions of and responses to AIDS. However, a survey of 100 members of a cohort of gay men revealed that in early 1986, 56 per cent reported obtaining 'a lot of useful information' about the epidemic from gay newspapers and magazines.[80] Only physicians and other healthcare personnel were considered more informative (which almost certainly reflects these gay men's participation in the cohort), and even voluntary organizations such as the Terrence Higgins Trust, which are widely recognized as having had a substantial impact at this time, were acknowledged by only 43 per cent of the sample. The seriousness with which the gay media treated AIDS, the regularity with which it addressed the issue (in stark contrast to mainstream press reporting, which was derived from a very different and unhelpful sense of the 'newsworthiness' of AIDS and gay men), and the provision of a forum for often heated debates and discussion of the new realities can only have made a positive contribution to the development of a culture among gay men which recognized the epidemic as a matter of great concern, and legitimized safer sex as an essential innovation by and for gay men, rather than a restriction imposed from without.

Between about 1989 and 1991 there was something of a hiatus in gay media discussion and promotion of safer sex. However, one of the most significant recent developments in Britain has been the publication of *Boyz*, a weekly free newspaper for young gay men on the commercial scene. As Simon Watney describes it:

> it affirms a defiantly cheerful, sexually confident youth culture, focused closely on the pleasures of being young – fashion, sport, holidays, dancing and music, but above all relationships and sex ... Indeed, it is perhaps the only gay paper in Britain which evidently has a clear, consistent policy on HIV prevention issues, presenting HIV as a very important question which is constantly addressed, but as a reminder rather than with a sledge-hammer, always around, but never obtrusively.[81]

Although its editorial approach is one of light-hearted hedonism, in many respects *Boyz* can be seen as representing a uniquely mature, consolidatory response to the epidemic, in which safer sex, with all its attendant complexities, is a fact of late twentieth-century gay life. In this way, the gay press continues to contribute to a gay culture which provides a supportive environment for the uptake and sustaining of safer sex.

● *Activities on the commercial gay scene*

In the early and mid-1980s, many gay and AIDS organizations placed a high priority on meeting the needs of gay and bisexual men for accurate information and practical advice about AIDS. In gay centres such as New York, London, Sydney and San

Francisco, community-based groups provided a wide range of printed materials, discussion forums and roadshow events in gay pubs and clubs. From as early as 1983, London Gay Switchboard, as it was then known, instituted a policy of raising the subject of safer sex with as many callers as possible. As a means of providing early safer sex education to men who were just in the process of coming out as gay, and as a demonstration to other callers of the seriousness and importance with which the epidemic was viewed by an influential gay institution, this tactic is described by many men as having been highly significant. From about 1985, interactive group workshops were offered by a number of AIDS organizations.[82] Initially, these aimed to build upon the provision of factual information about risk reduction, by exploring and dispelling psychological doubts, fears and stresses, and reinforcing confidence in safer sex. Later workshops have focused more on 'the social context of the health crisis, and on the interpersonal realities of living in a community changed by AIDS'.[83] Although workshops continue to be a staple component of American safer sex programmes, relatively few have ever been offered in Britain.

A related model which aimed to reinforce a sense of social support for changing to and sustaining safer sex was the influential Stop AIDS Project in San Francisco.[84] This began in 1985 and ran until 1989, when it was felt that its work was done. It was characterized by aggressive recruitment on the street and in bars, in which a member of the Project would approach gay men and ask if they had heard of the Stop AIDS Project, or whether they would like to attend a discussion of AIDS in their community. Even this form of peer contact is thought to have been influential in reinforcing the view that AIDS and safer sex are important issues for gay men. Those who were willing were signed up to attend a specific group meeting, which would be held in someone's home rather than at a more impersonal meeting-place. There would follow a facilitated discussion of topics such as 'What do you think of the AIDS crisis?', 'How are you coping?', 'How are your friends coping?', 'What kinds of behavior changes have you made: what has been easy, what has been hard?', and 'Where do you think we are now as a community?'. Similar initiatives have been implemented in Berlin, Sydney, New Zealand and, most recently, London; however, one study has suggested that this model's reliance on participants' perception of HIV as a strong personal threat and their direct experience of AIDS within their communities may render it less efficacious in low prevalence areas as compared with the hard-hit city of San Francisco.[85]

Other activities have included specialized interventions in events or other aspects of gay culture, such as the annual Sydney Gay and Lesbian Mardi Gras, a month-long festival culminating in a street parade watched by over 200,000 people and followed by an all-night dance party catering for over 15,000:

> During this period special safe sex campaigns are run, featuring the usual posters and pamphlets, special disco songs, and video clips in gay-community venues, and thousands of condoms are distributed in special flip-top packages. Floats in the parade, costumes and street theatre by groups such as the Safe Sex Sluts – a group of educators in 'radical drag' – exhort gay men to practise safe sex to protect themselves and their community. ... It is the construction of a safe sex culture, where collective action is mobilised as one way of helping men to sustain safer sex.[86]

Similar projects have set about training gay bar-staff to raise the topic of safer sex, or have intervened in institutions such as the American Mr Leather competition, in which a gay man chosen through regional and later national contests is mandated by the organizers to spend his winning year doing safer sex education.[87] Outreach activities of this kind, which originate from within the gay communities, work on a number of different levels. By providing up-to-date, accessible and sex-positive advice about HIV, they can help meet the basic need for factual information, particularly among those new to the gay scene. Moreover by their very presence they strengthen the sense of safer sex as a community norm which is both expected and supported.

However, subsequently safer sex work on the gay scene became a somewhat stigmatized activity in HIV prevention circles. Workers on the Newcastle MESMAC project have described how in mid-1990 they took the view that:

although many gay men on the commercial scene still had many needs around HIV and safer sex, they had to a certain extent been 'privileged' in so far as they had received some HIV prevention work, whereas other groups of men who had sex with men had received little or nothing apart from inappropriate national campaigns aimed at the 'general population'.[88]

However, the project's work with men who identified as gay made it 'increasingly clear that any notion of gay scene users having been sufficiently "dealt with" was erroneous'.[89] Instead, the project came increasingly to recognize the role of the commercial scene as a resource. Condoms distributed in pubs and clubs were found used and discarded in parks and public sex environments, indicating the shortcomings of simplistic distinctions between men on the out gay scene and those who make use of non-gay identified sexual sites.

● Commercial sex venues

There can be little doubt that one of the factors which facilitated the rapid spread of HIV among gay men in the gay centres of the United States during the late 1970s and early 1980s, before anyone knew that the virus even existed, was the existence of bath-houses and backrooms as designated sex facilities. The debate about the enforced closure of most of the baths in San Francisco in September 1984 and in New York in 1985 has been thoroughly documented elsewhere.[90] It is impossible to know which (if either) side in this debate was correct – whether those who argued that the baths 'promote and profit from the spread of AIDS',[91] or those who considered that the baths offered an opportunity to reach the most sexually active gay men with safer sex messages.

It is surely significant, however, that AIDS organizations such as GMHC generally favoured keeping the baths open. Speaking in 1985, a spokesman for GMHC described gay sex places as 'our classrooms. As they close them down, they disperse the very guys we need to reach. That creates an underground, destroys the possibility of education, and ups the risk.'[92] Indeed, in cities such as Amsterdam, the widespread adoption of safer sex in the mid-1980s almost totally inhibited the further spread of HIV, despite the gay saunas remaining open. In New York, some baths stayed open by appointing 'committed, articulate "Lifeguards" to assure their patrons play safe', and hiring out their premises on a not-for-profit basis for safer sex events.[93]

Robin Hardy has highlighted what is perhaps the most important objection to the closing of the baths – namely, that it represented an authoritarian approach to HIV prevention that was in stark contrast to strategies devised by gay men for gay men, which emphasized self-determination and self-empowerment in the face of the health crisis:

> Safer sex began out on the hustings: in sex clubs, in s&m activist organizations. Promiscuous gay men committed to safer sex became role models for slow learners, and sex parties became forums for safer practices. ... By acquiescing in the closure of the bathhouses and sex clubs in 1985, the gay community implicated itself in the silencing of a vibrant sexual culture.[94]

Myths about behaviour change

Popular accounts of gay men's response to AIDS often fail to acknowledge the importance of community-based education initiatives such as those discussed above. Instead, the widespread adoption of safer sex is frequently attributed to mythical factors such as the effect of seeing friends and lovers dying, the impact of widespread HIV antibody testing, or the success of state-funded campaigns targeting the population as a whole. Some do not even accept that the decreased incidence of HIV infection resulted from changes in sexual behaviour, preferring to believe that all the gay men who practised anal sex became infected, leaving the virus with no further opportunities for spread.

● Saturation

The concept of 'saturation' is the only explanation other than sexual behaviour changes which might account for the decline in HIV transmission among gay men. This hypothesis proposes that new infections declined only because most of the gay men likely to become infected had already done so. So within cohort studies, for example, the number of men becoming infected with HIV each year may have fallen over time because all the cohort members who were having unsafe sex became infected early in the epidemic, rather than because participants changed to safer sex.[95]

This theory cannot be conclusively ruled out in large American studies such as the 1034-member San Francisco Men's Health Study,[96] due to the extremely high prevalence of HIV in such cohorts, as discussed in Chapter 1. However, the levelling off in infection rates among gay men which is consistently seen in studies around the world occurred at different levels of seroprevalence in different countries. As Michael Rooney and Peter Scott have argued:

> In US cities, where HIV had longer to establish itself before HIV/AIDS was recognized and thus before behaviour changes could begin, rates of HIV infection appear to have reached significantly higher levels amongst gay men before levelling off. Clearly, saturation cannot account for a levelling off at much lower levels of HIV infection in the UK given that this did not happen at those levels in the USA.[97]

Similarly, researchers in Amsterdam concluded that the observed decline in HIV transmission in two cohorts of gay men from 1985 onwards was likely to be a result of sexual behaviour changes, rather than a saturation effect, 'given that 60% of the participants were still not infected'.[98]

The saturation theory also fails to take account of the shifting nature of the population of gay men at risk. For example, a Health Education Authority survey in 1991 found that 40 per cent of men using gay pubs and clubs had come out onto the scene during the previous five years.[99] A large proportion of men on the gay scene are therefore unlikely to have experienced directly the safer sex campaigns of the 1980s, or even to have been sexually active at that time. Thus there clearly continues to be a large number of susceptible individuals, a fact also reflected in the recent evidence of increasing HIV transmission among gay men, which is discussed in Chapter 4.

● *The role of state campaigns*

Sexual behaviour changes by gay men throughout the western world generally took place *before* governments began national education campaigns. As described elsewhere in this book, the British public awareness advertisements did not begin until 1986, and even then, specific advice for gay men was not produced until 1989, much to the concern of groups such as the Terrence Higgins Trust. This is not to say that community organizations were not greatly assisted by the provision of state funding. In Australia, such funding was (inconsistently) available from the earliest days, when factual information about safer sex was being promoted for the first time. In Victoria, a leaflet entitled 'AIDS: trying to reduce the risk' was distributed in 1984, financed by the Health Department of Victoria, although this was not publicized at the time; however, the 'Rubba Me' campaign in Sydney at the same time was paid for by fundraising from the gay community, after the New South Wales Health Department withdrew support at the last moment on account of the 'explicit nature' of the materials.[100] In San Francisco, the Department of Public Health provided substantial financial support for HIV prevention and education programmes for gay men from the beginning of the epidemic: expenditure rose from $48,200 in the financial year 1982–83, to $2,536,136 in 1986–87.[101]

All in all, there are very few identifiable examples of successful safer sex interventions for gay men which were not clearly identified with overtly gay or gay-focused organizations or publications. This has clear implications for the development of ongoing prevention campaigns, particularly in the context of the professionalization of AIDS education within local government or other statutory health agencies which has taken place throughout the world since the late 1980s. In Britain, however, the development of the National Health Service 'contracts culture', with a division of roles between purchasing and providing agencies, and the government's commitment to building 'healthy alliances' in health service provision, offer the prospect of fruitful collaborative approaches in which prevention work is funded by statutory agencies, but actually implemented and fronted by groups which are clearly identified with the gay population. This is discussed in more detail in Chapter 7.

● *The presence of death and illness*

Addressing the British Association for the Advancement of Science in 1992, Sir Donald Acheson, the former government Chief Medical Officer, warned that there were signs that a growing number of gay men were practising unsafe sex, and concluded that 'The loss of friends and the fear of death has but a temporary effect on behaviour'.[102] In reality, however, there is little or no evidence that gay men's adoption of safer sex in the 1980s was significantly motivated by the witnessing of the deaths or illness of other gay men. While some American studies did suggest that men who knew someone who had AIDS were more likely to have adopted safer sex than others, the behaviour changes took place on too vast a scale for personal acquaintance with people who were sick to have played a significant role. This is particularly true in relatively low prevalence countries such as Britain, where, as Michael Rooney and Peter Scott have explained:

> By the end of 1985, for example, 227 gay men with AIDS had been reported to the CDSC [Communicable Disease Surveillance Centre]. If these men were close friends of as many as 30 other gay men each (probably an overestimate) this still means that the awareness of AIDS based upon personal contact would have intimately affected less than 7,000 gay men. This is a tiny proportion of the estimated number of gay men in the UK. In other words we may conclude that intimate personal knowledge, whilst a possible motivator for some, cannot have been the engine for the major observed behaviour changes in the wider population of gay men.[103]

It is also important to remember that, as discussed below, most gay men adjusted to safer sex in the years *before* the HIV antibody test became available, when reports of the magnitude of the epidemic were based solely on those cases of AIDS that had already developed, rather than on knowledge of HIV seroprevalence.

Certainly fear of the disease may have motivated many men to take initial steps intended to reduce their personal risk. However,

fear is considered to be largely ineffective as a motivator for constructive and long-term behaviour change.[104] Indeed, in the 1990s
there is an emerging body of evidence to suggest that the stress of
living in a community heavily affected by the epidemic, a form of
guilt at surviving when so many have not survived, and fatalism
about one's own chances may actually encourage some uninfected
gay men to practise unsafe sex.[105]

● *HIV antibody testing*

There has been considerable controversy over the role of
HIV antibody testing in relation to sexual behaviour changes.[106]
Advocates of widespread testing, including those politically on the
authoritarian right, have argued that individuals who found that
they were infected would be motivated to adopt safer sex or safer
drug injecting practices, while those uninfected would be motivated
to protect themselves from future exposure. Some doctors have
even proposed that 'standards for safe sex should be tailored to the
person's HIV-infection status ... HIV status is the single most
important piece of information for use in planning the scope of
one's sexual activities'.[107] This position is based on the view that
'[t]he primary goal of our educational programs on [AIDS] must be
to modify behavior enough that the risk of HIV infection is eliminated', rather than on the tried-and-tested risk reduction approach
eventually developed by gay men.[108]

For opponents of testing, however, an individual's antibody
status is irrelevant to the issue of behaviour change, since everyone
should be practising safer behaviours to protect either himself or his
partners.[109] Moreover, they argue, a positive test result could have
serious psychological consequences, and merely taking the test,
regardless of its outcome, could expose an individual to discrimination in a huge variety of settings. Besides, as Cindy Patton has
pointed out, '[t]he gay community had been coping with AIDS for
three years before testing became available as a mechanism for
making social and personal adjustments to AIDS, and in the
absence of treatment, testing was initially of mixed benefit'.[110] In
the mid-1980s, therefore, most gay organizations urged caution on
testing, with some going as far as actively discouraging gay men

from taking the test.[111] Predictably, this stance attracted strong criticism from the Moral Right.[112]

Data on the effects of antibody testing on sexual behaviour can be difficult to interpret. In western countries, HIV antibody testing is often accompanied by extensive pre- and post-test counselling, regardless of the outcome of the test. In these circumstances, it may not be possible to distinguish between the effects of learning one's antibody status and the effects of one-to-one counselling about safer sex. However, a number of studies have shown differences in behaviour following a test which are dependent on the outcome of the test. If one assumes that safer sex recommendations will have been provided equally to all study participants, regardless of the test result, it is not unreasonable to assume that these differences do indeed reflect the impact of discovering one's antibody status.

The evidence from cohort studies confirms that radical reductions in gay men's practice of unprotected anal sex took place in the early 1980s, the years during which testing was unavailable or, on its introduction, viewed with suspicion. For example, the Baltimore/Washington SHARE (Study to Help the AIDS Research Effort) examined changes in the sexual behaviour of 1001 gay men, both during the year between 1984 and 1985 when participants were unaware of their HIV status, and during the following 6 months when two-thirds had been informed of a test result.[113] During the initial year, participants reduced both the total number of their sexual partners and the number of partners with whom they had receptive anal sex by one-third, leading the researchers to conclude that '[m]uch of the striking decline in overall sexual activity since 1984, measured by the numbers of partners and also by specific high-risk practices such as anal intercourse, therefore occurred in the absence of individual knowledge of HIV serologic status'. A study which pooled data on 134 American and 139 Danish gay men who were participating in three separate cohorts was 'unable to detect any major difference in sexual behavior that was attributable only to knowledge of one's own HIV status'; instead, most of the behaviour changes reported between 1982 and 1987 'occurred prior to the availability of HIV test results in 1985 and [are] a testament to the effectiveness of the "safe sex" education efforts in the homosexual community'.[114]

This was not the only study which failed to find any detectable difference in the uptake of safer sex between men who test HIV-positive, those who test negative, and those who decide not to take the test. In the San Francisco City Clinic cohort, changes in the sexual behaviour of 181 men who chose to learn their serostatus between 1985 and 1987 were compared with those of 128 men who preferred not to know. Between 1983/84 and 1986/87, similar declines in unprotected anal sex were seen throughout the cohort, regardless of whether an individual had tested positive, tested negative, or had chosen not to be tested.[115] An evaluation of the effects of counselling and testing upon gay men in Denver between 1988 and 1991 also found 'no substantial differences in sexual behavior or condom use between HIV-seropositive and HIV-seronegative men', either at their initial visit or after one year.[116] Among 270 gay men attending a Boston community health centre, discovering their antibody status was 'not associated with reduction of unprotected receptive anogenital contact, either in seropositive or seronegative men' – in other words, men who found that they were negative were no more likely to avoid unprotected receptive anal sex thereafter than those who were told that they were already infected. However, '[i]ndividuals who learned of a positive antibody result were more likely to eliminate unprotected insertive anogenital contact than either unaware seropositive men, or men who learned of a negative antibody result'.[117]

Other studies have also suggested that men who learn that they are HIV-positive may make the greatest reductions in unsafe sex. Researchers following a group of gay men in San Francisco since November 1984 found that, by 1986, only 12 per cent of those who tested positive continued having unprotected anal sex, compared with 22 per cent of those who tested negative and 30 per cent of untested men. By 1987, the differences were even more significant: only 5 per cent of infected men had unsafe sex, compared with 18 per cent of those who were uninfected or untested.[118]

In the SHARE study described above, the trends to fewer sexual partners and less anal sex continued during the 6 months after disclosure of test results, but men who knew that they were HIV-positive showed significantly greater decreases in unprotected receptive and insertive anal sex than those who either were HIV-negative or had chosen not to know their status. However, those most likely to have unsafe sex during this period were men who knew that they were uninfected, leading to the worrying conclusion that 'disclosure of a negative test may have implied to a study participant that he was in some way "protected" because previous sexual practices did not lead to HIV infection'. Thus, while learning their HIV antibody status may lead to greater adoption of safer sex among men who discover that they are infected, it may also result in a lower uptake of safer sex, or even an increase in risky behaviour, among those who test negative.

This finding has been duplicated by a number of subsequent studies. The AIDS Behavioral Research Project in San Francisco, comparing the sexual behaviour of 508 men in 1984 and 1988, also reported that 'knowledge of seronegative status was associated ... with increased practices of unprotected anal intercourse'.[119] Another report focused on 361 men enrolled in the Vancouver Lymphadenopathy-AIDS Study. Information gathered in questionnaires between April 1984 and March 1985 was compared with the same men's reported sexual behaviour approximately 18 months later. During this period, marked decreases in the number of men reporting unprotected anal sex and the average number of sexual partners were observed. With regard to the relevance of antibody status, the researchers noted that 'the marked overall behavior change exceeded any differences between serological groups', suggesting that 'the effects of societal influences, such as community education and media coverage, may have outweighed any marginal additional effect of knowledge of serological status'. But again, there was evidence that testing negative can result in a smaller uptake of safer sex:

> We did observe some differences, however, between the serologic groups. Although seronegatives practised receptive anal intercourse with casual partners less often than seropositives, it was disconcerting to note that when they did engage in this practice, seronegatives utilized condoms less often than did seropositives. Although it may be that seronegatives were more selective in the choice of their casual partners, the possibility remains as suggested by others that some seronegatives may infer from their status some form of

protection and this may act as a disincentive to behavior change.[120]

For the UK, Project SIGMA reported that of the 930 participants recruited in 1987/88, those who had taken the HIV antibody test were significantly more likely to practise anal sex than those who were untested.[121] Given the relatively low prevalence of HIV among gay men in Britain compared with the USA, it is likely that most of these men who took the test received a negative result. However, SIGMA also demonstrated that the relatively small number of men who believed, suspected or knew themselves to be HIV antibody positive were significantly more likely always to use a condom for insertive anal sex than participants who believed, suspected or knew themselves to be antibody negative.[122] The researchers point out that '[t]his suggests that those respondents who perceive themselves to be HIV antibody positive are more conscientious at protecting their partners than those who perceive themselves to be antibody negative are at protecting themselves'.[123]

The patterns in these data can be summarized thus. First and foremost, learning one's HIV antibody status is by no means a necessary component of safer sex campaigns and, for seronegative men, may in some cases actually result in a *lower* uptake of safer sex compared with untested men. The most substantial behaviour changes occurred among gay men during the years in which antibody testing was not available or was discouraged by community organizations.

Secondly, however, for those who are infected, knowledge of serostatus *may* lead to more consistent practice of safer sex. This is presumably motivated by a wish to avoid infecting others. In terms of behaviour changes, therefore, the balance of risks and benefits from antibody testing may also depend on the prevalence of HIV in a given population. In cities such as New York, where a large proportion of the gay populations are infected, widespread testing *may* result in higher levels of safer sex practice; in relatively low prevalence settings, such as the UK, the great majority of gay men would test HIV antibody negative; here, then, widespread testing might be expected to have little positive effect on the adoption of safer sex, and possibly even to result in more unprotected anal sex.

Since the late 1980s, a growing number of community-based AIDS groups have adopted a policy of recommending antibody testing, to enable HIV-positive people to take advantage of available treatments as early as possible.[124] The San Francisco treatment organization Project Inform, which has always been a strong advocate for early and aggressive anti-viral and prophylactic treatment, has encouraged testing since as early as 1985.[125] In 1989, the San Francisco AIDS Foundation undertook an advertising campaign specifically directed 'to all gay and bisexual men who have *not* taken the HIV antibody test', urging them to 'seriously consider voluntary, anonymous testing'.[126] The State of New York distributed posters and leaflets in October 1991 declaring categorically that 'A test for the AIDS virus might add years to your life!'.[127] Among those advised to get tested were all homosexually active men, anyone who had ever had herpes, syphilis, gonorrhea or other sexually transmitted diseases, and anyone who had ever had anal sex. In Australia in early 1990, a policy of active encouragement of HIV antibody testing for gay men was endorsed by the AIDS Council of New South Wales, while the decision of the Victorian AIDS Council to continue with a policy of having 'no policy' on testing was strongly criticized in the lesbian and gay press as being 'both wrong in principle and a serious abdication of an AIDS Council's responsibility to give proper advice to gay men'.[128] European AIDS service organizations have been much less convinced of the wisdom of testing, reflecting a parallel scepticism among clinicians about the advantages of early anti-viral treatment.[129] In Britain, for example, the *National AIDS Manual*, the standard information resource used by advisors, has consistently maintained a policy of presenting the arguments for and against testing as being roughly balanced.

It is important to be aware that these broad changes in attitude to the risk/benefit ratio in testing *have nothing to do with prevention of HIV transmission*. While at the time of writing it seems increasingly clear that the medical advantages from knowing if one is HIV-positive may now outweigh the psychological and social disadvantages, this does not mean that testing should also now be seen as a component of safer sex strategies. However, it does mean that campaigns which start from the assumption that their target audience is mostly untested, especially those using the favourite British strategy of making an implicit altruistic appeal to the majority of untested gay men to assume that they may be infected and therefore protect their sexual partners by using condoms for anal sex, will become increasingly out of touch with a reality in which a growing number of gay men do take the test, and the majority test HIV-negative.[130]

Health education: theory and practice

HIV/AIDS prevention initiatives are often discussed carelessly under the general term of 'health education', implying that anything and everything done with the aim of preventing the transmission of HIV is 'health education'. In fact, the ways in which people may be educated about health have been the subject of considerable formal analysis and description, and paradigms within which health education can take place have been meticulously defined. French and Adams have identified three approaches: the behaviour change model, which seeks to 'improve health by changing people's behaviour'; the self-empowerment model, which aims to 'improve health by developing people's ability to understand and control their health status to whatever extent is possible within their environmental circumstances'; and the collective action model, which attempts to 'improve health by changing environmental, social and economic factors through community involvement and action'.[131] Homans and Aggleton have further proposed that the collective action model may be understood in terms of two kinds of community action: community-orientated models, which 'suggest that people should collectively identify and act upon the environmental and community-based factors that affect their health', and social transformatory models, which 'have the potential to enhance individual health and well-being and to bring about far reaching social change throughout society' by addressing four interrelated aspects of society: ideas, social relations, political processes and resource allocation.[132]

As Homans and Aggleton observe, attention to the strengths and limitations of these various approaches to health education is important, in order to ensure that interventions are efficiently and effectively designed and executed. However, it is also important to remember that many of the earliest AIDS education initiatives that were devised by gay men in the early 1980s, or which happened spontaneously, were not meticulously planned and often did not reflect conscious adoption of formal health education models. Instead, as this chapter describes, the highly successful adoption of safer sex by gay men was influenced by a host of more or less haphazard factors, many of which were simply the result of gay men using their knowledge of their own and their peers' lives to devise intuitive, common-sense ways to limit the spread of AIDS. Although with hindsight these activities can largely be described as employing variations on the community-orientated model of health education, this does not mean that they were formally planned and executed as such.

Critics have argued that in practice, 'the health education industry has failed gay men' by privileging academic models of health education and failing to learn from the successful grass-roots activities of the 1980s.[133] Peter Scott, editor of the *National AIDS Manual*, has argued that central to the problems facing health professionals who now wish, within the constraints of their institutions, to collaborate in prevention work with affected communities is 'the danger of a professionalisation of community development activities (based upon the greater resources and power of public institutions) leading to the clouding of original understandings and agenda and the imposition of inappropriate or ineffective methods'.[134] Cindy Patton has maintained that the shift from the early spontaneous initiatives to more conventional ones may have been harmful because:

> the professionalisation of safe sex education in 1985–86 led people to believe they could not come up with a personal safe sex plan based on a few facts and a lot of common sense. Professionalised health education displaced authority for understanding and enforcing safe sex standards from the people who engage in sex, and placed that authority instead in the hands of medical experts ... Professionalised education programs ignored or let atrophy the more innovative grassroots programs because they did not fit traditional

models and because they could not be evaluated by traditional pencil and paper tests or statistical methods.[135]

In the 1990s, most of the spontaneous, self-organized HIV education at a gay community grass-roots level has undoubtedly been lost. Moreover, for reasons discussed later in this book, many of those with responsibility for AIDS education in the UK today have little or no experience in targeting gay men. It has thus become all the more essential that new initiatives *are* properly assessed, planned, executed and evaluated, in an attempt to recreate and sustain deliberately the successful changes that occurred intuitively in the 1980s.

Conclusion

During the early 1980s, gay men invented safer sex as a community response to the emerging epidemic. Risk reduction guidelines were modified over time as HIV was discovered and its routes of transmission clarified. The initial advice to reduce the number of one's sexual partners is likely to have been relatively ineffective in the areas of the United States in which HIV had already reached a high prevalence, and where unsafe sex with only a small number of partners carried a significant risk of infection. However, in the low prevalence setting of the United Kingdom, early behaviour changes consisting of partner reductions appear to have had a significant impact on the course of the epidemic.

During the 1980s, safer sex became the established community norm within gay social networks throughout much of the industrialized world. This peer endorsement of safer sex, reinforced by educational interventions by groups recognized as a part of that community and by the gay press, played a key role in helping gay men put factual information about safer sex into practice. Contrary to popular wisdom, this unprecedented mass behaviour change owed little or nothing to the actions of governments or others outside the gay community, or to HIV antibody testing, or to the application of theory-based health educational models. Rather, it was founded upon gay men's sense of shared interests and responsibility for each other, and upon individual and collective determination to overcome this latest threat.

Notes

1. Working Group on Homophobia and AIDS, 'Health-from-below: the response of gay and lesbian communities to AIDS', *Homophobia, Heterosexism and AIDS*, p. 43. Canadian AIDS Society, Ottawa, 1991.

2. Maria L. Ekstrand *et al.*, 'Maintenance of safer sexual behaviors and predictors of risky sex: the San Francisco Men's Health Study', *AJPH*, 80(8): 973–7 (1990).

3. Quoted in John Seabrook, 'Letter from London: The AIDS Philosopher', *Vanity Fair*, p. 111, December 1990.

4. Harold W. Jaffe *et al.*, 'National case control study of Kaposi's sarcoma and pneumocystis carinii pneumonia in homosexual men: Part 1, epidemiological results', *Ann. Int. Med.*, 99: 145–51 (1983).

5. However, some men had explored the use of condoms or alternatives to anal sex to protect themselves or their partners against hepatitis B infection. Some commentators have argued that if gay men and public health agencies had taken the risks of hepatitis B seriously, and launched education campaigns similar to those prompted by HIV, the impact of the AIDS epidemic upon gay men would have been very much reduced.

6. Victor de Gruttola *et al.*, 'AIDS: has the problem been adequately assessed?' (editorial), *Reviews of Infectious Diseases*, 8(2): 295–305 (1986).

7. *Ibid.*

8. *Ibid.*

9. Lawrence A. Kingsley *et al.*, 'Risk factors for seroconversion to human immunodeficiency virus among male homosexuals', *The Lancet*, i (8529): 345–9 (1987).

10. Godfried J. P. van Griensven *et al.*, 'Risk factors and prevalence of HIV antibodies in homosexual men in the Netherlands', *Am. J. Epidem.*, 125(6): 1048–57 (1987).

11. Leon McKusick *et al.*, 'Reported changes in the sexual behavior of men at risk for AIDS, San Francisco, 1982–4 – the AIDS Behavioral Research Project', *Public Health Reports*, 100(6): 622–9 (1985).

12. Cladd E. Stevens *et al.*, 'Human T-cell lymphotropic virus type III infection in a cohort of homosexual men in New York City', *JAMA*, 255(16): 2167–72 (1986).

13. Donald E. Reisenberg, 'AIDS-prompted behavior changes reported', *JAMA*, 255(2): 171–2 (1986).

14. Leonard H. Calabrese *et al.*, 'Persistence of high risk sexual activity among homosexual men in an area of low incidence for acquired immunodeficiency syndrome', *AIDS Research*, 2(4): 357–61 (1986).

15. Eric Presland, 'This is arrant racism' (letter), *Capital Gay*, 8 February 1985.

16. S. W. Burton *et al.*, 'AIDS information' (letter), *The Lancet*, ii: 1040–1 (1986).

17. C. A. Carne *et al.*, 'Prevalence of antibodies to human immunodeficiency virus, gonorrhoea rates, and changed sexual behaviour in homosexual men in London', *The Lancet*, i: 656–8 (1987).

18. CDC, 'Prevention of acquired immune deficiency syndrome (AIDS): report of inter-agency recommendation', *MMWR*, 32(8): 101–3 (1983).

19. See Randy Shilts, *And the Band Played On*, pp. 257–9. Penguin, London, 1987.

20. Even after HIV was isolated, it took a number of years before the relevant experiments were done to provide hard evidence that condoms were an effective barrier against the virus: see Marcus Conant *et al.*, 'Condoms prevent transmission of AIDS-associated retrovirus', *JAMA*, 255(13): 1076 (1986); P. Van de Perre *et al.*, 'The latex condom: an efficient barrier against sexual transmission of AIDS-related viruses', *AIDS*, 1(1): 49–52 (1987). For a discussion of condoms for anal sex, see Chapter 3.

21. See, for example, Stevens, *op. cit.*; van Griensven, *op. cit.*

22. The Dutch safer sex campaigns and similar messages in early materials from Scottish AIDS Monitor are discussed in Chapter 3.

23. John L. Martin, 'The impact of AIDS on gay male sexual behavior patterns in New York City', *AJPH*, 77(5): 578–81 (1987).

24. Martin T. Schechter *et al.*, 'Patterns of sexual behavior and condom use in a cohort of homosexual men', *AJPH*, 78(12): 1535–8 (1988).

25. Roger Detels *et al.*, 'Seroconversion, sexual activity, and condom use among 2915 HIV seronegative men followed for up to 2 years', *J. AIDS*, 2(1): 77–83 (1989).

26. A. J. Hunt *et al.*, 'Changes in sexual behaviour in a cohort of homosexual men in England and Wales, 1988–1989', *BMJ*, 302: 505–6 (1991).

27. Project SIGMA, *Update*, London, March 1992.

28. *Ibid.*, p. 6.

29. P. M. Davies *et al.*, *Longitudinal Study of the Sexual Behaviour of Homosexual Males under the Impact of AIDS. A Final Report to the Department of Health*, p. 152. Project SIGMA, London, April 1990.

30. *Ibid.*, p. 167.

31. Project SIGMA, *op. cit.*, p. 6.

32. van Griensven, *op. cit.*

33. Paul Jenkins *et al.*, 'Synergistic effect of behaviour changes on HIV transmission risk among homosexual men', *VII International Conference on AIDS*, Florence, abstract W.C.3007 (1991).

34. *Kaposi's Sarcoma in Gay Men*. Bay Area Physicians for Human Rights, San Francisco, 1982.

35. *Towards a Healthier Gay Lifestyle: Kaposi's Sarcoma, Opportunistic Infections and the Urban Gay Lifestyle, What You Need to Know to Ensure Your Good Health*. Citizens for Human Equality, Houston, 1982.

36. Documented in 'The history of Gay Men's Health Crisis, Inc.', pp. 16–21 in the programme for *The Biggest Gay Event of All Time*, Ringling Brothers and Barnum & Bailey Circus benefit for GMHC, New York, 30 April 1983.

37. Described in Dennis Altman, *AIDS and the New Puritanism*, p. 161, Pluto Press, London, 1986, and Shilts, *op. cit.*, p. 325. Michael Callen attributes this leaflet to the Sisters of Perpetual Indulgence, an order of gay male nuns in San Francisco, in the Introduction (footnote 15) to *Surviving AIDS*. HarperCollins, New York, 1989.

38. Richard Berkowitz and Michael Callen, *How to Have Sex in an Epidemic: One Approach*. News From the Front Publications, New York, 1983.

39. John L. Martin, 'AIDS risk reduction recommendations and sexual behavior patterns among gay men: a multifactorial categorical approach to assessing change', *Health Education Quarterly*, 13(4): 347–58 (1986).

40. Gay Men's Health Crisis, *Newsletter*, New York, July 1982.

41. CDC, *op. cit.* These guidelines were updated in 1986 to include advice on avoiding 'contact with the blood, semen, urine, faeces, saliva, cervical secretions, or vaginal secretions' of any possibly infected person. The recommendations continued to advocate 'reducing the number of partners. A stable, mutually monogamous relationship with an uninfected person eliminates any new risk of sexually transmitted HTLV-III/LAV infection' (CDC, 'Additional recommendations to reduce sexual and drug abuse-related transmission of human T-lymphotropic virus type III/lymphadenopathy-associated virus', *MMWR*, 35(10): 152–5 (1986).

42. Berkowitz and Callen, *op. cit.*, p. 17.

43. S. J. Tovey, 'Condoms and AIDS prevention' (letter), *The Lancet*, i: 567 (1987).

44. Berkowitz and Callen, *op. cit.*, p. 3.

45. Karolynn Siegel *et al.*, 'AIDS risk-reduction guidelines: a review and analysis', *Journal of Community Health*, 11(4): 233–43 (1986).

46. *Ibid.*

47. Michael Shernoff *et al.*, 'Designing effective AIDS prevention workshops for gay and bisexual men', *AIDS Education and Prevention*, 3(1): 31–46 (1991).
48. Peter Weatherburn *et al.*, *HIV Education: The Effect on the Sexual Behaviour of Gay Men*, Project SIGMA Working Paper Number 30, p. 6, London.
49. Siegel, *op. cit.*
50. Burton, *op. cit.*
51. Mitchell Cohen, 'Using theoretical frameworks to evaluate HIV prevention programs', *VII International Conference on AIDS*, Florence, 1991.
52. *Ibid.*
53. *Ibid.*
54. Bruce Parnell, 'Changing behaviour', in *AIDS in Australia* (eds E. Timewell, V. Minichiello and D. Plummer). Prentice-Hall, Australia, 1992.
55. Simon Watney, 'Safer sex as community practice', in *AIDS: Individual, Cultural and Policy Dimensions* (eds P. Aggleton, P. Davies and G. Hart). Falmer Press, London, 1990.
56. Thomas J. Coates *et al.*, 'Behavioral factors in the spread of HIV infection', *AIDS*, 2 (Suppl. 1): S239–S246 (1988).
57. Carol-Ann Emmons *et al.*, 'Psychosocial predictors of reported behavior change in homosexual men at risk for AIDS', *Health Education Quarterly*, 13(4): 331–45 (1986).
58. Research & Decisions Corporation, *Designing an Effective AIDS Prevention Campaign Strategy for San Francisco: Results from the First Probability Sample of an Urban Gay Male Community*. San Francisco, 1984.
59. Research & Decisions Corporation, *Designing an Effective AIDS Prevention Campaign Strategy for San Francisco: Results from the Second Probability Sample of an Urban Gay Male Community*. San Francisco, 1985.
60. *Ibid.*
61. R. W. Connell, 'AIDS: the "Social Aspects of Prevention of AIDS" (SAPA) Project', in *The Social Sciences and Health Research* (eds Daly and Willis). Public Health Association of Australia, 1990.
62. Susan Kippax *et al.*, 'The importance of gay community in the prevention of HIV transmission: a study of Australian men who have sex with men', in *AIDS: Rights, Risk and Reason* (eds P. Aggleton, P. Davies and G. Hart). Falmer Press, London, 1992.
63. Emmons, *op. cit.*; Jill G. Joseph *et al.*, 'Magnitude and determinants of behavioral risk reduction: longitudinal analysis of a cohort at risk for AIDS', *Psychology and Health*, 1: 73–96 (1987).
64. Robert B. Hays *et al.*, 'Understanding the high rates of HIV risk-taking among young gay and bisexual men: the Young Men's

Study', *VII International Conference on AIDS*, Florence, abstract FC 722 (1991). This is discussed in Chapter 4.

65. Joseph, *op. cit.*

66. Joseph, *op. cit.*, p. 94.

67. Ron Stall *et al.*, 'Sexual risk for HIV transmission among singles-bar patrons in San Francisco', *Medical Anthropology Quarterly*, 4(1): 115–28 (1990).

68. Joseph A. Catania *et al.*, 'Changes in condom use among homosexual men in San Francisco', *Health Psychology*, 10(3): 190–9 (1991).

69. Jeffrey A. Kelly *et al.*, 'Psychological factors that predict AIDS high-risk versus AIDS precautionary behavior', *Journal of Consulting and Clinical Psychology*, 58(1): 117–20 (1990).

70. Ronald O. Valdiserri *et al.*, 'AIDS prevention in homosexual and bisexual men: results of a randomized trial evaluating two risk reduction interventions', *AIDS*, 3: 21–6 (1989).

71. Michael Rooney and Peter Scott, 'Working where the risks are', in *Working Where the Risks Are: Issues in HIV Prevention* (eds B. Evans, S. Sandberg and S. Watson). Health Education Authority, London, 1991.

72. The range of community responses of this kind is discussed in more detail in Peter Scott, 'HIV/AIDS health education', *National AIDS Manual* (Spring 1993 edition), Ch. A2. NAM Publications, London, 1993.

73. Valdiserri, *op. cit.*

74. Simon Watney, 'A common tragedy: the politics of AIDS', *Gay Times*, 130, July 1989.

75. Paul van Reyk, 'Never turning back: gay men's response to AIDS in Sydney', *National AIDS Bulletin*, pp. 12–14, July 1992.

76. Larry Kramer, 'A personal appeal', *New York Native*, 19, 24 August 1981, reprinted in *Reports from the Holocaust: The Making of an AIDS Activist*. Penguin, London, 1990.

77. Richard Berkowitz and Michael Callen, 'We know who we are: two gay men declare war on promiscuity', *New York Native*, New York, 8 November 1982.

78. Larry Kramer, note to 'Where Are We Now?' (first published in *GMHC Newsletter*, 2, February 1983), in *Reports from the Holocaust*.

79. Weatherburn, *op. cit.*

80. Carne, *op. cit.*

81. Simon Watney, 'Emergent sexual identities', in *AIDS: The Second Decade* (eds P. Aggleton, P. Davies and G. Hart). Falmer Press, London, 1993.

82. Shernoff, *op. cit.*

83. *Ibid.*, p. 56.

84. This description is based on Chuck Frutchley, 'The role of com-

munity-based organizations in AIDS and STD prevention', in *Promoting Safer Sex* (ed. M. Paalman), pp. 81–92. Swets & Zeitlinger, Amsterdam, 1990.

85. Brian Robert *et al.*, 'Evaluation of the efficacy of AIDS education interventions for homosexually active men', *Health Education Research*, 5(3): 299–308 (1990).

86. G. W. Dowsett, 'The sociological context', in Timewell, Minichiello and Plummer, *op. cit.*

87. Cindy Patton, *Inventing AIDS*, p. 145, n. 28. Routledge, London, 1990.

88. S. Bartlett *et al.*, in *A Report on the Distribution of Free Condoms and Lubricant in Gay Bars in Newcastle-upon-Tyne* (ed. D. Miller), p. 11. MESMAC Tyneside, Newcastle, 1993.

89. *Ibid.*

90. The most balanced discussion of this issue is contained in Altman, *op. cit.*, pp. 147–155. Shilts, *op. cit.*, offers a partisan view which privileges the perspective of those who agreed with the closure of the baths.

91. Dr Mervyn Silverman, San Francisco Department of Health, quoted in Altman, *op. cit.*

92. Quoted in Darrell Yates Rist, 'Policing the libido', *Village Voice*, p. 19, New York, 26 November 1985.

93. Committee for Stare Decisis, 'Wanted: lifeguards', advertisement, *New York Native*, 160, p. 19, 12 May 1986.

94. Robin Hardy, 'Risky business – confronting unsafe sex', *Village Voice*, pp. 35–8, New York, 26 June 1990.

95. The 'saturation' effect is a variation on conventional epidemic theories of infectious diseases spread by contact. These argue that epidemics are self-limiting because susceptibles are exhausted from an affected population by acquisition of immunity after infection, making them unable to transmit the agent or to be infected by it. As HIV infection does not provide immunity, declining rates of transmission are attributed to changes in the susceptible population for other reasons, such as saturation or behaviour change. This is discussed in Warren Winkelstein Jr. *et al.*, 'The San Francisco Men's Health Study: III. Reduction in human immunodeficiency virus transmission among homosexual/bisexual men, 1982–6', *AJPH*, 76(9): 685–9 (1987).

96. *Ibid.*

97. Rooney and Scott, *op. cit.*

98. van Griensven, *op. cit.*

99. *Research in Gay Bars 1991*, unpublished report, Health Education Authority and British Market Research Bureau, 1992.

100. Parnell, *op. cit.*; Garry Bennett, 'The problem of safe sex campaigns within the gay communities and the rationale for the Rubba Me campaign in the Sydney gay community', in *Proceedings*

of the Second European Gay Health Conference, London, 31 May–2 June 1985. Terrence Higgins Trust, London, 1985.

101. Patricia E. Evans, 'Does health education work? Publicly funded AIDS education in San Francisco, 1982–1986', *IV International Conference on AIDS*, Stockholm, abstract 6044 (1988).

102. Reported in Tom Wilkie and Ruth McKernan, 'Heterosexuals "unwittingly spreading AIDS"', *The Independent*, p. 6, 27 August 1992.

103. Rooney and Scott, *op. cit.*

104. R. F. Soames Job, 'Effective and ineffective use of fear in health promotion campaigns', *AJPH*, 78(2): 163–7 (1988).

105. Walter Odets *et al.*, 'Unconscious motivations for the practice of unsafe sex among gay men in the United States', *VIII International Conference on AIDS*, Amsterdam, abstract PoD 5191 (1992); Charles Kaiser, 'Tempting the virus', *QW* magazine, New York, pp. 23–6, 1 November 1992.

106. Two reviews of research on this topic have been published: Thomas J. Coates *et al.*, 'AIDS antibody testing, will it stop the AIDS epidemic? will it help people infected with HIV?', *American Psychologist*, 43(11): 859–64 (1988); Donna L. Higgins *et al.*, 'Evidence for the effects of HIV antibody counseling and testing on risk behaviors', *JAMA*, 266(17): 2419–29 (1991).

107. James J. Goedert, 'Sounding board: what is safe sex?', *NEJM*, 316(21): 1339–1441 (1987).

108. James J. Goedert, reply to Paul R. Gustafson, 'What is safe sex?' (letter), *NEJM*, 317(19): 1222–3 (1987).

109. See, for example, the six posters translated from Dutch originals by the Terrence Higgins Trust in 1987, with the slogan 'Safer sex – keep it up! Positive or negative, it's the same for all'.

110. Patton, *op. cit.*, pp. 36–7.

111. See, for example, the Gay Counselling Service of Western Australia's leaflet 'Beware the test!!', published in 1985, and reproduced in the Australian Federation of AIDS Organisations' *National AIDS Bulletin*, p. 22, July 1992.

112. See, for example, 'The Sun says: gay – and wicked!' (editorial), *The Sun*, 15 January 1987, which argued that members of the Campaign for Homosexual Equality 'deserve to be locked away where they can do no more harm' for advising gay men not to take the HIV antibody test.

113. Robin Fox *et al.*, 'Effect of HIV antibody disclosure on subsequent sexual activity in homosexual men', *AIDS*, 1: 241–6 (1987).

114. Stefan Z. Wiktor *et al.*, 'Effect of knowledge of human immunodeficiency virus infection status on sexual activity among homosexual men', *J. AIDS*, 3: 62–8 (1990).

115. Lynda S. Doll *et al.*, 'High-risk sexual behaviour and knowledge of

HIV antibody status in the San Francisco City Clinic cohort', *Health Psychology*, 9(3): 253–65 (1990).

116. D. L. Cohn *et al.*, 'Changes in sexual behavior and condom use associated with a risk-reduction program – Denver, 1988–1991', *MMWR*, 41(23): 412–14 (1992).

117. Jane McCusker *et al.*, 'Effects of HIV antibody test knowledge on subsequent sexual behaviors in a cohort of homosexually active men', *AJPH*, 78(4): 462–7 (1988).

118. T. J. Coates *et al.*, 'Consequences of AIDS antibody testing among gay men', *JAMA*, 258: 1889 (1987).

119. Leon McKusick *et al.*, 'Longitudinal predictors of reductions in unprotected anal intercourse among gay men in San Francisco: the AIDS Behavioral Research Project', *AJPH*, 80(8): 978–83 (1990).

120. Martin T. Schechter *et al.*, 'Patterns of sexual behavior and condom use in a cohort of homosexual men', *AJPH*, 78(12): 1535–8 (1988).

121. P. M. Davies, *op. cit.*, p. 138.

122. *Ibid.*, p. 165.

123. Peter Weatherburn *et al.*, *The Sexual Lifestyles of Gay and Bisexual Men in England and Wales*, p. 23. HMSO, London, 1992.

124. Martin Delaney, 'Staying alive: making the ultimate political statement. New reasons to consider taking the antibody test', *The Advocate*, pp. 32–7, 28 February 1989.

125. *The Case for Antibody Testing*, factsheet. Project Inform, San Francisco, 1989.

126. 'Think about it', poster. San Francisco AIDS Foundation, 1989.

127. 'A test for the AIDS virus might add years to your life!', leaflet and poster. State of New York Department of Health, New York, October 1991.

128. Adam Carr, 'VAC and ACON on HIV testing', *Outrage*, pp. 54–5, March 1990.

129. See, for example, Anne-Marie Swart *et al.*, 'Early HIV infection: to treat or not to treat?', *BMJ*, 301: 825–6 (1990).

130. See Edward King, 'What is safer sex?', in *Risks Worth Taking: Developing Effective HIV Prevention Work with Gay Men and Other Men Who Have Sex with Men* (ed. Michael Rooney), report from a conference in December 1991. North-West Thames Regional Health Authority, London, 1992. These issues are discussed in more detail in Chapter 4.

131. J. French and L. Adams, 'From analysis to synthesis', *Health Education Journal*, 45(2): 71–4 (1986). These models are excellently discussed in relation to HIV prevention in Hilary Homans and Peter Aggleton, 'Health education, HIV infection and AIDS', *Social Aspects of AIDS*. Falmer Press, London, 1988.

132. Homans and Aggleton, *op. cit.*

133. Peter Scott, 'How the health education industry has failed gay men', oral presentation at *Sixth Social Aspects of AIDS Conference*, London, May 1992.

134. Peter Scott, 'Community development and the challenges of the HIV crisis', oral presentation at *Action For Change – Community Development Approaches to the HIV Crisis Conference*, London, July 1991. The abstract is reprinted in the Association of Community Workers' newsletter, *Community Work*, 144, September 1991.

135. Patton, *op. cit.*, pp. 42–3.

Chapter three

Promoting Safer Sex

... safe sex was viewed by early AIDS activists, not as a
practice to be imposed on the reluctant, but as a form
of political resistance and community building that
achieves both sexual liberation and sexual health.

● *Cindy Patton,* Inventing AIDS, *p. 42*

THE accumulated experience of more than a decade of the
AIDS crisis has taught many important lessons on successful safer
sex education for gay men. As described in Chapters 1 and 2,
community-based interventions have resulted in unprecedented
sexual behaviour changes which have undoubtedly saved many
thousands of lives. However, those interventions remain largely
undocumented in mainstream health literature, with the danger
that the lessons to be learned from the successful interventions of
the 1980s will be ignored, and that valuable time and resources will
be wasted on inappropriate models of working. The overview of
some of those lessons presented here examines the rationale behind
the use of a number of specific messages and techniques in HIV
prevention work for gay men.

Some general principles

The scope of this chapter does not allow it to extend to the
technicalities and practicalities of planning and undertaking HIV
prevention activities for gay men.[1] Rather, it is intended to present

an overview of key issues relating to the targeting and content of such interventions. Nevertheless, it is informed by a number of fundamental underlying principles of good practice in safer sex education.

First, it is based on a recognition of the importance of targeting health education. As the *National AIDS Manual* points out:

> Too many messages have been addressed to an undifferentiated 'general public', apparently without any assessment of the varying needs of the different groups that make up the whole population. This has led to campaigns based on bland generalities that tell most people nothing useful or practical.[2]

By contrast, the behaviour changes documented in Chapters 1 and 2 appear to have been the result of largely spontaneous activities by and for gay men, activities which were based on a direct understanding of gay lifestyles and culture and instinctively designed to be acceptable and influential in those settings. Targeted interventions recognize that strategies that work for one social group may be ineffective or even counter-productive for other groups. While many observers believe that those planning HIV education campaigns for other sections of society can learn much from the unprecedented successes achieved by gay men, this book is primarily intended to document the history and help to inform the future of safer sex initiatives specifically for gay men; its recommendations and conclusions should therefore be read in translation in relation to the specificities of other social groups.

Secondly, it reflects the view that AIDS educators have a responsibility to aim only for the minimum necessary changes in individuals' lives which are needed to reduce the risk of giving or getting HIV. The purpose of safer sex is simply to minimize the chances of the transmission of a virus; in the process of promoting safer sex, health educators should aim to cause as little disruption as possible to gay men's lives. This has important implications for educational strategies and messages. For example, the known effectiveness of condoms in preventing HIV transmission during anal sex means that the appropriate intervention for gay men who enjoy fucking is to encourage condom use, rather than to attempt to persuade them to abandon anal intercourse in favour of non-penetrative forms of sex. (Advice about anal sex is discussed in more detail later in this chapter.) Likewise, it is relatively common-place to read accounts of the ways in which the impact of AIDS has changed the way gay men relate to each other, with more emphasis now being placed on friendship and relationships, and less on sex. While this may or may not be the case, and may or may not be a desirable outcome, it is important to recognize that such changes cannot in themselves be considered legitimate aims of HIV education.

In this context, it is essential to recognize the difference between the notions of *safer sex*, which is based on the drastic reduction of risk to a level which is generally perceived as accept-able, and that of *safe sex*, which aims for the total elimination of any degree of risk. The distinction between these approaches is considered in more detail later in this chapter; however, it should be noted here that, historically, risk reduction strategies have been the dominant model in successful HIV prevention campaigns for gay men, and that this book is based on the conviction that, on the grounds of pragmatism and to maximize their effectiveness, initiat-ives should have the goal of encouraging safer, rather than safe, sex.

Finally, in a book of this length and scope it is unfortunately impossible to discuss the range of possible interventions that may be undertaken by AIDS educators. Again, these issues are dealt with well elsewhere.[3] Ideally, prevention activities should involve a number of mutually reinforcing approaches, such as the production or provision of materials which address specific local circum-stances, the provision of educational events in public settings such as pubs and clubs, the use of peer education and other outreach methods and the development of a supportive community environ-ment. The discussion of the aims and content of safer sex education for gay men which is contained in this book may be of help in informing all these different activities.

Defending anal sex

For many gay men, anal sex was and is not just another form of sex. In addition to being the most enjoyable act in many men's sexual repertoire, anal sex has also come to have deep symbolic significance.[4] As the object of anti-sodomy laws throughout the world, asserting its legitimacy became a key goal in campaigns for law reform and in the gay liberation movement's claims for sexual freedom. Moreover, as Dr Joseph Sonnabend has insisted:

> The rectum is a sexual organ, and it deserves the respect a penis gets and a vagina gets. Anal intercourse has been the central activity for gay men and for some women for all of history ... We have to recognize what is hazardous, but at the same time, we shouldn't undermine an act that's important to celebrate.[5]

Safer sex guidelines therefore have to reconcile advice intended to enable gay men to avoid giving or getting HIV with the continuing emotional, physical and symbolic value of anal sex in those men's lives.

Writing in their 1983 booklet *How to Have Sex in an Epidemic: One Approach*, Richard Berkowitz and Michael Callen sounded a note of caution about safer sex messages relating to anal sex. They noted that 'because of the ridiculous and dangerous stereotype that being "passive" and getting fucked are somehow "unmanly", some gay men tend to be defensive about any warnings concerning the medical hazards of passivity. Remember that the issue is disease – not sex. The risk isn't getting fucked; the risk is getting exposed'.[6] Thus they acknowledged that safer sex education should not be concerned primarily with deterring gay men from fucking, but instead with enabling gay men to make their own informed decisions about risk reduction.

This was a key distinction, and one which it is increasingly important to make. In the earliest years of the epidemic, when the cause of AIDS was still a matter of speculation and the idea that gay men should use condoms was little more than a joke,[7] safer sex guidelines first recommended reducing the number of one's sexual partners, and later, avoiding anal sex. It was soon established that anal sex was by far the most risky activity for HIV transmission, and that men who do not practise anal sex face at most a tiny risk of giving or getting HIV. The priority for HIV prevention must therefore be to provide the necessary information and support to help those who enjoy fucking to reduce the risk to themselves and their partners. There are two possible approaches to this: either the correct use of appropriate condoms and lubricant can be encouraged, or those men can be urged to stop having anal sex.

It is only comparatively recently that most AIDS agencies have begun to give positive messages about condom use; however, their health-preserving potential was recognized even before HIV was identified. As a leaflet produced by the Dallas Gay Alliance argued:

> It must be emphasized that there aren't any guarantees. Nobody knows for sure that a condom is going to prevent AIDS, but the chances are fairly good. ... When we definitely find out what causes AIDS, then more definite advice can be given. In the meantime, however, we can say that condoms probably help prevent AIDS, as well as all sorts of other sexually transmitted diseases, like gonorrhoea, syphilis, and hepatitis.[8]

Rather than recommending condom use, however, early safer sex advice tended to err on the side of caution. In autumn 1983 the Terrence Higgins Trust adopted a policy (reaffirmed as late as February 1987) that 'prior to any material referring to condoms it should be stated that: Anal sex with or without a condom is dangerous. If you choose to continue having anal sex condoms may offer some worthwhile protection'.[9] Julian Meldrum described the early disagreements between individuals over the use of condoms: 'One very sane and reasonable gay man I know finds condoms a sexual turn-on and can't see why they aren't more widely adopted. Another says he would have to think seriously about resigning from the Terrence Higgins Trust if ever it endorsed them as a protective measure against AIDS'.[10] In 1987, the Trust's safer sex policy group, under the strong influence of the Medical Group, went so far as to recommend against the distribution of condoms by Trust 'roadshow' events, because:

> Provision of condoms effectively negates any health education that is saying screwing with or without a condom is risky ... By handing out condoms the trust would be seen to be saying 'safer sex is wearing a condom.' If that resulted in

someone getting the virus through condom failure when they would not otherwise have been screwed, the trust would be morally, if not legally responsible.[11]

Tony Whitehead explained the reasons for the Trust's caution in his regular column in *Capital Gay* newspaper in 1987:

> Fucking with condoms is not as safe as sucking and a host of other erotic activities. Yet heavy promotion of condoms can be perceived as suggesting that the use of condoms IS safe. This in turn can discourage many men from exploring other activities which are truly much safer.[12]

In the Netherlands, the typical advice in safer sex leaflets for gay men throughout the 1980s was 'Anal sex is best left alone. It is by far the most dangerous, even with a condom. If you really cannot do without anal sex, use a condom suitable for the purpose'.[13] Materials from Scottish AIDS Monitor in Edinburgh were among the most hostile to condoms, declaring that 'Screwing is Out. If gay guys stop getting fucked in the ass they will no longer be exposed to the virus. *Screwing is the most dangerous thing ... you can do ...* Even the strongest [condoms] can break during screwing. They are a very thin line of defence against infection ... The best defence against the virus is – *don't get screwed*'.[14] These materials typically aimed to encourage men to explore other means of sexual satisfaction, and often provided 'shopping lists' of suggested low-risk activities.

In materials from the United States and Australia, this level of hostility to anal sex *per se* is unusual. *How to Have Sex in an Epidemic: One Approach*, while pointing out that 'rubbers are not designed for assholes and might rip apart during penetration', nevertheless made them the central plank of risk reduction during anal sex.[15] In an addendum written in December 1983, its authors bluntly observed that 'Short of sexual abstinence, rubbers provide sexually active gay men with the best protection currently available. To discourage their use by those who have decided to continue sexual activity during this health crisis verges on the irresponsible'.[16] For a number of years the San Francisco AIDS Foundation ran a campaign with the slogan 'Be a rubberman ... Use condoms every time'. In Los Angeles the L.A.CARES project produced billboards, posters and gay press adverts depicting a mother waving a wooden spoon at a young man with the message 'Don't forget your rubbers', and published leaflets such as 'Mother's handy sex guide', which contained explicit safer sex stories including protected anal sex.[17] In 1986 the Victorian AIDS Council in Australia produced an exhaustive 16-page gay consumers' guide to condoms entitled 'It's black & white ... condomwise',[18] and the AIDS Council of New South Wales (ACON) published the leaflet 'Cum inside ... a condom'.[19]

As described in Chapter 2, it is far from clear to what extent the adoption of condoms, as opposed to avoidance of any anal sex, was responsible for the decline in new HIV transmissions during the 1980s. Today, however, condom use is the bottom line of virtually all gay men's safer sex materials. It has now been clearly established that HIV is primarily transmitted through unprotected anal sex, and that strong condoms used with additional water-based lubricant do provide a high level of protection for anal as well as vaginal intercourse. It is also evident that very many gay men either do not want or find it too much of a sacrifice to give up anal sex altogether. It is these gay men who are the most at risk of HIV infection. It is also these men who are likely to be placed at greatest risk by messages which undermine their confidence in condoms.

In a critique of a campaign based on a policy of 'stress[ing] the potentially life-saving option of totally eliminating anal intercourse from sex practices' on account of the 'alarming dangers of protection failure through condom breakage, undetected faults and/or improper usage', Michael Callen has highlighted three major objections to this strategy.[20] First, he points out that '[i]t is an equivocation. If they believe ... that anal sex even with a condom poses a great likelihood of killing you, they should say so outright and aggressively urge everyone to stop having anal sex entirely.' This analysis can be taken further. There is every reason to believe that a significant proportion of gay men would not find it acceptable to give up anal sex altogether. Even during the earliest prevention campaigns which did recommend abstinence from fucking, at a time when the relatively recent emergence of the epidemic, the lack of knowledge about the disease and the total absence of treatments meant that alarm and fear about AIDS were at their height, substantial numbers of gay men continued to have anal sex. A campaign which insists that condoms are unreliable is likely to lead those gay men who carry on having anal sex to conclude that they may as well take their chances with unprotected sex, if condoms are so worthless. Moreover, it will inevitably diminish the self-esteem of gay men who do enjoy anal sex, so leading to guilt, fear and an unwillingness to raise the issue of condom use when negotiating safer sex. Thus, this approach may well undermine educational messages that have demonstrably succeeded in cutting HIV transmission between gay men over the last decade, and thus *increase* rather than reduce the incidence of HIV transmission.[21]

Secondly, Callen argues that adopting the goal of eliminating anal sex is an easy option – a complacent failure both of imagination and of political will to find realistic responses to the epidemic:

> Instead of urging gay men to pull out before they cum (even if they're wearing a condom); instead of demanding stricter standards for condom manufacture and inspection (or even manufacturing our own condoms, as a Swiss AIDS organization has done); instead of redoubling efforts to educate gay men about the *proper* use of condoms; instead of demanding a national AIDS educational campaign which speaks bluntly in non-clinical language that people can understand, they have come to the same conclusion as the fundamentalists (albeit for very different reasons) and have decided to 'stress' that the best solution to the problem of AIDS is to give up anal sodomy entirely.[22]

His third objection is to the casually homophobic way in which it is considered reasonable to recommend that gay men should live without anal sex, when it would clearly be unthinkable to counsel heterosexuals to abandon vaginal sex. As discussed later, there is little or no conclusive evidence that strong condoms, used properly, are more prone to breakage during anal sex than during vaginal use. Thus, anti-anal sex messages implicitly treat gay men's sexual pleasures as though they are inherently less important and significant than those of heterosexuals.

In contrast, responsible safer sex education works with the realities of people's sexual desires and impulses, and indicates ways in which individuals can continue to do whatever they enjoy in sex, but more safely. With regard to anal sex, that means the provision of clear information about choosing condom brands, and using them properly. To enable gay men to take properly informed decisions, it is important that condom use is understood to be a risk reduction strategy, although, as will be discussed in the case of oral sex, it is equally important that the small degree of risk which remains is seen in perspective alongside the considerable degree of protection which condoms can offer.

Even today, however, the development of straightforward safer sex advice on the use of condoms for anal sex is complicated by the contradictory messages which emanate from health educators, condom manufacturers and regulatory bodies such as the British Standards Institution. At the time of writing, the only recognized standard for condom manufacture in this country is a specification for condoms intended for vaginal use. The legal and institutional complexities which underlie this regrettable state of affairs are discussed next.

Unacceptable standards: condoms for anal sex

The ability of condoms to prevent HIV transmission during anal sex has been established in controlled studies. In 1989, data from the 2915 men in the Multicenter AIDS Cohort Study (MACS) revealed:

> a very significant difference in the seroconversion rate among men who reported using condoms with all of their partners as opposed to those reporting use with none of their partners suggest[ing] that condoms *as used during this period by the MACS participants* did provide significant, although not complete, protection against infection with HIV-1.[23]

Seven men seroconverted despite reporting condom use with all of their sexual partners; it was unestablished whether these were due to 'condom failure, improper usage, occasional nonuse, errors in recall, or other types of sexual activity'.

Studies have also investigated the incidence of and reasons for condom failure during anal sex. In the mid-1980s, Dutch researchers recruited 17 gay couples who had never used condoms before to evaluate 7 combinations of different condoms and water-based lubricants for both safety and acceptability. They found that the condoms least likely to rupture during anal use were the stiffest ones, at least 80 μm in thickness and able to withstand inflation with over 27 litres of air in laboratory tests.[24] These tests were used by the Dutch division of the London Rubber Company (LRC) in manufacturing the Duo condom, which has been marketed to gay men in the Netherlands since June 1986.

In late 1986, Dutch researchers investigated the failure rate of Duo and Gay Safe condoms compared with other brands of condom which were not designated for anal use. The failure rate of these two brands was 3 per cent, whereas vaginal condoms failed on 9 per cent of occasions in which they were used anally. Failure of designated anal condoms was more often due to them slipping off rather than tearing.[25] Ignoring the differences between brands and factors such as the use of oil-based lubricants, the overall failure rate in 1986 was 8 per cent, but declined to 4 per cent in 1991, presumably reflecting greater experience in both the choice and proper use of condoms.[26]

In a postal survey of 229 British gay men, 97 reported condom use during the preceding year, of whom 30 had experienced one or more breakage. Overall, the mean breakage rate was 4.73 per cent; however, this cannot easily be interpreted since no distinction between standard vaginal condoms and stronger brands was reported in the analysis. Participants believed that 'powerful thrusting during anal intercourse' was the commonest reason for condom failure.[27]

The competence of the user is almost certainly a highly significant factor in determining the safety of condoms, but is not something that lends itself to easy measurement. However, in an Australian study of the breakage rate of condoms used by 30 male and 4 female prostitutes, who may be assumed to be expert in their use, only 3 breaks were reported out of 664 usages, giving a failure rate of 0.5 per cent. Two of the three breakages were associated with the use of oil-based lubrication.[28] American researchers interviewed 25 men who experienced repeated failure of condoms during vaginal or anal sex, yet who answered correctly a set of questions about the proper use of condoms. They found that while all 25 claimed only to use water-based lubricants, 23 identified their usual lubricant as an oil-based product; however, they had assumed that it was water-based because it easily washed away with tap-water. The researchers concluded that there was little evidence that condoms failed when used properly with water-based lubricant, and that 'differences in frictional stress between anal and vaginal intercourse may not suffice to account for breakage'.[29]

The most recently presented data come from questionnaires completed by participants in two Dutch cohort studies during late 1990 or early 1991.[30] The overall failure rate of condoms during anal sex was 3.7 per cent; 2 per cent were due to condom breakage, and 1.7 per cent to the condom slipping off during sex. The failure rate for condoms designed for vaginal sex was 4.6 per cent, significantly higher than the 3.1 per cent rate for designated anal condoms. When oil-based lubricants were used, 10.3 per cent of condoms failed, compared with only 1.7 per cent when water-based lubrication was employed.

A similar breakage rate was demonstrated in a smaller study[31] which used Durex Extra Strong condoms.[32] Of 760 condoms used, 12 broke during anal sex, representing a failure rate of 1.6 per cent. The researchers observed that: 'This compares favourably with the breakage rates reported for standard condom use during anal sex which range from around 4% to 10.5%, and is very similar to the 1.8% breakage rate reported in a study of vaginal intercourse.'

On the basis of all this research, gay men are usually advised to use stronger condoms than those recommended for vaginal sex. In practice, this means using thicker condoms. The additional latex used in thicker condoms may result in a greater inconsistency in the thickness of the wall of an individual condom when compared with standard condoms, and the condom may be liable to break due to stress at one of these thinner patches; however, in these condoms such patches are still likely to exceed the thickness of standard condoms.[33] In some countries such stronger condoms have been specifically manufactured and marketed to gay men, such as Gay Safe or Duo condoms from the Netherlands, HT Special condoms from Germany, or Hot Rubber condoms manufactured in Switzerland in conjunction with the national AIDS service organization.

The stronger condoms available in Britain are Durex Extra Strong, manufactured by LRC Products Ltd, and Mates Superstrong, from Ansell. These are manufactured to essentially the same specifications as overseas brands such as HT Special: they are smooth, plain shaped and lubricated condoms of at least 0.09 mm thickness. Consequently it is these brands which have been specifically recommended by health agencies as being the best available on the British market for anal sex.[34]

At the time of writing, manufacturing and testing requirements for British condoms are defined in a standard known as BS 3704, which was drawn up by the British Standards Institution (BSI). This is not a compulsory standard, and condoms which do not meet its specifications may still legally be sold. Condom manufacturers may also claim on the packaging of their condoms that the product conforms to the standard, without that claim having been independently verified. However, the BSI operates a certification scheme whereby a manufacturer may agree on an ongoing basis to have its condoms randomly sampled and tested by BSI technicians. Condoms which are assessed in this way and are found to be manufactured to the requirements of BS 3704 may then carry a symbol called the Kitemark on their packaging. Accordingly, health agencies usually recommend that consumers only use Kitemarked products.

However, BS 3704 is described as a Standard which specifies requirements for natural rubber latex condoms 'designed and intended for use during vaginal sexual intercourse'.[35] As part of the information which must be given either on the condom packaging or in a leaflet within the pack, manufacturers must include 'a statement that the standard to which compliance is claimed ... is a specification for condoms designed for vaginal use'.[36] There is no equivalent British Standard for anal sex.

Thus, although both LRC and Ansell either repackage their condoms or produce specific condom brands to appeal to particular population groups,[37] the glaring omission in the manufacturers' marketing strategies is that of a condom specifically for gay men, or for anal sex between men and women. As if this were not bad enough, all these manufacturers' condoms currently carry the warning 'For vaginal use only' on the packaging, a label which can only deter gay men from using these condoms and undermine their confidence in the protection such condoms may offer.

This very strong directive against the use of condoms for anal sex is not required by BS 3704; indeed, manufacturers would be acting entirely within the requirements of the Standard if they were to advise their customers that a suitable condom was produced in accordance with the specification for vaginal use, *but also offered a significant level of protection during anal sex*. However, manufacturers choose actively to discourage the use of their condoms for anal sex because of their fears of liability under the Consumer Protection Act 1987.

Essentially, the Consumer Protection legislation means that it would be an offence to produce or supply a defective product. A product is 'defective' if the safety of the product is not such as persons generally are entitled to expect in all the circumstances. The 'circumstances' include 'the manner in which, and purposes for which, the product has been marketed ... and any instructions for or warnings with respect to doing or refraining from doing anything with or in relation to the product'. Since the British Standard is for condoms for vaginal sex, and since there is no equivalent standard for anal sex, manufacturers argue that they cannot vouch for the safety of their condoms during anal sex and therefore must discourage their use in this way.[38]

These legal concerns would not arise if there were a recognized Standard for condoms for anal sex. But unfortunately, the British Standards Institution and the condom manufacturers claim that they do not know how to formulate one. The standard for condoms for vaginal sex was not based on scientific principles, but simply evolved over time and was accepted as being a reliable standard. It has therefore been argued that there is no precedent for developing a new standard. However, the marketing of the Femidom, a 'female condom' manufactured by Chartex International which lines the vagina rather than covering the penis, has prompted work on a British Standard for female condoms, a product whose nature is surely far more unprecedented than the relatively straightforward adaption of 'male' condoms for anal use. Moreover, it could be argued that an acceptable standard for anal sex condoms has evolved just as that for vaginal sex condoms evolved, through the development and marketing of brands such as HT Special, Gay Safe and Duo in Europe.

Recently a pan-European condom standard, which is deliberately not described as a standard for condoms for vaginal sex only, has been developed at the request of the EC. This standard, known as the CEN standard, is intended to become the norm throughout Europe in 1993, replacing existing national standards. Unlike the existing British Standard, it is compulsory; condoms which do not conform to this standard will not be permitted to be sold in Europe. It also includes explicit additional specifications for condoms which make claims of extra strength or safety. It remains to be seen whether this standard for extra strong condoms will provide manufacturers with the assurance they appear to require to enable them to market condoms for anal sex.

In the meantime, some gay men have experimented by using the female condom.[39] This consists of a transparent polyurethane tube held open at one end by a round springy plastic rim about 3 inches across. The other end is sealed; inside sits another loose transparent plastic ring. The bag lines the vagina, using the flexible internal ring to hold it in place above the pubic bone, while the outer ring stays outside the body to prevent the condom from getting pushed inside. In December 1991, the Toronto lesbian and gay newspaper *Xtra!* reported that a local AIDS counsellor, Bill Downer, had been testing an American version called the Aegis Barrier for anal sex.[40] He stated that: 'when I was doing the fucking, I did notice the interior ring a bit at first, until it got pushed out of the way. But in terms of sensation, it was great. When I was being fucked, it didn't feel as if there was a device in me at all.' According to *Xtra!*, the American manufacturers sponsored a small study of 14 male couples which found no leaks or tears in any of the pouches used, although 'all of those responding found design and usage difficulties with the Aegis condom during anal intercourse, which were primarily due to lack of experience and knowledge of the Aegis condom'. It remains to be seen whether anal use of the female condom has a practical role to play in safer sex: the *Xtra!* reporter added that 'even after a good 20 minute struggle I was utterly unable to get the thing up my far from virgin bum – and I almost put my back out trying'. Manufacturers are also interested in using polyurethane in the manufacture of conventional 'male' condoms. The difficulties in this largely revolve around the perceived need to produce a product which does not have a seam, which might split under stress.

Oral sex

One of the most controversial areas in safer sex advice is the issue of the degree of risk involved in oral sex. It is widely believed by AIDS educators that it is impossible to give firm advice about HIV transmission by this route. However, there is reliable epidemiological evidence to show that the risk of HIV transmission through oral sex is very small, and that the practice can, happily, be described as a form of safer sex. Objections to this classification stem largely from misconceptions or discomfort with the notion of risk reduction – as opposed to risk elimination – which is implicit in the concept of safer sex.

Some of the disagreements about the riskiness of oral sex are derived from misunderstandings of the basis for our knowledge about the ways in which HIV is transmitted in practice. As described in Chapter 2, safer sex guidelines were originally formulated before the cause of AIDS was established. At that time the most prominent three theories focused either on factors relating to gay men's 'lifestyle' such as drug use; or on the effects of repeated infection with known pathogens such as cytomegalovirus (CMV); or on a new transmissible agent, either alone or in conjunction with co-factors. Safer sex advice was based on the latter two, and assumed that the cause or causes of AIDS was or were sexually transmitted, and that transmission could be stopped by preventing one partner's body fluids from entering the other's body. While these guidelines have proved to be essentially correct, accumulating epidemiological evidence has provided increasingly clear indications of the relative risk of particular sexual acts, and allowed educators to become more sophisticated in their recommendations for safer sex.

It is not the case that our understanding of the ways in which HIV can be transmitted is based on laboratory research. Although test-tube studies are able to identify which body fluids contain HIV at infectious levels, they provide little or no information on the risk of transmission through particular acts. Discussing the possibility of oral transmission of HIV, Canadian researchers pointed out that:

> The isolation of HTLV-III in a body fluid or tissue does not prove that the fluid or tissue represents a mode of transmission. Factors which determine whether infection is transmitted include the concentration and viability of the agent within the fluid or tissue, access to a port of entry for the fluid or medium, the presence of receptors at the site of entry, and natural host defences near the site of entry.[41]

The physical mechanisms by which HIV enters someone's body and infects him or her are still not fully understood, and there is still no entirely convincing non-human animal model for researchers to study; laboratory scientists therefore tend to rely on epidemiology to indicate the ways in which infection occurs in practice, and then adjust their theories accordingly.[42] The assertion that more research is needed to understand particular issues in HIV transmission, which is most commonly made in relation to woman-to-woman transmission, is thus highly misleading if it is taken to refer to bench science as opposed to epidemiological surveillance.

Gerald Oppenheimer has described how epidemiologists established the routes by which HIV is transmitted among gay men, essentially by identifying those men in cohort studies who were HIV-positive, and then analysing how their sexual behaviour had differed from men who were not infected:

> [Risk factors] included sexual contact with a person known to have AIDS and participation as the receptive partner in anal intercourse, a risk that increased with the number of persons with whom one acted as the anal receptive partner. These behaviours heightened the chances of viral transmission. Implicated as well was a history of anal douche use. In the population studied, therefore, HIV infection is an

STD in which anal mucosa appears to be an inefficient barrier to infection, especially when traumatised by frequent contact. These results were consistent over many epidemiological studies.[43]

The potential difficulty is that of distinguishing between a high-risk activity, such as receptive anal sex, and a lower-risk activity such as oral sex. In these studies, the vast majority of the men who have practised unsafe anal sex have also had oral sex, which may seem to make it hard to know which activity is actually responsible for transmitting HIV. However, in virtually all such studies, a large number of *uninfected* men also report having had oral sex. It is the fact that HIV transmission is typically not shown to occur unless someone has unprotected anal sex, regardless of whether or not he also has oral sex, which proves that anal sex carries by far the greatest risk, and that any risk in oral sex is very low indeed.

Another means by which it may be possible to distinguish between activities with different levels of risk is through multivariate analysis. This is a statistical approach which makes explicit adjustments to its calculations to take account of this type of possible confounding effect. Virtually all of the studies described below used multivariate analysis in demonstrating that there is little or no risk of HIV transmission associated with oral sex.[44]

For example, in 1984, Danish researchers analysed the correlation between specific sexual acts and risk of HIV infection among 250 gay men, and found that '[t]he number of acts as the recipient of anal intercourse correlated with seropositivity whereas being a recipient of oral intercourse ... did not appear to be important', or if anything was 'slightly protective', since men who did not practise sucking proved to be more likely to have passive anal sex.[45]

A study of 304 gay men in London during 1985 found that 'the swallowing of semen did not show any significant relationship with anti-HTLV-III/LAV seropositivity'.[46] Researchers in San Francisco reported that there was 'no significantly increased risk of HIV infection by ... oral/genital contact with ejaculation'. To check this conclusion, they collected data on 64 men who reported no anal sex or only oral sex since June 1982, and found that the 14 who were HIV-positive all reported having had receptive anal sex before June

1982. They concluded that '[t]he data from the San Francisco Men's Health Study confirm that receptive anal/genital contact is the major mode of transmission of HIV infection. In fact, there was no evidence of epidemic spread due to any other sexual mode of transmission'.[47]

Very similar findings were reported from the Canadian cohort of 700 gay men known as the Vancouver Lymphadeno-pathy-AIDS Study, in which, 'in multivariate analyses, no risk associated with oral sexual contact was detected'. As confirmation, researchers studied 21 uninfected gay men who reported no receptive anal sex during the year prior to enrolment in the study or during subsequent follow-up: all still practised oral sex. They concluded that:

> The sexual practices of the 21 men we studied, the number of their partners and the prevalence of HTLV-III seropositivity in homosexual men in Vancouver (at least 35%) combine to suggest that during the observation period these men received frequent oral exposure to HTLV-III. Yet only 1 man seroconverted and this probably happened through insertive anal intercourse, a known mode of transmission. Our findings corroborate the lack of oral transmission of HTLV-III.[48]

No significant risk of HIV infection was found to be associated with oral sex in the Multicenter AIDS Cohort Study in the USA. Of 147 men who performed oral sex with at least one partner during a 6-month period, but who reported no anal sex during the preceding year, not a single seroconversion occurred. All but 3 of the 95 men who did become infected during this period had had unprotected passive anal sex during the 12 months before they tested HIV-positive, and the remaining 3 had been the insertive partner during unprotected anal sex.[49] In 1989 an update on the seronegative gay men in the Multicenter AIDS Cohort Study reported that:

> an increasing number of men over the course of follow-up in the MACS have given up anal–genital intercourse while continuing to practise other sexual activities. If these prac-

tices were associated with an appreciable risk of infection over time, we should have observed seroconversions due to these other exposures ... There was only one man in this study who appears to have been infected by sexual activities other than anal–genital intercourse. The accuracy of this report is, of course, dependent upon the accuracy of recall of the individual. The motivation for denial of anal–genital intercourse increases as it becomes more and more apparent to the homosexual community that this is the major route of infection.[50]

The researchers came to the conclusion that, on the basis of this individual's report, 'such transmission is possible, albeit rare'.

This assessment is also confirmed by the patterns of HIV transmission seen since large numbers of gay men started practising safer sex. Surveys show that although many men have avoided unprotected anal sex, whether by using condoms or by giving it up altogether, considerable numbers have continued to practise oral sex. As early as 1984, researchers in Vancouver reported that over a 3-month period, '[s]pecific sexual practices were more likely to have decreased than increased, except for oral–genital contact'.[51] Although the proportion of gay men who avoid getting semen in their mouth has increased,[52] only a tiny number have started to use condoms during sucking. In a sample of 229 sexually active British gay men who responded to a questionnaire in 1988, 180 (79 per cent) had practised oral sex during the previous year, 117 to ejaculation. Of these, 103 (88 per cent) never used a condom, the commonest reason being that they did not feel that it was necessary.[53] In some studies oral sex has become much more common in recent years: in Project SIGMA, the proportion of men who had oral sex in the month before they were interviewed rose from about 60 per cent in 1988 to about 75 per cent in 1991.[54]

But nevertheless, HIV transmission rates have fallen dramatically, in line with the reduction in unprotected anal sex. As Adam Carr has pointed out:

oral sex is now a far more common practice among gay men than unprotected anal sex. In cities like San Francisco and Sydney, sexually-active gay men are statistically likely to have frequent sexual encounters with HIV-infected partners. Seroconversions due to unprotected anal sex with HIV-infected partners continue to be documented; the Sydney study documented 55, or 8.5 per cent of their total cohort, within four years. This makes the lack of documented seroconversions among the large majority of gay men who do not practise unprotected receptive anal sex with casual partners, but who do practise receptive oral sex, all the more striking.[55]

In virtually every instance, gay men who become infected with HIV today report having had unprotected anal sex. For example, in 1991 researchers on Project SIGMA reported that:

> no-one in the study who has not engaged in fucking is HIV antibody positive and all the men who are positive have engaged in fucking. In a case study of the 7 sero-conversions which have happened during the course of the Project's first 4 years, 5 of them can be linked to being fucked without a condom and the other 2 to fucking someone else without a condom.[56]

Despite the increase in oral sex among study participants, SIGMA found 'no statistical relationship between HIV status and the general number of sexual partners, which if sucking were implicated would be the case'.[57] Similarly, investigators with the cohort study at St Mary's Hospital in London concluded in summer 1992 that '[t]he observation of declining rates of seroconversion despite the fact that a large proportion of seronegative subjects (>75%) have continued to practise oral sex suggests that this practice carries very little or no risk for HIV transmission'.[58]

It is also helpful to reflect on the established modes of transmission of hepatitis B virus (HBV). In a two-and-a-half year prospective study of gay men recruited into the Pittsburgh arm of the Multicenter AIDS Cohort Study, it was established that HBV is transmitted 8.6-fold more efficiently than HIV between gay men, but nevertheless, no association between receptive oral sex and HBV transmission could be detected.[59] This is consistent with earlier research on HBV transmission,[60] and suggests that the risk of HBV transmission during oral sex is at best very small, and that the risk of HIV being passed on in this way is likely to be even lower.

It is on these data that safer sex advice should be based. Much of the confusion about oral sex may derive from the varying advice given in safer sex materials published by different organizations in different countries at different times. However, rather than reflecting confusion and uncertainty, the evolution of those messages should actually be seen as an indication of increasing knowledge and growing confidence that oral sex can be considered to be safer sex.[61]

Early safer sex advice, developed during the years before HIV was discovered, erred on the side of caution by advising against exposure to any body fluid, including saliva during kissing. For example, in *How to Have Sex in an Epidemic: One Approach*, Callen and Berkowitz warned that 'sucking is a moderate risk for CMV ... If you suck, you can reduce your risk for CMV by preventing your partner from coming in your mouth ... Apart from CMV, sucking can of course transmit other diseases such as syphilis and gonorrhea and in certain settings amoebas'.[62] By 1985, it had been established that the recently discovered HIV, then known as HTLV III or LAV, was indeed transmitted in blood or semen, but there was still doubt about the infectivity of other body fluids like saliva and urine. The Terrence Higgins Trust guidelines on safer sex from that time ranked both oral sex and deep kissing as 'medium risk', in what was described as an 'educated guess'.[63] The precise means by which someone could become infected with HIV was still a complete mystery at this time. Did the virus merely have to come into contact with mucous membranes (and if so, did the mucous membranes of the mouth differ from those of the rectum), or did it actually have to enter the bloodstream through cuts, sores or abrasions? The contradictory opinions on this are reflected even in different Terrence Higgins Trust materials from 1985: the *Medical Briefing* simply warned against letting HIV 'enter the body',[64] while the 'Sex ...' leaflet for gay men was less stringent, advising that 'Sucking is OK – but cum or pre-cum in the mouth is risky if there are cuts or sores on your cock or gums'.[65]

By 1988, AIDS organizations in Canada, Australia and the UK – but not the USA – were sufficiently persuaded by the consistent data emerging from cohort studies for their advice about oral sex to be relaxed significantly. London Lesbian and Gay Switchboard, whose advice on oral sex had classified it as only a possible low risk for some years, now placed full-page advertisements in the gay press encouraging gay men to 'SUCK'. The Canadian AIDS Society convened a panel of experts which reclassified oral sex as low risk; in the words of one researcher, the Canadian government 'decided to give oral sex back to gay men'.[66] The AIDS Committee of Toronto designed a major campaign with erotic leaflets and posters to reassure gay men about sucking; their director of education maintained that they 'could not equate the risk of unprotected anal sex with unprotected oral sex ... Oral sex is closer to no-risk'.[67] In Germany, Deutsche AIDS-Hilfe published an explicit poster illustrating sucking, with the slogan '*Nicht in den Mund Spritzen*' – 'Don't cum in his mouth'.

The two remaining contentious areas were the significance of cuts or sores around the mouth or gums, and the advice about getting semen or pre-ejaculatory fluid in the mouth. The latter is the most straightforward. It is clear that HIV cannot be transmitted from the skin of the penis, and that there is no risk of infection when there is no contact with cum or pre-cum. However, HIV is present in both fluids, although it is not known whether the levels in pre-cum are sufficiently high to be infectious.[68] Some advice has therefore made a quite reasonable distinction between oral sex in which no cum or pre-cum is taken into the mouth, when HIV transmission is impossible, and sucking to ejaculation, where there are at least grounds for suspicion that infection could occur. Most researchers appear not to have performed separate analyses of the risk associated with oral sex both with and without the ingestion of semen. However, it is reasonable to assume that a fair proportion of incidents of oral sex in the studies described earlier will have involved ejaculation into the mouth, yet nevertheless, very little or no risk of infection was observed. Moreover, in some studies the acts of 'oral receptivity' and swallowing semen *have* been differentiated, without revealing evidence of transmission of HIV.[69]

One factor which may play a role in preventing HIV transmission through oral sex is the inhibitory properties of saliva. In

May 1988 the *Journal of the American Dental Association* reported that an unidentified component of saliva prevented HIV infection of lymphocytes, even when greatly diluted.[70] It has also been demonstrated that HIV is rapidly destroyed by bile in the intestines, and researchers assume that the digestive enzymes and changes in pH (acidity/alkalinity) in the stomach which inactivate other viruses would also kill HIV. Surveys have shown that many gay men have based their decision to continue having oral sex on these pieces of evidence.[71]

The remaining question, however, is concerned with whether any risk as a result of getting semen in the mouth is increased if there are cuts or sores in the mouth. First, it should be remembered that oral sex has been shown to be associated with very little or no risk of infection in cohort studies, and that it is reasonable to assume that in terms of their oral hygiene, the men in those cohort studies will not have had significantly more or fewer cuts and sores in their mouths than any other cross-section of the gay population. As described by a Briefing Paper on oral transmission prepared for advisors working on the National AIDS Helpline in Britain:

> The mouth is an entry point into the digestive system where enzymes in saliva are secreted to begin the task of digesting food. It is very thick compared with the mucous membrane in the rectum, and fluids stay in contact with it for a very short time because swallowing clears the mouth regularly. Thus the likelihood of semen, blood or vaginal fluid being absorbed through damaged tissue is minimal.[72]

However, in the isolated case reports in which infection is claimed to have taken place through oral sex, poor oral health has been reported on a number of occasions.[73] It may therefore be reasonable to distinguish between the low risk from getting cum or pre-cum in a healthy mouth, and a possibly slightly greater but still low risk if the tissue of the mouth is damaged. Some reports have also suggested that any risk of infection through oral sex may also be somewhat increased if the mouth or throat are compromised in other ways, such as through inflammation due to conditions such as pharyngitis[74] or gonorrhoea.[75]

It is those case reports which have caused the greatest amount of confusion and concern about the safety of oral sex. As Nicholas Mulcahy has observed:

> A case study is the tale of an individual – in this instance, one who evidently becomes infected with HIV from sucking cock. Because it personalizes an issue, a case study can have a more powerful effect on the imagination than a study with hundreds of participants. However, the sexual histories of ten individuals are not a good basis for determining the riskiness of oral sex. Large-scale epidemiology studies reduce the chance that errant or omitted details in a person's sexual history will distort a larger reality.[76]

Reports of such case studies are usually made in letters to medical journals, which unlike formal articles are not peer-reviewed. Thus, some have included such eccentricities as the suggestion that HIV transmission may take place *from* the partner performing the sucking.[77] Moreover, they rely on the testimony of individuals, who may be understandably reluctant to admit to practices about which they feel guilty or embarrassed, especially if they have had unsafe anal sex, which is increasingly stigmatized among gay men. One Dutch study assessed the sexual activities of 102 HIV-positive gay men for whom the date of infection was known. In a written questionnaire, 20 men denied having had receptive anal sex during the 6–9 months before seroconversion; however, in face-to-face interviews, 11 subsequently contradicted this. A further 5 had been the active partner in anal sex. The researchers concluded that 'orogenital transmission of HIV does appear to occur, but a psychological barrier in reporting the practice of anogenital receptive intercourse may lead to an overestimation of the transmission rate'.[78]

Thus, these isolated cases often attract attention which is out of all proportion to their significance, while the more reliable conclusions from large cohort studies are overlooked. Doctors have been known to argue that just a single case of alleged oral transmission is sufficient 'to show that we can't assume that it's safe any more'.[79] This reflects a fundamental misunderstanding of what is meant by the term safer sex, as opposed to 100 per cent safe sex, which is discussed next.

Safer sex versus safe sex

As mentioned earlier, American AIDS organizations have been much more reluctant than those in Canada, Australia and Europe to recognize oral sex as an acceptable part of safer sex. This reticence appears to stem from a different approach to giving advice about the risk of HIV transmission during particular sex acts, which is also reflected in the differences between the terms 'safe sex' and 'safer sex'.[80] In the USA, where safe sex is the order of the day, guidelines emphasize the *presence* of risk, albeit a low one, in acts such as oral sex; consequently, American safer sex materials often read as though they are aiming at the total elimination of any possibility of HIV infection.[81] However, the model of safer sex advice used elsewhere focuses more pragmatically on the *relative* risk of transmission, and offers advice that is intended drastically to reduce the risk of HIV transmission, but not necessarily to remove that risk altogether.[82]

The reasons for this variance in approach are not immediately apparent. Wayne Blackenship of the San Francisco AIDS Foundation suggests that they include: 'the higher incidence of AIDS in America (thus making the disease more frightening), [American] cultural puritanism (thus making sex more frightening) and American politics (AIDS service organizations, fearing a right-wing backlash, have been conservative in their prevention programs).'[83] Michael Callen, who in part established the risk-reduction model in the booklet *How to Have Sex in an Epidemic: One Approach*, agrees that subsequent developments in the USA have not necessarily been informed primarily by a concern for the sexual health of gay men:

> [R]ather than admit that oral sex is actually reasonably safe, U.S. AIDS educators would rather thousands of gay men suffer unnecessary guilt and anxiety over oral sex than risk being sued by the one individual who gets HIV from the exclusive practice of oral sex. What's missing from the cal-

culations is a fair assessment of the emotional and psychological importance to individuals of particular forms of sexual expression.[84]

Oral sex cannot be endorsed in the safe sex model because it almost certainly is not 100 per cent safe. Although the reliability of case reports in which oral transmission is alleged is questionable, and although the cohort studies consistently find little or no risk in sucking, there remains a very real possibility that there is a small chance of infection through oral sex with an HIV-positive partner. Literature from American AIDS organizations such as Gay Men's Health Crisis (GMHC) in New York therefore recommends men and women to 'Wear a rubber when you have sex and cum (semen) could get inside your mouth, vagina or ass (in oral, vaginal or anal sex)'.[85] This kind of generalization can only obscure the very great difference in the magnitude of the risk of transmission through vaginal or anal sex in comparison with sucking. In 1990 Robin Hardy observed that: 'In New York, safer sex "guidelines" remain the most conservative in the world. GMHC's Maggie Reinfeld seems almost evasive when she states, "We say it is safest to use a condom during oral sex".'[86] Subsequent leaflets from GMHC reflect a shift in this position; now oral sex is clearly defined as 'low risk for HIV transmission', although again, the contradictory recommendations to 'put a condom on that cock' or '[k]eep your head off the head of his dick' are still made.[87] According to the *Village Voice* newspaper, however, American gay men have made up their own minds about sucking:

> One thing gay men have worked out is sucking. Not too far into the crisis, men realized that going down on a condomed dick is as pleasurable as wrapping lips around a roll of Saran Wrap. No one likes to talk about it, but read their lips: Most gay men are doing it without rubbers.[88]

Since the late 1980s, countries which work on the risk-reduction model have included oral sex as a legitimate form of safer sex. This approach aims to modify gay men's sexual behaviour by bringing about a shift away from the very risky practice of anal sex without a condom and towards acts which, although not entirely free of risk, are still highly unlikely to result in HIV transmission. From this perspective, gay men should be actively encouraged to take the informed decision to practise oral sex, rather than to have unprotected anal sex.

This does not mean that these materials mislead gay men by pretending that oral sex is 100 per cent safe. Most do advise that the option of avoiding getting semen in the mouth, perhaps by using a condom, is a legitimate response for people who wish to aim for complete safety. The important thing is that this element is not allowed to dominate the message, the predominant tone of which is that of reassurance. Thus, the Terrence Higgins Trust's most recent factual leaflet for gay men explains that:

> No-one can be absolutely sure that virus in cum or pre-cum can't get through the linings of the mouth or throat.
>
> A small number of people think they have been infected through sucking. However, when the sexual behaviour of thousands of gay men has been studied over a number of years, sucking hasn't shown up as a risk. So if there is a risk, it's very small. But the risk may be higher if your mouth is sore or bleeding.
>
> You might choose to use condoms and avoid getting any cum or pre-cum in the mouth.
>
> Some men get just as turned on by nuzzling and licking the cock and balls without taking them in the mouth.[89]

None of this is to say that it may not be *theoretically* possible to become infected with HIV by getting cum in the mouth during oral sex just once. It is a matter of putting that risk in perspective. As Adam Carr points out:

> A South African doctor has reported a case of HIV seroconversion in a gay man who had practised only mutual masturbation (possibly by using his partner's cum as lubricant). The odds on this must be about one in a million ... Does this mean that mutual masturbation cannot be described as 'safe'? ... Most of us happily do things which carry a small but statistically measurable risk of leading to death. Anyone who has undergone surgery, flown to the United States,

driven from Sydney to Melbourne or sniffed amyl has probably run a higher risk of death than has a gay man who has sucked even quite a lot of cocks. Yet we accept these activities as being 'safe', since the risk of death, while real, is so small that we judge it to be acceptable in exchange for the benefits we get from doing these things.[90]

Thus, the existence of cases where HIV infection appears to have occurred as a result of oral sex in no way undermines the classification of sucking as being a safer sex practice. If the risk of infection through a single occasion of oral sex with an HIV-infected person is, say, 0.1 per cent, one would expect a growing number of cases of infection to be reported as more and more time passes and more occasions of oral sex occur. But the detection of these cases does not mean that the actual level of risk in a single occasion of oral sex with an infected person has changed at all, or that safer sex advice is wrong to define oral sex as low risk. Similarly, if the failure rate of condoms during anal sex were 0.1 per cent, a growing number of cases of infection by this route would be reported as time went by. This would not mean that condoms had become any more or less reliable, or that the advice about the advisability of using condoms for anal sex would need to be revised.

For example, in September 1991 doctors at St Bartholomew's Hospital in London reported in a letter to *The Lancet* on a case in which a gay man appeared to have become infected with HIV and gonorrhoea simultaneously through oral sex. They concluded from this single case that 'Health education should advise the use of condoms during fellatio, and the safety of oral sex should be questioned'.[91] A more realistic and helpful approach would have observed that even if it is authentic, this is the only case of oral transmission that has ever been reported at St Bartholomew's, which has seen many thousands of gay men in its genitourinary medicine clinic in the years since 1982; indeed, it is one of only a handful of cases that have ever been reported in the UK, where, at time of writing, extrapolation suggests that nearly 150,000 gay men to date may have taken the HIV antibody test. Such an exceptionally low incidence should properly be seen as a reassuring confirmation that oral sex, if not entirely risk free, is a very low-risk activity for HIV transmission. The tendency for doctors and journalists to suggest that safer sex guidelines may need revision every time there is a new case report of alleged infection through oral sex is one of the most unhelpful and misleading phenomena in the field of HIV prevention, and has doubtless been the cause of much unnecessary anxiety or, worse, of fatalism on the part of gay men who may despair of the possibility of avoiding infection.

By any definition, safer sex necessarily requires the long-term avoidance of unprotected anal sex, except possibly between men who are certain that they both have the same HIV antibody status. This is inevitably a considerable sacrifice for many men, including those who find condoms completely unerotic, those who value greater spontaneity, and those who resent having a latex barrier between them and their partner. As discussed earlier, gay men are unlikely to adopt safer sex unless they feel that it is possible, practical and enjoyable. Thus, the benefits of the more realistic approach to HIV prevention are not simply that gay men are 'allowed' to continue with forms of sex that they find pleasurable. The less restrictive the definition of safer sex, the less likely it is that avoiding HIV transmission will be considered either impossible, unrealistic or simply not worth the trouble.

It is not surprising, therefore, to learn that research has shown that gay men who overestimate the risk of HIV transmission by oral sex may be more likely to have unprotected anal sex. A study presented at the *VIII International Conference on AIDS* in Amsterdam in 1992 analysed correlations between individuals' estimates of the riskiness of various practices and the likelihood that they practised anal sex without a condom. All 330 men knew that there was a very high risk of infection through unprotected anal sex. Of those who actually had oral sex relatively often and estimated the risk of oral sex to be high, 75 per cent practised unsafe anal sex. Among the men who actually practised oral sex relatively often but considered its riskiness to be low, only 50 per cent practised unsafe anal sex. The authors concluded that men who had an exaggerated sense of the riskiness of oral sex:

> had the idea that reducing the risk of infection by quitting unsafe anal sex is relatively futile. They will have the impression that through their frequent practicing of oral sex, they will have run relatively much risk anyway ... Messages

[about the potential risk of oral sex] may lead to an increase instead of a decrease in the practice of unsafe anal sex ... [and] should therefore be issued with great care.[92]

In other words, by aiming too high, unrealistic HIV prevention guidelines run the risk of missing the target altogether.

Eroticism and prevention

A characteristic feature of many community-based HIV prevention campaigns for gay men has been their use of sexually explicit language and imagery to promote safer sex. This approach has been highly controversial in some countries, and even sparked federal restrictions on AIDS education in the USA. In the UK, the obscene publications legislation has, until recently, greatly inhibited the development of erotic safer sex materials, although it should perhaps be stressed that explicit sexual images *have* been used in British safer sex information for gay men since the early days of the epidemic.[93] Given the controversy which seems inevitably to attend the production of frank materials, it is important to remember that health educators' desire to use eroticism in prevention campaigns is not motivated by radicalism or a wish to shock, but because of the proven efficacy and sound educational value of such an approach.

Risk reduction advice aims to persuade its target audience of two factors. First, the existence of safer alternatives to risky behaviour must be communicated. This requires the provision of information about the ways in which HIV is and is not transmitted, allowing individuals to identify whether their own sexual practice is putting them or their partners at risk, and if so, what changes may be necessary to reduce that risk. For gay men, this means identifying unprotected anal sex as the primary risk activity, and recommending either the proper use of strong condoms or the avoidance of anal sex altogether. (The relative merits of these two different approaches is described in Chapter 2, and below.) It also means providing reassurance about sex acts which are considered to be safer sex, such as oral sex and rimming. Although surveys repeatedly show that there remains much confusion about the safety of oral sex, it is clear that the majority of gay men are well informed about the risks in unprotected anal sex and the degree of protection provided by condoms.

Secondly, safer sex must be presented as both an achievable and a desirable option. The latter is perhaps the key component in this. As Dennis Altman has described it, to understand the significance of gay men's adjustments to the presence of HIV:

> requires an understanding of the way gay men have developed a particular set of values and behavior around sexuality which AIDS seemed to throw into question. During the 1970s the growth of gay assertion and a commercial gay world meant an affirmation of sex outside of relationships as a positive good, a means of expressing both sensuality and community ... [I]n general, sexual adventure became a central tenet of gay life. 'Whenever I threw my legs in the air,' one person with AIDS subsequently remarked, 'I thought I was doing my bit for gay liberation.'[94]

Anal sex in particular became a fiercely protected act, the target of anti-sodomy legislation throughout the world, but remaining almost a defining practice of confident homosexuality for many gay men. The task facing AIDS educators was to find acceptable ways in which to bring about substantial changes in this fundamental and intensely politicized area of gay men's lives.

Altman has documented how community organizations were in effect faced with two different approaches to behavioural change, although they have rarely been articulated as being distinct, and in practice, safer sex campaigns have tended to include elements of both. The first approach was to argue for fewer partners, presumably with monogamy being the ideal. As described in Chapter 2, this strategy is likely to be of little value in high prevalence areas where there is a significant chance that one or other of the monogamistic partners may already be infected with HIV. The other strategy was 'the creation of a sexuality which might still involve numbers of partners, but which was based on "risk-free" sex'.[95] This is the tactic which has become most common among community-based organizations. Douglas Crimp has argued that:

[Gay men] were able to invent safe sex because we have always known that sex is not, in an epidemic or not, limited to penetrative sex. Our promiscuity taught us many things, not only about the pleasures of sex, but about the great multiplicity of those pleasures. It is that psychic preparation that has allowed many of us to change our sexual behaviors.[96]

To this extent, community-based safer sex education aims to draw upon the strengths of gay men's confident and imaginative attitude to sex as developed in the 1970s, emphasizing continuity with the objectives and achievements of gay liberation in the possibility of still enjoying pleasurable and satisfying sex, while also preventing HIV transmission. *Capital Gay* argued in 1986, 'The fight for gay liberation and the freedom to have sex with whoever we want, whenever we want it, does not have to be forgotten because of AIDS'.[97]

As Mark Barnes has written of the USA:

explicit sexual images and the freedom to create and use them has been essential to the emergence of gay and lesbian cultures and identities over the past four decades. Explicit sexual images have allowed gay men and women to develop new eroticisms, to dismantle the view of homosexuality as pathological, to define a new culture apart from the dominant heterosexual ideal, and to establish new sets of norms and expectations. Censorship of sexual images – in the context of AIDS as much as in other contexts – therefore threatens the vitality and even the survival of gay culture.[98]

In Britain, the development of a similar culture of sexual frankness has to some extent been inhibited by a web of legislation, which is described later in this chapter. Nevertheless, there is a huge market in male erotica in the UK, ranging from legal soft porn pin-up magazines to imported materials from abroad. Moreover, the restricted availability of such images probably *increases* their appeal to gay men. And in recent years, homoeroticism has become a mainstream component of advertising, as commercial enterprises have recognized that they can use eroticism to help them sell their product. Gay men have become used to seeing the male body used in advertisements ranging from underwear to nightclubs, from jeans to telephone sex lines, from holidays to health spas. Likewise, health educators have discovered that eroticism can sell the concept of safer sex. While risk-reduction guidelines can in themselves seem sterile and appealing, explicit safer sex materials can demonstrate that, in practice, they offer genuinely enjoyable alternatives to riskier sex. Writing in the *New England Journal of Medicine*, Dr John Whyte declared that:

> Many people think of safe sex as unfulfilling, boring or unsatisfying ... [F]actual information may impart knowledge about what is safe, but it does not change attitudes about what is satisfying and erotic. Explicit materials can show people how to adopt safer sexual practices through a process of adaptation rather than a lifetime of self-sacrifice. The dramatic changes in sexual behavior in the gay community argue that explicit, culturally tailored materials can benefit public health substantially.[99]

Mark Barnes has highlighted another important use of the vivid depiction of safer sex, namely, 'to educate low-income or disadvantaged populations in which college-level education should not be presumed'.[100]

> Indeed, censorship of safe sex materials may do more harm to these populations than to more educated and affluent persons at high risk for HIV infection. If so, legal prohibitions on the explicitness of AIDS education in fact will discriminate between low and high-income populations, between the less and the better-educated, and between the less than literate and the fully literate.[101]

However, this rationale should be weighed in the light of Australian research on the acceptability of safer sex materials to working-class gay men, which found that these men 'preferred pamphlets and posters that conveyed images of intimacy, closeness and relational connotations ... They disliked raunchy, sexually explicit material.'[102]

Despite the inherent difficulties in evaluating the effectiveness of specific educational interventions, the efficacy of safer sex materials which use erotic imagery has been demonstrated through sound scientific research. In 1987, Gay Men's Health Crisis in New York sponsored research which compared the impact of four different educational techniques on the sexual behaviour of a cohort of 619 gay men.[103] One of the groups saw and discussed an explicit film showing gay men practising safer sex, while the others received printed safer sex guidelines or heard a man with AIDS talk about the disease. After 2 months, men who had seen the film had reduced by one-third the number of occasions in which they had sex without using condoms, while in the other groups, no changes in sexual behaviour were seen, except that some men temporarily gave up sex but were no more likely to practise safer sex when they resumed.

The rationale for the use of eroticism can be taken further, to identify how specific emphases in explicit portrayals of safer sex can maximize their effectiveness. In Australia, gay community AIDS education programmes have found that:

> a strategy which also promotes the sleazy attributes of sex (in the 'safe' practices) is more successful than one which simply eroticises it as 'hot' or wholesome. The idea of *sleaze* capitalises on the fact that sexual desire has an element of the unknown, the racy and daring, which constitutes part of its excitement. This approach invokes a subcultural metaphor – it is (homo) sex as transgression – rather than as an individualistic search for pleasure ... Most gay men who have changed their sexual practices know that there are no substitutes for what they have lost; but an emphasis of a collective pursuit of the 'naughty' and the 'illicit' in safe sex has been helpful in dealing with this sense of sexual loss.[104]

Unfortunately, the provision of appropriate safer sex materials for gay men has been hampered in many countries by the view that such materials are intended to 'promote' homosexuality. As Dr Frank Rhame has observed, 'The reluctance of governmental institutions to produce materials that are candid about gayness doubtless arises because segments of our society believe that acknowledging and accepting gayness is equivalent to encouraging it. To such persons, nothing that concedes the reality of gayness ... is permiss-ible'.[105] In Britain, the most notorious use of this terminology is enshrined in Section 2(a) of the Local Government Act 1986 – as inserted by Clause 28 of the 1988 Act – which states that a local authority shall not 'intentionally promote homosexuality or pub-lish material with the intention of promoting homosexuality', or 'promote the teaching in any maintained school of the acceptability of homosexuality as a pretended family relationship'.[106] Although Section 2(a) does specify that it does not prohibit 'the doing of anything for the purpose of treating or preventing the spread of disease', there can be little doubt that it has contributed to a climate of fear and inhibition both in teaching about homosexuality and AIDS and in the wider circles of local-government-funded health promotion.

Legal restrictions on safer sex education

In 1986, Gay Men's Health Crisis produced a series of *Safer Sex Comix*, which used cartoon stories of sexual encounters be-tween gay men as a vehicle for safer sex advice. The leaflets are archetypal examples of pro-sex gay health education, which places a primary focus on the authentic sexual satisfaction in the (safe) practices depicted, rather than on the motivation of avoiding HIV transmission. In materials such as these, gay sex *is* safer sex, and vice versa. This equation is made explicit in the title of the Terrence Higgins Trust's leaflets entitled *Tales of Gay Sex*, published in 1991. Within the limits of British obscenity legislation, these aimed to illustrate safer sex as a negotiated interaction between two (or more) individuals, using not cartoons but photographs, with genuine locations and volunteers from the gay scene as models, in order to ground the materials and their message in the recognizable, everyday reality of gay men's lives. The debt owed by the Trust leaflets to the GMHC *Safer Sex Comix* is unmistakable.

However, GMHC's leaflets came to the attention of Republican Senator Jesse Helms, who sent copies to 15 or 20 other Senators. They were '[w]ithout exception ... revolted' and suggested that the President be informed about what was being done 'under the pretence of AIDS education'.[107] A few days later, Helms introduced an amendment to a Labor, Health and Human Services, and Education Bill, which included allocations for AIDS education and research in the financial year 1988–89. In its final approved form, passed in the Senate by a vote of 94 senators for and only 2 against, the amended Act declared that:

> none of the funds made available under this Act to the Centers for Disease Control shall be used to provide AIDS education, information, or prevention materials and activities that promote or encourage, directly, homosexual sexual activities ... Education, information, and prevention activities and materials paid for with funds appropriated under this Act shall emphasise –
> (1) abstinence from sexual activity outside a sexually monogamous marriage (including abstinence from homosexual activities) and
> (2) abstinence from the use of illegal intravenous drugs.[108]

Contributions to the House of Representative's debate on this amendment were also highly illuminating. Referring to one of the GMHC leaflets, Representative Dornan commented that:

> What is offensive, outrageous, about any Federal money being spent on this, is that, like all pornography – the writing of whores, in this case male prostitutes – it is to stimulate sexual desire. It is written lustfully. It talks glowingly of how fantastic the sexual high is of these contacts between Ed the Jock and Julio the Pump Boy.[109]

This is, of course, absolutely correct, in that the sex-positive approach to AIDS education does indeed aim to persuade its readers of the pleasurability of safer sex. The wording of the Helms amendment with its emphasis on abstinence, and comments such as Representative Dornan's, reflect the gulf between state-sanctioned methods of HIV prevention and those designed at a grass-roots, community level by gay men who are genuinely informed about effective means of communicating with and influencing their peers.

For Helms and his colleagues, gay sex which is risk free in terms of HIV transmission is still morally lethal, and AIDS education materials which encourage safer gay sex are in fact 'promot[ing] sexual activity, homosexual activity ... the very thing we want to stop'.[110]

The Helms amendment was finally overturned in 1992, after the American Civil Liberties Union and the Center for Constitutional Rights filed a legal challenge based on the first amendment. However, its existence for four years sent a clear signal to AIDS educators, including those who did not receive funding from the Centers for Disease Control (CDC) and were therefore not affected by the legislation: according to Congress, sex-positive AIDS education was unworthy of funding, and to support gay men in adopting and sustaining safer sex (as opposed to giving up sex altogether) was to exacerbate the AIDS epidemic.

Writing about this and other explicit federal restrictions on the content of AIDS education, Mark Barnes has concluded that 'lives have been sacrificed solely to allow for the denial that certain disgusting things do happen and to promote the hope that those things will never happen again'.[111] The clearest means by which the specificities of gay men's health education needs are obliterated by the mandate of the heterosexual majority have been funding regulations which judge educational programmes by their acceptability to the 'man in the street'. For instance, in 1986 the CDC's directive about materials for group education sessions included the guideline:

> Such terms or descriptors used should be those which a reasonable person would conclude should be understood by a broad cross-section of society, or which when used to communicate with a specific group like gay men about high risk sexual practices would be judged by a reasonable person to be unoffensive to most reasonable persons beyond that group.[112]

To Dr Harvey Fineberg of the Harvard School of Public Health, '[t]his kind of restriction on graphic, direct communication is an added handicap that public health officials do not need and that our society can no longer afford'.[113] Yet in 1988 the CDC announced that it would only fund projects whose content is judged by 'a reasonable person to be unoffensive to most educated adults'.[114] Materials were specifically not to include overt depictions of sexual activity. Funding recipients were each to draw up a review panel and submit materials to it for approval before dissemination; this panel was to consist of 'a reasonable cross-section of the general community, not drawn predominantly from the target group'.[115]

These and similar requirements in which the educational value or the social acceptability of safer sex campaigns is to be assessed by those for whom they are not intended, and by whom they would probably otherwise never be seen, makes a mockery of the notion of targeted interventions. An AIDS educator's primary responsibility must be to those in need of advice, information and support to avoid giving or getting HIV, regardless of the sensibilities of others. Yet these regulations simply make explicit the compromises and self-censorship which many HIV prevention workers find themselves forced to make every day. Whether it is in a CDC-funded project, or in a British local authority which is scared of media criticism if it undertakes targeted work for gay men, or in a non-governmental AIDS organization which is determined not to be seen as a 'gay organization' or to jeopardize its statutory funding, gay safer sex campaigns are routinely inhibited by considerations which should be deemed irrelevant.

Explicit educational materials and British law

There is no doubt that fear of controversy and loss of funding can be major obstacles to the development of erotic safer sex campaigns for gay men. However, prevention workers may also feel that the use of explicit materials is impossible due to legal restrictions, particularly in a country such as Britain where, as the Obscene Publications Squad of the Metropolitan Police is proud to point out, sexual materials are subject to stricter controls than anywhere else in Western Europe.[116] But in reality, current legislation leaves AIDS educators with significant leeway to make use of sexually explicit materials. In particular, common-sense considerations about the purpose of and intended audience for materials are taken into account when deciding if materials are to be considered obscene. Thus, the biggest obstacle facing HIV prevention workers may be that of self-censorship: it is always worthwhile to seek specific legal advice from a solicitor who is knowledgeable in this area, rather than simply to assume that the law prevents erotic safer sex campaigns.[117]

The Obscene Publications Act 1959 includes a definition of the test for obscenity, namely that the effect of the article taken as a whole must be to 'tend to deprave and corrupt a [significant proportion] of persons who are likely ... to read, see or hear the matter contained' in the article. Attempts have been made to define the terms 'deprave' and 'corrupt', but according to solicitor Angus Hamilton, who has advised the Terrence Higgins Trust and other AIDS organizations in matters of obscenity:

> In practice the legislation is applied by having an effective blacklist of forbidden images. Text is, since a number of unsuccessful prosecutions, left largely untouched. The blacklist is not static, however, but constantly changing as publishers seek to push the boundaries of permitted images forward and the prosecuting authorities seek to re-impose what they feel to be the acceptable limits.[118]

The apparent absence of controls on text therefore allows the use of explicit descriptions of safer sex, perhaps in the form of erotic stories or books. However, since the early 1980s, British gay magazines have become less and less explicit in their use of erotic fiction; one publisher has described how stories which used to *start* at the bedroom door now tend to *end* there. This trend may have given the wrong impression to safer sex campaigners: materials such as the AIDS Action Committee of Boston's 'Hot off the streets' leaflet, containing safer sex stories, could probably be used perfectly lawfully in Britain. It was on the basis of this advice that the Terrence Higgins Trust produced the *Tales of Gay Sex* story booklet in summer 1992, featuring eight narratives describing gay men enjoying safer sex in various contexts and settings.

In relation to images, the Obscene Publications Act contains a number of potentially helpful concepts. First, 'it is arguable that careful targeting of a specified audience (for example, only distributing safer sex material for gay men at gay venues) will lessen the risk of prosecution since the Act requires the corruption of persons who are "likely to", as opposed to "conceivably might" see the article'.[119] This provision is in stark contrast to the CDC's requirement that the acceptability of educational materials should be assessed by 'a reasonable cross-section of the general community, not drawn predominantly from the target group'. However, the argument that, in effect, gay men are already depraved and corrupted and may therefore safely be exposed to any and all images may not be accepted by the courts: the Act is also concerned with preventing the *further* corruption of those already less than innocent.

Secondly, the test of obscenity must be applied to the article as a whole, requiring sexually explicit content to be judged in its context. Hence, videos such as *The Gay Man's Guide to Safer Sex*[120] or *Getting It Right*[121] would have to be judged not only on their sex scenes, but also on their lengthy introductory material, captions and voice-overs about HIV transmission and safer sex. Similarly, a sexually explicit image used to illustrate one part of a larger publication, or to catch the attention of the reader, could not be used in isolation to argue that the item as a whole was obscene.

The Obscene Publications Act also allows a 'public good' defence, which states that the publication of an article, even though it may be judged to be obscene, may be justified as being for the public good 'if it is in the interests of science, literature, art or learning, or other objects of general concern'. This defence was used successfully, for example, on behalf of *Lady Chatterley's Lover*, which was judged to be of ethical and Christian merit, of educational and sociological merit, and to make a contribution to human relations. Hamilton points out that '[s]ome of the case law on this section appears to be unhelpful to the application of the "public good" defence to sexually explicit material',[122] as in 1977 the Court of Appeal rejected an application to call expert evidence to establish whether certain magazines had merit in the field of sex education, and ruled that the provision of information about sexual matters did not fall within the scope of the 'public good' defence. However, he concludes that:

it is arguable that th[is] ruling was largely expedient and sought principally to control pornography dressed up as sex education material. Safer sex information may still be regarded as possessing scientific interest if it extends an existing body of knowledge or presents known facts in a systematic way. It would certainly be arguable that safer sex information should be within the scope of the 'public good' defence.[123]

A further provision in the Act allows material which the authorities consider to be obscene to be seized without prosecution, placing the onus on the person who possessed the material to take (potentially expensive) legal action to recover it. However, this provision does not apply to material which is not distributed for gain, so safer sex leaflets which are circulated on a non-commercial basis are not vulnerable.

Happily, current moves in relation to sexually explicit images appear to be in the direction of a relaxation of the law. Hamilton points out that:

it was considered, until relatively recently, that an image of an erect penis was not permissible. The early 1990s, however, have seen an explosion of sexual guidance videos, which contain such images and yet have been certificated by the British Board of Film Classification, and have to date not been the subject of any prosecutions.[124]

While British Board of Film Classification (BBFC) certification does not exempt these videos, which include safer sex films for gay men, from prosecution for obscenity, it may reflect an endorsement of the educational value of some erotic material. Sir James Ferman, director of the BBFC, has publicly declared that he sees the certification of these films as part of a 'deliberate campaign to decriminalize certain sexually explicit images'.[125] The sex education tapes have been granted '18' certificates, allowing them to be sold to those aged 18 or older in standard video outlets including high-street record stores, rather than the now little-used '18R' certificate, which marks videos which may only be sold in licensed sex shops. During this unofficial campaign, the BBFC has taken an even-handed view of homosexuality, agreeing that they would apply the same criteria to sex acts between two women or two men (provided both are over the homosexual age of consent) as they apply to those between a man and a woman.

Guidance to video producers from the BBFC advises that the more sexually explicit an image, the more clearly educational its context must be. Scenes of penetrative sex of any kind should not be lingering, and require voice-overs or captions which describe, for example, the correct method of condom use or the low risk of HIV transmission during oral sex. In consultations over the script for *The Gay Man's Guide to Safer Sex* prior to filming, the BBFC also warned against showing sexual positions which might be considered gratuitous.

British law contains other provisions which may hamper erotic safer sex education. Some legislation uses the concept of indecency rather than obscenity. Indecency is accepted to be a wider concept than obscenity, and items which are not considered to be obscene may therefore still be judged to be indecent. Legislation which uses the test of indecency does not include the 'public good' defence of the obscenity law, meaning that material can be judged regardless of its overall purpose. The Post Office Act 1953 makes it an offence to send any 'offending, shocking lewd or indecent' article through the post, although in 1981 the Director of Public Prosecutions took the view that material which is judged to be indecent, but can nevertheless be sold over the counter because it is not obscene, could also be ordered and sent by post. Future prosecutions would be confined to cases where indecent material was visible on the outside of the package or the material was sent unsolicited. The Unsolicited Goods and Services Act 1971 makes it an offence for a person to send someone publications which describe or illustrate human sexual activity unless they have been requested. The Customs and Excise Management Act 1959 prohibits the importation into the United Kingdom of obscene or indecent material, although the dawning of the single European market has meant that material imported from other EC member states must be judged by the Obscene Publications Act's test of obscenity, rather than that of indecency. Finally, the Indecent Displays (Control) Act 1981 is designed to prevent the public display of any indecent item. However, it is important to know that at the time of writing there have been no prosecutions of safer sex materials under any of these laws.

Conclusion

The purpose of this chapter has been to provide reassurance and guidance in three of the more vexed areas of safer sex promotional work. Messages about oral sex have for years been confused and unclear, and rarely based on a rational reading of the medical literature in the context of a risk reduction strategy. Unhelpful absolutism has also inhibited the vigorous promotion of condoms for anal sex. Uncertainty about the law and a mistaken self-censorship have rendered health educators over-cautious in employing explicit erotic images in safer sex materials, despite the sound rationale for their use.

The challenge for HIV prevention workers now is to build on the successes and redress the shortcomings of the past. Initiatives to encourage the initial adoption of safer sex continue to be essential; additional strategies to support gay men who have been practising safer sex for some years are also needed. Recent data suggest that there may have been an increase in unsafe sex and in new HIV infections among gay men since the late 1980s. The evidence and possible explanations for this are discussed next.

Notes

1. Helpful resources dealing with these issues include: Michael Rooney and Peter Scott, 'Working where the risks are', in *Working Where the Risks Are: Issues in HIV Prevention* (eds B. Evans, S. Sandberg and S. Watson). Health Education Authority, London, 1992; 'Beginning HIV prevention work with gay and bisexual men', in *Healthy Alliances in HIV Prevention* (eds B. Evans, S. Sandberg and S. Watson). Health Education Authority, London, 1993; Edward King, Michael Rooney and Peter Scott, *HIV Prevention for Gay Men: A Survey of Initiatives in the UK*. North-West Thames Regional Health Authority, London, 1992; Peter Scott, 'HIV/AIDS health education', *National AIDS Manual* (April 1991 edition), vol. 1, Ch. H1. NAM Publications, London, 1991, Ronald Valdiserri, *Preventing AIDS*. Rutgers University Press, London, 1989.

2. Scott, *op. cit.*

3. See the sources listed in note 1.

4. See the discussion in Chapter 4.

5. Joseph Sonnabend, 'Looking at AIDS in totality: a conversation', *New York Native*, 129, 7 October 1985.

6. Richard Berkowitz and Michael Callen, *How to Have Sex in an Epidemic: One Approach*, p. 21. News From the Front Publications, New York, 1983.

7. However, from the late 1970s gay men who were 'super-carriers' of hepatitis B were recommended always to use condoms for anal sex. The prevention of hepatitis B transmission was never seen as a community-wide gay health concern, unlike the prevention of HIV.

8. 'Condoms and gay men: information and advice', leaflet. Dallas Gay Alliance, USA, undated.

9. Minutes of Terrence Higgins Trust Safer Sex Policy Group meeting, 4 February 1987. I am grateful to Simon Watney for bringing these to my attention.

10. Julian Meldrum, 'Barrier methods', *Capital Gay*, 28 September 1984.

11. Minutes of Terrence Higgins Trust Safer Sex Policy Group meeting.

12. Tony Whitehead, 'Safer sex and gay men – disputes and dilemmas', *Capital Gay*, 299, 3 July 1987.

13. Buro GVO, 'On vacation? Keep it safe!', leaflet in English, German, French, Italian, Dutch and Spanish, May 1989.

14. Scottish AIDS Monitor, 'Living gay, loving safe', undated leaflet (emphasis in original).

15. Berkowitz and Callen, *op. cit.*, pp. 19–22.

16. Richard Berkowitz and Michael Callen, *Condom Update*, addendum to second edition of *How to Have Sex in an Epidemic*, December 1983.

17. Los Angeles Cooperative AIDS Risk Reduction Education Service (L.A.CARES), 'Mother's handy sex guide', 8-page undated booklet.

18. Victorian AIDS Council and Gay Men's Community Health Centre, 'It's black & white ... condomwise', 16-page leaflet, November 1986.

19. AIDS Council of New South Wales, 'Cum inside ... a condom', undated leaflet.

20. Michael Callen, 'In defense of anal sex', *PWA Coalition Newsline* (New York), 41: 37–43 (1989).

21. See Edward King, 'Defending anal sex', *The Pink Paper*, 153, 15 December 1990.

22. Callen, *op. cit.*

23. Roger Detels *et al.*, 'Seroconversion, sexual activity, and condom

use among 2915 HIV seronegative men followed for up to 2 years',
J. AIDS, **2**(1): 77–83 (1989).

24. Lode Wigersma *et al.*, 'Safety and acceptability of condoms for use by homosexual men as a prophylactic against transmission of HIV during anogenital sexual intercourse', *BMJ*, **295**: 94 (1987).

25. G. J. P. van Griensven *et al.*, 'Failure rate of condoms during anogenital intercourse in homosexual men', *Genitourinary Medicine*, **64**: 344–6 (1988).

26. John de Wit *et al.*, 'Failure rate of condoms among gay men', *VIII International Conference on AIDS*, Amsterdam, abstract PoD 5178 (1992).

27. Susan Golombok *et al.*, 'Condom failure among homosexual men', *J. AIDS*, **2**: 404–9 (1989).

28. J Richters *et al.*, 'Low condom breakage rates in commercial sex', *The Lancet*, **ii**: 1487–8 (1988).

29. B. Voeller *et al.*, 'Persistent condom breakage', *V International Conference on AIDS*, Montreal, abstract W.A.P.99 (1989).

30. de Wit, *op. cit.*

31. Susan Golombok *et al.*, 'Evaluation of an extra strength condom in anal intercourse', *VIII International Conference on AIDS*, Amsterdam, abstract PoC 4792 (1992).

32. Privileged communication.

33. 'Can you rely on condoms?', *Consumer Reports*, pp. 135–42 (Consumers Union, New York), March 1989; Nick Dale, LRC Products Ltd, personal communication, January 1990.

34. See, for example, the advice in the Health Education Authority's fact card 'They're everywhere!', or in the Terrence Higgins Trust's leaflet 'Safer sex for gay men', both published in 1991.

35. *British Standard specification for natural rubber latex condoms* (BS 3704: 1989), paragraph 1. British Standards Institution, London, 1989.

36. *Ibid.*, paragraph 9.3.2.2 (e).

37. For example, Durex Assure and Ladymates are intended for women, and PlayMates and Durex SafePlay are promoted for young people.

38. It is, however, arguable that manufacturers would have a defence against compensation claims based on the Consumer Protection Act if they simply went to the trouble of generating research data proving the effectiveness of condoms during anal sex and assisted in the development of a British Standard specifically for condoms for anal sex. This is because section 54 (1) (e) of the Consumer Protection Act provides a 'development risks defence': 'In any civil proceedings by virtue of the first part of the Act against any person in respect of a defect in a product it shall be a defence ... to show that the state of scientific and technical knowledge at the relevant

time was not such that a producer of products of the same description as the product in question might be expected to have discovered the defect if it had existed in the products while they were under his control.'

39. See Edward King, 'Up yours?', *The Pink Paper*, 250, 4 November 1992.

40. Gerald Hannon, 'A bum wrap', *Xtra!*, 6 December 1991.

41. Martin T. Schechter *et al.*, 'Can HTLV-III be transmitted orally?' (letter), *The Lancet*, i: 379 (1986).

42. See, for example, Thomas Lehner *et al.*, 'Mucosal transmission of HIV', *Nature*, 353: 709 (1991), in which researchers trying to understand how HIV can be transmitted across undamaged mucous membranes adjust their theories to take account of the epidemiological fact that 'there is no convincing evidence that HIV particles in seminal fluid ejaculated during oral sex gain entry through the oral mucosa'.

43. Gerald M. Oppenheimer, 'Causes, cases and cohorts: the role of epidemiology in the historical construction of AIDS', in *AIDS: The Making of a Chronic Disease* (eds E. Fee and D. M. Fox), pp. 49–83, University of California Press, Berkeley, CA, 1992.

44. In 1988, a team of researchers from Toronto pointed out that 'In the [two] studies that have reported elevated risk [from oral sex], the analysis was univariate in nature' (Randall A. Coates *et al.*, 'Risk factors for HIV infection in male sexual contacts of men with AIDS or an AIDS-related condition', *American Journal of Epidemiology*, 128(4): 729–39 [1988]).

45. Mads Melbye *et al.*, 'Seroepidemiology of HTLV-III antibody in Danish homosexual men: prevalence, transmission and disease outcome', *BMJ*, 289: 573–5 (1984).

46. B. A. Evans *et al.*, 'Sexual lifestyle and clinical findings related to HTLV-III/LAV status in homosexual men', *Genitourinary Medicine*, 62: 384–9 (1986).

47. Warren Winkelstein *et al.*, 'Sexual practices and risk of infection by the human immunodeficiency virus', *JAMA*, 257(3): 321–5 (1987).

48. Schechter, *op. cit.*

49. Lawrence A. Kingsley *et al.*, 'Risk factors for seroconversion to human immunodeficiency virus among male homosexuals', *The Lancet*, i: 345–9 (1987).

50. Detels, *op. cit.*

51. M. T. Schechter *et al.*, 'Changes in sexual behaviour and fear of AIDS' (letter), *The Lancet*, i: 1293 (1984).

52. See, for example, Leon McKusick *et al.*, 'Reported changes in the sexual behavior of men at risk for AIDS, San Francisco, 1982–84 – the AIDS Behavioral Research Project', *Public Health Reports*, 100(6): 622–9 (1985); CDC, 'Self-reported behavior changes

among homosexual and bisexual men – San Francisco', *JAMA*, **254**(18): 2537–8 (1985); John L. Martin, 'The impact of AIDS on gay male sexual behavior patterns in New York City', *AJPH*, **77**(5): 578–81 (1987).

53. S. Golombok *et al.*, 'Condom use among homosexual men', *AIDS Care*, **1**(1): 27–33 (1989).

54. Project Sigma, *Update*, London, March 1992.

55. Adam Carr, 'Swallowing the evidence – is oral sex (or anything else) safe?', *Outrage*, pp. 50–3, January 1991.

56. Andrew Hunt *et al.*, 'Coming to blows' (letter), *Capital Gay*, London, 15 November 1991.

57. *Ibid.*

58. R. K. W. Lau *et al.*, 'Trends in sexual behaviour in a cohort of homosexual men: a 7 year prospective study', *International Journal of STD and AIDS*, **3**: 267–72 (1992).

59. Lawrence A. Kingsley *et al.*, 'Sexual transmission efficiency of hepatitis B virus and human immunodeficiency virus among homosexual men', *JAMA*, **264**(2): 230–4 (1990).

60. M. T. Schreeder *et al.*, 'Hepatitis B in homosexual men: prevalence of infection and factors related to transmission', *J. Inf. Dis.*, **146**: 7–15 (1982).

61. See Edward King, 'Is it safe?', *The Pink Paper*, 146, 27 October 1990.

62. Berkowitz and Callen, *How to Have Sex in an Epidemic*.

63. *AIDS and HTLV III – Medical Briefing* (second edition). Terrence Higgins Trust, London, 1985.

64. *Ibid.*

65. 'Sex . . .', leaflet, Terrence Higgins Trust, London, 1985.

66. Maria Ekstrand, quoted in Robin Hardy, 'Risky business: confronting unsafe sex', *Village Voice*, 26 June 1990.

67. Ed Jackson, quoted in *ibid.*

68. See Gerald Ilaria *et al.*, 'Detection of HIV-1 DNA sequences in pre-ejaculatory fluid' (letter), *The Lancet*, **340**: 1469 (1992); Jeffrey Pudney *et al.*, 'Pre-ejaculatory fluid as potential vector for sexual transmission of HIV-1', *The Lancet*, **340**: 1470 (1992).

69. For example, see Andrew R. Moss, 'Risk factors for AIDS and HIV seropositivity in homosexual men', *Am. J. Epidem.*, **125**(6): 1035–47 (1987).

70. P. C. Fox *et al.*, 'Saliva inhibits HIV-1 infectivity', *Journal of the American Dental Association*, **116**: 635–7 (1988). See also P. N. Fultz, 'Components of saliva inactivate human immunodeficiency virus', *The Lancet*, ii: 1215 (1986).

71. Martin P. Levine and Karolynn Siegel, 'Unprotected sex: understanding gay men's participation', in *The Social Context of AIDS* (eds J. Huber and B. E. Schneider), pp. 47–71, Sage Publications, London, 1992.

72. Keith Alcorn, *Briefing Paper*. National AIDS Helpline, London, 1990.

73. Alan R. Lifson *et al.*, 'HIV seroconversion in two homosexual men after receptive oral intercourse with ejaculation: implications for counseling concerning safe sexual practices', *AJPH*, 80(12): 1509–11 (1991).

74. W. Chen *et al.*, 'Allergy, oral sex, and HIV' (letter), *The Lancet*, 339(8793): 627–8 (1992).

75. Alison B. Murray *et al.*, 'Coincident acquisition of *Neisseria gonorrhoeae* and HIV from fellatio' (letter), *The Lancet*, 338: 330 (1991).

76. Nicholas Mulcahy, 'The truth about oral sex', *QW* magazine, pp. 37–9, 29 November 1992.

77. W. Rozenbaum *et al.*, 'HIV transmission by oral sex' (letter), *The Lancet*, i:1395 (1988).

78. Ireneus P. M. Keet *et al.*, 'Orogenital sex and the transmission of HIV among homosexual men', *AIDS*, 6: 223–6 (1992).

79. Alison Murray, St Bartholomew's Hospital, London, quoted in 'Doctors warn against oral sex', *Capital Gay*, 514, 4 October 1991. Her comments relate to the publication of Murray, *op. cit.*

80. However, in Australia the term 'safe sex' is also used in preference to 'safer sex', but with the understanding that 'the term does not and cannot only mean sexual practices which carry absolutely no risk whatever of HIV infection. This definition would define the term out of existence'. See Carr, *op. cit.*

81. For an extreme example, see the discussion of the San Francisco AIDS Foundation's poster 'An important message for gay and bisexual men ...', in Chapter 4.

82. This distinction is well discussed by Mulcahy, *op. cit.*

83. Quoted in Mulcahy, *op. cit.*

84. Callen, *op. cit.*

85. 'The safer sex condom guide for men and women', leaflet. Gay Men's Health Crisis, New York, 1987.

86. Hardy, *op. cit.*

87. Untitled 40-page leaflet for gay men in English and Spanish. Gay Men's Health Crisis, New York, 1991.

88. Hardy, *op. cit.*

89. 'Safer sex for gay men' leaflet. Terrence Higgins Trust, London, 1991.

90. Carr, *op. cit.*

91. Murray, *op. cit.*

92. Ernest de Vroome *et al.*, 'Overestimating the risk of a low-risk sexual technique increases or decreases behavioral risk, depending on mediating factors'; and handout, 'Overestimating the risk of orogenital sex may increase unsafe anogenital sex', *VIII Inter-*

national Conference on AIDS, Amsterdam, abstract PoD 5125 (1992).

93.   See, for example, the double-page spread, 'The new joy of gay sex' in *Capital Gay*, 23 May 1986, including photographs of erect penises with condoms.

94.   Dennis Altman, *AIDS and the New Puritanism*, pp. 142–3, Pluto Press, London, 1986.

95.   *Ibid.*, p. 156.

96.   Douglas Crimp, 'How to have promiscuity in an epidemic', in *AIDS: Cultural Analysis, Cultural Activism* (ed. Crimp), p. 253, MIT Press, Cambridge, MA, 1988.

97.   'The new joy of gay sex', *Capital Gay*, 23 May 1986.

98.   Mark Barnes, 'Toward ghastly death: the censorship of AIDS education', *Columbia Law Review*, 89(3): 698–724 (1989).

99.   John Whyte, 'Teaching safe sex' (letter), *NEJM*, **318**(6): 387 (1988).

100. *Ibid.*

101. *Ibid.*

102. G. W. Dossett *et al.* 'Working class homosexuality and AIDS', *Psychology and Health*, 6: 313–24 (1992). Thanks to Keith Alcorn for drawing this to my attention.

103. J. E. D'Eramo *et al.*, 'The "800 Men" Project: a systematic evaluation of AIDS prevention programs demonstrating the efficacy of erotic, sexually explicit safer sex education on gay and bisexual men at risk for AIDS', *IV International Conference on AIDS*, Stockholm, abstract 8086 (1988). See also Gina Kolata, 'Erotic films in AIDS study cut risky behavior', *New York Times*, p. C3, 3 November 1987.

104. Gary Dowsett, 'Reaching men who have sex with men in Australia. An overview of AIDS education: community intervention and community attachment strategies'.

105. Frank S. Rhame, 'More on "Safe Sex"' (letter), *NEJM*, **318**: 1760 (1988).

106. Section 28 is well discussed in relation to the AIDS epidemic by Simon Watney, 'Taking liberties: an introduction', in *Taking Liberties: AIDS and Cultural Politics* (eds E. Carter and S. Watney). Serpent's Tail, London, 1989.

107. *133 Congressional Record*, S14203 (daily edition, 14 October 1987), Statement of Senator Helms.

108. *Ibid.*, H12478 (daily edition, 21 December 1987), Section 514.

109. *Ibid.*, H8801 (daily edition, 20 October 1987), Statement of Representative Dornan.

110. *Ibid.*, H8802 (daily edition, 20 October 1987), Statement of Representative D. Burton.

111. Barnes, *op. cit.*

112. Quoted by Dr Harvey Fineberg, 'Public health and private rights: health ethical and social perspectives', in *AIDS: Impact on Public Policy – An International Forum: Policy, Politics and AIDS* (eds R. F. Hummel, W. F. Leavy, M. Rampolla and S. Chorost), p. 21, Plenum Press, New York, 1986.

113. *Ibid.*

114. 'Centers for Disease Control cooperative agreements for acquired immunodeficiency syndrome (AIDS) health education and risk reduction programs', *51 Federal Register*, 3431 (1986).

115. *Ibid.*

116. 'AIDS, pornography and the law' are discussed as the fourth chapter of Simon Watney's *Policing Desire* (second edition). University of Minnesota Press, Minneapolis, 1989.

117. For a thorough overview of legal considerations in promoting safer sex in Britain, see Angus Hamilton, 'HIV prevention and the law', *National AIDS Manual* (Spring 1993 edition), chapter A7. NAM Publications, London, 1993.

118. *Ibid.*

119. *Ibid.*

120. Pride Video Productions in association with the Terrence Higgins Trust, *The Gay Man's Guide to Safer Sex*, video, London, 1992.

121. Pride Video Productions in association with the Terrence Higgins Trust, *Getting It Right – Safer Sex and Young Gay Men*, video, London, 1993.

122. Hamilton, *op. cit.*

123. *Ibid.*

124. *Ibid.*

125. Sir James Ferman, comments at 'We should be seeing things: screen censorship and sexuality' seminar, Institute for Contemporary Arts, London, 25 April 1992.

Chapter four

Sustaining Safer Sex?

Th[e] notion of relapse threatens to inform the next generation of health education initiatives for gay and bisexual men, yet it remains a beguiling but imprecise idea that is conceptually untenable, empirically dubious and politically naïve.

● *Peter Davies and Project SIGMA*[1]

DURING the late 1980s, gay communities around the world were rightly congratulated on their unprecedented and extensive adoption of safer sex, and held up as evidence that responsible behaviour change in response to the threat of AIDS was indeed possible. However, from the end of 1989 until the present, the focus on the elements of success in gay men's behavioural modifications shifted somewhat, and a number of reports from both clinics and cohorts described evidence of continuing and increasing levels of unsafe sex among gay men. Outside the medical literature, Michael Rooney's *Gay Men: Sustaining Safer Sex?* (North West Thames Regional Health Authority, London, 1991) was very important in documenting and drawing attention to these new trends. Researchers responded by constructing theories to explain why some gay men might still be practising unsafe sexual activities, and defining subgroups of the gay and bisexual population in which unsafe sex might be particularly likely. Quickly, a new paradigm became established, characterized by the view that what was occurring could be accurately described as 'relapse' or 'slippage', as gay men were apparently unable to maintain safer sexual practices, perhaps due to the effects of drink or drugs, or perhaps on account of denial or reckless fatalism. This model has in turn been strongly criticized for a 'subtle homophobia',[2] which unhelpfully pathologizes gay sex.

Increasing levels of STDs at clinics

The article that first prompted the new attention to unsafe sex among gay men was published in *Morbidity and Mortality Weekly Reports* (*MMWR*), the bulletin of the US Centers for Disease Control (CDC). In November 1989, Dr Handsfield and colleagues from King County, Washington, reported that, as elsewhere, the incidence of gonorrhoea among gay or bisexual men attending sexually transmitted disease (STD) clinics had fallen from 720 cases in 1982 to 27 cases in 1988. However, during the first nine months of 1989, 71 cases were seen. There was no significant difference between the age or race of the men with gonorrhoea in 1989 and those presenting with the condition throughout the 1980s, suggesting that the increase was not limited to an easily definable subpopulation of gay or bisexual men. An editorial comment suggested that this tripling in gonorrhoea might reflect either the reintroduction of the *N. gonorroheae* organism to a subpopulation of gay men who had never consistently adopted safer sex, or an increase in the frequency of high-risk sex.[3]

During 1990, similar data were presented from STD clinics in the Netherlands and Victoria, Australia. In Amsterdam, cases of gonorrhoea among gay men increased in 1989 after seven years of consistent decline, and despite a continuing fall in the number of cases seen in all men and women attending clinics. Rectal gonorrhoea had been becoming increasingly uncommon since 1983, but also increased slightly in 1989. The number of cases of early syphilis among gay or bisexual men more than doubled in 1989 compared with the previous year.[4] These data seemed to parallel an increase in new HIV infections in the Amsterdam cohort study. The annual incidence of seroconversion fell from 8.9 per cent in 1985 to only 1 per cent, or 4 cases in 1989; however, it rose to 2.8 per cent in 1990.[5]

In Victoria, the proportion of cases of gonorrhoea which were among gay or bisexual men fell from an average of 13.2 per cent between 1983 and 1987 to a record low of 4.6 per cent in June 1987. However, in the third quarter of 1987 there followed a sharp rebound to 29.3 per cent of the total, which was sustained throughout 1988. In 1989 the proportion rose to 58.9 per cent by the second quarter, and remained as high as 37 per cent one year later. Although many of these isolates were from the urethra, and therefore may have been contracted through low-risk activities such as rimming or oral sex, the proportion of rectal isolates also increased. During this period, cases of gonorrhoea among women or heterosexual men were steadily declining. The clinicians described the trends among gay men as 'extraordinary'.[6]

The first half of 1991 saw a flurry of reports of increasing evidence of unsafe sex from STD clinics throughout the United Kingdom. In January, clinicians from Leicester Royal Infirmary reported a sharp increase in the incidence of rectal gonorrhoea acquired through homosexual sex, from 0 cases in 1988 to 13 in 1990, a level last seen in 1984. There was little evidence that these occurrences reflected a limited 'cluster' of the condition. Of these cases, 60 per cent were in men aged under 24 years old, and nearly 70 per cent were in men in relationships of 3 months' duration or longer.[7]

In the following month, doctors at Leeds General Infirmary reported that the frequency of gonorrhoea in gay or bisexual men, which had dropped significantly from 1984 to 1987, had now risen again; in 1990 they treated 34 cases, or 12 per cent of the total number of gonorrhoea cases seen at the clinic. This rate was the same as that for 1980, although the absolute number of cases both in heterosexuals and homosexuals had fallen to a third of the 1980 total.[8] At the John Hunter Clinic in London, doctors observed 'a considerable rise in new cases of gonococcal infection ... particularly in homosexual males, especially in the 20–30 year age group'. Among gay or bisexual men, 58 cases were seen over a 3-month period, compared with 19 during the same period in 1989. There was also evidence that a significant proportion of the 1990 cases was in gay men who knew that they were HIV-positive and had been 'repeatedly counselled and advised about safer sexual practices'.[9]

A collaborative study between St Mary's and the Middlesex

Hospitals in London revealed a similar increase in gonorrhoea, but questioned the extent to which it correlated with unsafe sex. Of 39 men presenting with rectal gonorrhoea between August and December 1990, 8 (21 per cent) had had no receptive anal sex, and a further 9 (26 per cent) had always used condoms during receptive anal sex. The only sexual risks for these men were oro-anal sex (rimming) or digital-anal sex (fingering), neither of which carries a significant risk of HIV transmission. Likewise, 31 out of 68 cases of urethral gonorrhoea were in men whose only risk factor was insertive oral sex, also low risk for HIV transmission. A further 10 of the 39 men (26 per cent) with rectal gonorrhoea had had unprotected anal sex within a regular relationship.[10]

A retrospective analysis of cases of gonorrhoea in gay or bisexual men attending St Mary's during 1985–88 showed that the median age of the men appeared to be remaining fairly stable at around 30 years old. This was interpreted as a sign that new cases of gonorrhoea were continuing to occur in younger men who were just beginning their sexual careers, rather than solely among a consistent group of older men who had never fully adopted safer sex. The clinicians argued that safer sex campaigns targeting younger gay men might therefore be more urgent than efforts designed to sustain behaviour changes in men who had already adopted safer sex.[11]

In April 1991, increases in syphilis and gonorrhoea among STD clinic attenders in Edinburgh, including gay or bisexual men, were reported. During the first 9 months of 1990, 15 cases of rectal gonorrhoea were seen, compared with 3 cases throughout 1989. Gonorrhoea at other body sites also increased. More cases of early syphilis in gay men occurred than in the preceding four years combined.[12]

All these data from STD clinics are subject to the cautions and provisos discussed in Chapter 1. In particular, the limitations of conclusions based on sexually transmitted diseases as surrogate markers for unsafe sex, as raised by clinicians from St Mary's and the Middlesex Hospitals, must be stressed. Nevertheless, these figures do paint a broadly consistent picture of rising levels of sexual activities which may give rise to increasing transmission of HIV among gay men. Indeed, the increases in these markers are paralleled to some extent by rises in unsafe sexual practices and new HIV infections in interview- and questionnaire-based studies such as the Amsterdam cohort mentioned above, and the studies discussed below.

Increasing unsafe sex and HIV transmission in studies

The San Francisco AIDS Behavioral Research Project continues to be one of the largest and most influential studies of gay men's sexual behaviour during the AIDS crisis. An analysis presented at the VI International Conference on AIDS in San Francisco in 1990, and subsequently published, stated that 69 per cent of high risk sex that occurred during a 1-month study period in 1988 'could be characterised as a relapse', in that the participants had previously reported the adoption of safer sex. In this analysis, high-risk sex was considered to be any anal sex with a casual partner, regardless of condom use, or anal sex without a condom within a relationship. This 'relapse' was reported by 19 per cent of the 397 men analysed. By contrast, only 9 men had consistently reported high-risk sex between 1984 and 1988. Out of 535 men, 256 had had unprotected anal sex during the preceding year, of whom 46 per cent were in mutually monogamous relationships, 18 per cent were in non-monogamous relationships and 35 per cent had no primary relationship. Further analysis revealed that:

> men in monogamous relationships are more likely to report having unprotected sex as a result of being in love and having the same HIV antibody status as their partner than men without primary relationships. Men without a primary relationship are more likely to report having unprotected sex as a result of being sexually aroused or due to a combination of sex and alcohol or drug use or a lack of condoms at the time that sex occurred than are men in monogamous relationships.[13]

The distinction between ongoing unsafe sex and a reversion from safer to unsafe sex was also made by researchers on the San

Francisco Men's Health Study. They reported that '16 percent and 12 percent of the subjects admitted to relapsing to unprotected insertive and receptive anal sex, respectively, while an additional 10 percent were stable high risk' between 1984 and 1988.[14] Analysis of a subsample of 300 men who were followed between 1987 and 1990 found that 62 per cent had had unprotected anal sex at least once during the three years, indicating that 'occasional "relapse" may be something that happens to most gay men in the study population over time'. However, two distinct patterns of unsafe sex were identified. Men who reported 6 or more instances of unsafe sex during the preceding year were likely to have the same HIV antibody status, to have practised unsafe sex together in the past, and to be in love. For these men, unprotected sex was essentially a planned, considered choice about which they therefore felt little unease. Men who reported less frequent unprotected anal sex were more likely to identify situational factors such as a lack of condoms or being particularly sexually aroused, or to have thought that 'once would be OK'. These men were more likely to feel guilty, worried or scared on account of having had unsafe sex.[15]

Data from the Chicago arm of the Multicenter AIDS Cohort Study (MACS) highlighted 'alarming rates of relapse' between 1986 and 1988. Although over this two-year period an increasing proportion of the cohort stopped having anal sex altogether, and fewer men reported never or inconsistently using condoms, the proportion who reported at least one occasion of unprotected anal sex increased to a total of 47 per cent.[16]

The British cohort study Project SIGMA reported that more participants had become HIV-positive in 1991 than in any year since the start of the study in 1987.[17] Between 1988 and 1989 there was a small net increase in the proportion of men who reported practising anal sex during the month before interview, from 41 per cent to 43 per cent;[18] there was also an overall increase in the mean number of sexual partners in 1989.[19] SIGMA, in common with many other studies, demonstrated that anal sex was much more common between regular partners than casual partners, and that unprotected anal sex was relatively rare outside regular relationships. It was calculated that 93 per cent of the increase in anal sex could be explained by a growing number of participants entering regular sexual partnerships;[20] moreover, of 11 men who tested

HIV-antibody negative in 1987–88 but were subsequently found to have become infected, 8 were clearly infected through sex with a regular partner, while only 1 could be confidently traced to a casual partner.[21] Nevertheless, there remained a significant underlying level of unprotected anal sex with casual partners: in the 1991 wave of interview, less than two-thirds of study participants always used condoms, and one-seventh never used them, when they had anal sex with casual partners.[22]

Another British cohort compared sexual behaviour reported by 356 gay men at two interviews, the first in the period mid-1987 to early 1989, with the follow-up 9–12 months later. In each case, the data refer to the year prior to each interview. Most of the participants either sustained safer sex (40 per cent), or changed from unsafe to safer behaviours (16 per cent); 37 per cent reported unprotected anal sex during both time periods, and 7 per cent changed from safer to unsafe sex. Again, men in regular relationships were significantly more likely to report unsafe sex than men with casual or non-regular partners.[23]

In early 1993, epidemiologists from the Communicable Disease Surveillance Centre (CDSC) published an overview of data relating to recent unsafe sexual behaviour among gay men in England and Wales.[24] The CDSC receives reports of all positive HIV antibody tests from clinics and laboratories throughout the country, and data on all HIV antibody tests, regardless of result, from a smaller number of centres. The paper reported that the number of gay men testing HIV-positive each year decreased between 1986 and 1988, but had subsequently risen, with more gay men testing positive in 1991 than in any year since 1987. If most of these reports had been of individuals who became infected some time ago, but had only now decided to take the test, the average age of those testing positive and the proportion who had already developed HIV-related symptoms at the time of testing would be expected to have increased; in practice, both of these measures had remained stable, suggesting that new infections among young men were still occurring. Each year there was an increasing number of reports of infection among gay men who had previously tested negative; moreover, 29 per cent of those who were known to have become infected between 1989 and 1991 were aged under 25. The proportion of gay men aged 19 or younger who tested HIV-positive had also increased significantly. Between 1987 and 1990, between 2.1 per cent and 2.7 per cent of gay teenagers who took the antibody test were found to be HIV-positive, while in 1991 this rose to 4.7 per cent. Other STDs had also become more common: rectal gonorrhoea among men increased five-fold in 1990 and remained at the same level in 1991, after a consistent decrease between 1982 and 1989. One of the motives behind the publication of these collected statistics was the epidemiologists' perception that AIDS educators, especially in the statutory sector, had been neglecting the need for continuing initiatives targeting gay men.[25]

There are several recurrent themes in these various reports. A number of clinic-based studies suggest that younger men may be particularly likely to practise unsafe sex. This finding is generally not seen in the cohort studies, although this may to some extent be due to their very nature, involving a fixed group of ageing participants rather than an uncontrolled selection from the sexually active gay population. Secondly, there is clear evidence of an association between regular relationships and unprotected anal sex. Thirdly, and relatedly, distinctions may exist between men who have consistently practised unsafe sex and men who revert to unprotected sex after a period of safer behaviour; these latter may also be divided into those who usually have safer sex but may occasionally 'lapse' into unsafe sex, and those who consciously and rationally choose to have unprotected anal sex in particular situations.

'Relapse' theory

These are the factors which many behavioural scientists have come to describe collectively as 'relapse'. Graham Hart and colleagues suggest that the term first came to prominence in presentations at the VI International Conference on AIDS in San Francisco in 1990, at which findings such as those from the AIDS Behavioral Research Project and the Chicago MACS cohort were presented.[26] It is worth remembering that in all the research on unsafe sex between men described above, participants were not asked whether they had 'relapsed'; rather, the terminology reflects the interpretation of the data imposed by some of the researchers.

Like 'men who have sex with men' (discussed in Chapter 5), 'relapse' is not a term that gay or bisexual men themselves employ.

British researchers such as Hart and the Project SIGMA team have taken a leading role in challenging the patterns of thought and interpretation from which the notion of 'relapse' is derived.[27] Linguistically, 'relapse' is used to describe the recurrence of the signs and symptoms of a disease, such as cancer or, indeed, the opportunistic infections of AIDS itself, after a temporary period of apparent resolution or remission. As Hart describes it:

> Relapse is therefore a term used frequently in medicine, and particularly psychiatric and psychological medicine in the treatment of alcohol and drug dependency, when periods of a patient's abstinence (when they are 'drug free') may be followed by a return to the use of the drug of addiction. Outside medicine, the term relapse is more clearly pejorative, and refers to backsliding, or slinking back to an unacceptable position. Relapse, then, is concerned with a return to bad behaviour or state of being. The use of such disease derived and negative language for behaviour (which itself is neutral until invested with meaning) reflects a medico-moral stance which many in the AIDS field have eschewed in favour of more positive language for discussions of sexuality and sexual activity.[28]

However, the significance of the terminology used to describe these phenomena is more than mere 'semantics', as some of the proponents of 'relapse' theory seem to believe.[29] Rather, it plays an active role in defining the nature of the phenomenon, and hence also influences perceptions of appropriate responses. For example, the close association between the concept of relapse and addiction models might well lead to the conclusion that providing 12-step programmes like those developed by Alcoholics Anonymous in the 1940s would be an appropriate assistance for gay men who are perceived as being relapsers, or at risk of relapsing. Indeed, relapse theory has emerged alongside the growing popularity in America and Australia of 'sex addiction' and 'sex compulsivity' movements, which do use the 12-step method.[30] In this way, gay men who are for some reason unhappy about their own sexual behaviour –

perhaps because they have been brought up in societies which refuse to accept the legitimacy of lesbian and gay lives, or perhaps because they feel bad about episodes of unsafe sex – are encouraged to regard themselves as being sick or addicted, and to seek treatment as if for a physical disease or a chemical dependency.

Moreover, the interpretation of gay men's continued practice of unsafe sex which is suggested by 'relapse' theory may actively obscure the true nature of the phenomenon. As Project SIGMA spells out, use of the term 'relapse':

> says that gay and bisexual men are unable to maintain the patterns of safer sexual behaviour for which they have been widely praised. They are, the term asserts, falling victim again to their urges, unable to resist a damned good fuck in the interests of their individual safety and the greater good.[31]

Implicit in the term are two particularly misleading suggestions: first, that unsafe sexual behaviour is the result of individual factors such as ignorance, complacency, poor social skills or loss of control, particularly due to drug or alcohol use, rather than the action of two or more individuals; and second, that making the choice to practise unprotected anal sex is necessarily always wrong and to be actively discouraged by AIDS educators, or, worse still, that anal sex is unhealthy *per se*. What is more, the assumption that the increasing levels of STD markers or the direct evidence of increasing unsafe sex and HIV infection among gay men are due to an inability to sustain behaviour change also threatens to obscure the need for continuing basic safer sex education among gay and bisexual men, as men of all ages discover the scene and become sexually active for the first time.

Reasons for having unprotected sex

The discourse of relapse and the explanatory approach which it encourages shed little (if any) light on the true range of very practical considerations which are likely to be the most influential factors in determining why some gay men have unprotected anal sex.

First, it is important to remember that unsafe sex was by no means totally eliminated among gay men even at the peak of the widespread adoption of safer sex during the 1980s. As reviewed in Chapter 1, the very studies which were at that time hailed as evidence of gay men's sexual behaviour changes nevertheless also showed continuing unprotected anal sex by anywhere between 3 per cent and 64 per cent of participants. It may therefore be fundamentally misleading to assume that there has been a clear transition from a successful period of behaviour change to an era of 'relapse'. Instead, what has changed to some extent is the emphasis placed upon pieces of research data. Where in the past a paper might enthusiastically have reported, say, 50 per cent adoption of safer sex among a cohort of gay men, it is likely today to highlight the other 50 per cent of men who may not be consistently practising safer sex.

Hence, many of the components of what has now widely become labelled as 'relapse' have been reported in the literature on AIDS-related sexual behaviour changes since the earliest days, but have only recently been specifically highlighted. For example, since the beginning of the epidemic, studies which have collected data on the link between partner status and safer sex have shown, almost without a single exception, that gay men in regular partnerships, particularly monogamous relationships, are far more likely to practise unprotected anal sex than men with casual sexual partners.[32] Yet it has only been in recent years, since new attention began to be paid to unsafe sex among gay men, that this factor has been seized upon as an important phenomenon and has received attention from researchers and those responsible for planning and prioritizing educational interventions.

One of the more obvious, yet easily overlooked, reasons why someone may have unsafe sex is that they may simply be unaware either of the need for or the meaning of safer sex. Gay men who have come out since about 1987 will probably have emerged into a milieu of bars, clubs and other meeting places in which the issues of HIV and safer sex have a relatively low profile, in contrast to the years earlier in the decade when the initial behaviour changes were effected. And if the neglect of educational initiatives targeting 'out' gay men has been considerable in recent years, the neglect of interventions designed to reach gay men who have not yet emerged or may never emerge onto the scene has been almost total. As Richard Turner has written of the situation in Australia:

> Of the young gay men I talked to, none had gained either an adequate knowledge of AIDS and safe sex or a gay perspective until they came out and had spent some time in gay environments. Their sources of information were material produced by ACON [the AIDS Council of New South Wales] and the gay papers ... A study carried out by the Sydney West Education Unit revealed that youth workers and teachers responsible for sex education are ill prepared to provide information. Over 50 per cent of study participants had gained their knowledge of AIDS from the mainstream media, and a great many had accepted common misconceptions about transmission and proper safe sex practices.[33]

In this context, awareness of the need for safer sex should also be understood not merely in terms of a general cognizance of the existence of the AIDS epidemic, but in terms of each individual's specific, personal realization of the potential threat posed to him by HIV. This is one of the main reasons why the heterosexualization of the epidemic (described in Chapter 5) may be directly harmful to gay men's health, in that it risks leaving some gay men with the mistaken impression that the likelihood of infection through unprotected sex has decreased, when in reality it is continually increasing.

Gay men's risk perception may also be directly or indirectly compromised by the content of educational messages about HIV intended for other population subgroups, or for a general population which is assumed to be wholly heterosexual. There is no doubt that the most substantial changes in gay men's sexual behaviour occurred before the state-funded education campaigns began, and some observers, such as doctors at the West London Hospital in 1989, have suggested that since then there has been a 'reduced trend' towards safer sex among gay men, perhaps 'attributable to the government's reluctance to target the homosexual community in its subsequent publicity'.[34] Government advertisements have also used messages which may inadvertently place gay men at greater risk from HIV. In general terms, Michael Rooney and Peter Scott have argued that 'the heterosexualisation of the response to the epidemic may have had the unfortunate side effect of "swamping" gay men's messages'.[35] More specifically, for example, advertisements have placed considerable faith in monogamy or reduced numbers of sexual partners – strategies which may indeed significantly decrease the risk of infection to someone having unprotected sex in a low prevalence environment, such as the vast majority of heterosexuals in Britain. But as discussed in Chapter 2, having unprotected sex with fewer partners is likely to be of little protection to a gay man when up to 1 in 4 of his potential sexual partners may already be infected and infectious. This kind of heterosexual message becomes even more dangerous when monogamy is presented as a simple, clear-cut *alternative* to condom use. For example, Tony Newton, Health Minister in 1986, summarized safe sex as 'Avoid "sleeping around", and stick to a stable relationship with someone you trust. The more people you have intercourse with, the bigger risk you run. If you DO have casual sex, make sure a condom is used. It cuts the risk down'.[36] As Robin Hardy has pointed out:

> The myth that romance can protect gay men from a virus may be the most ominous instance of a cultural collision between mainstream values and gay male sexuality. Men are coupled now far more than they were in the '70s, sometimes going to tortuous lengths to sustain relationships. Says Maggie Reinfeld, director of education at [Gay Men's Health Crisis in New York], 'We are bombarded by education that says the solution to HIV transmission is marriage. And a lot of gay men appropriate that in a very, frankly, dangerous way'.[37]

The most recent research, summarized earlier in this chapter, suggests that many, and possibly most, gay men becoming newly infected may be in regular relationships in which they do not use condoms – perfectly in accordance with governmental advice.

There are other aspects of safer sex education aimed at heterosexuals or women which may also inadvertently damage interventions for gay men. Despite the false history now apparently endorsed – to its shame – by the Terrence Higgins Trust,[38] antibody testing has played no significant role in prevention campaigns. The test did not even become widely available until well after the most substantial initial behaviour changes among gay men had been made, and even in the first years of its availability, testing was actively discouraged by gay community institutions in America and Australia, and regarded with considerable scepticism by AIDS organizations in the UK. No clear relationship between testing and behaviour change has ever been established.[39] Yet the promotion of antibody testing as a response to a perception of personal risk has become one of the staple components of state-sponsored AIDS education. In Britain and the USA, this myth has now become institutionalized, as state funders such as the Medical Research Council[40] and the Centers for Disease Control (CDC)[41] have come to require education or behavioural research programmes to offer testing to participants as a condition of financial support. In contrast, educational strategies designed by and for gay men have typically stressed the irrelevance of HIV antibody status when safer sex is practised, and have encouraged a sense of solidarity between HIV-positive and HIV-negative gay men with slogans such as 'Positive or negative, it's the same for all'.[42] Such campaigns may have been undermined by a climate in which those who believed that they might be HIV-positive were being urged to take the HIV antibody test, as though there were different responsibilities or safer sex guidelines for the infected as opposed to the uninfected.[43]

Likewise, there has been a growing trend for AIDS education messages to move away from the tried-and-tested risk reduction approach to *safer* sex developed and perfected by gay men over a number of years, and towards strategies which seem to aim for total risk elimination in the form of *safe* sex. As Simon Watney has argued:

> Exceeding any demonstrably necessary precautions against HIV transmission, Safe Sex becomes little more than an instrument for exercising social control of people's sexual behaviour through the use of fear. Such an approach typically tends to whip up anxieties about oral sex for example, and is always ready to tell people not to have sex.[44]

While gay health educators have felt both an ethical and a practical imperative to cause only the minimum necessary disruption to gay men's sexual practices in the interests of reducing or preventing HIV transmission, and have refined their safer sex messages in line with these principles as increasingly reliable information becomes available, non-community-based AIDS education is characterized more by a distrust in the reliability of condoms and a tendency to absolutism. Government safer sex advice has been tinged with a pragmatic hypocrisy, which warns that condoms do not provide 100 per cent protection during either vaginal or anal sex, but then discourages only anal sex,[45] as though it expects gay men to put up with restrictions which it knows would be unacceptable for hetero-sexuals. Similarly, safer sex advice which exaggerates the very low risk of HIV transmission through oral sex not only undermines interventions for gay men which are designed to encourage such alternatives to anal sex,[46] but may also increase the likelihood that gay men will feel fatalistic or helpless about the possibility of avoid-ing HIV infection, and so be more likely to practise unsafe anal sex.[47]

At a time conspicuously coinciding with the emergence of 'relapse' theory, there has been an increasing tendency for edu-cational messages for gay men also to adopt an unhelpful, absolu-tist position of risk elimination. For example, materials produced by MeSMAC Manchester (a community development project for 'men who have sex with men' based on, but unrelated to, the Health Education Authority's MESMAC projects described in Chapter 5) have aimed to encourage non-penetrative 'Fucking alternatives' (as one of their leaflets is called), in which condoms are promoted only for bizarre activities – 'Fill it with whipped cream and use it as a chef's piping bag' and 'Draw a face on it and use it for a puppet show' – while their use for making anal sex safer is ignored.[48] This leaflet and others typically also advocate the use of condoms for oral sex and dental dams or other barriers for rim-ming. There is an unhelpful internal logic at work here, which requires that the very low or even non-existent risk of HIV trans-mission through sexual activities such as rimming or oral sex be reduced to zero by the use of latex barriers, and which denies the legitimacy of anal intercourse using condoms as a form of safer sex because it cannot be guaranteed to be 100 per cent safe. It seems highly probable that, on some conscious or subconscious level, this shift in gay men's health education is a response to the renewed attention drawn by 'relapse' theory to unsafe sex among gay men, as though it is felt that new and more drastic measures are now needed. The link is made explicit in some campaigns, such as the 'An important message for gay and bisexual men ...' poster from the San Francisco AIDS Foundation, which preaches that: 'Research has shown that some gay men still have unsafe sex. Unsafe sex must be eliminated completely if we are to triumph over AIDS. There are no excuses.'[49]

Men who are having difficulty always sticking to safer sex, for example because of antipathy to condoms, are bluntly and unsympathetically told to 'Get over it ... If you have any unsafe sex – STOP NOW.' The definition of unsafe sex which it provides is predictably extreme, and includes oral sex to ejaculation, rimming and fisting without a glove. Reactions such as these are ultimately likely only to obscure the most important fact that virtually every new case of HIV infection can still, of course, be attributed to unprotected anal sex, and that the principled, pragmatic approach should encourage condom use by gay men who enjoy anal sex, rather than pressure them into giving up anal sex altogether and create unnecessary alarm about other sexual activities.

There remain two predominant themes in discussions of continuing unprotected anal sex among gay and bisexual men, namely, the behaviour of the specific subgroups of younger gay men and men in relationships. These will now be discussed in turn.

Young gay men

In the eyes of the media at least, the explanation for unsafe sex among young gay men is obvious. The headlines say it all: 'New Aids fear as young gays shift away from condoms';[50] 'Number of VD cases soars as Aids advice for safe sex ignored';[51] 'Young homosexuals "giving up safe sex in setback on Aids"';[52] 'Young gay men spurn safe sex';[53] 'Old enough to know he could die, but too young to care'.[54] In these reports, young gay men are represented as consciously and culpably choosing not to practise safer sex, often in explicit defiance of their 'elders and betters'. It is precisely this kind of pathological view of youth that Ian Warwick and Peter Aggleton have condemned in their critique of contemporary social research on HIV which 'accepts a priori and without question the view that young people as a group are unknowledgeable, irresponsible in their relationships with others, immature and easily led'.[55]

Nevertheless, the research data do indicate that a significant proportion of young gay men practise unsafe sex. It may be the case that young gay men are not significantly more likely to have unprotected anal sex than older men, but that the fact that younger gay men tend to be more sexually active than older men has to some extent introduced unnoticed biases into the findings of some studies.[56] However, there is a trend in some of the data on STDs and in HIV seroconversions that suggests that younger men are forming an increasingly large proportion of those practising unsafe sex. This trend, if it is genuine, may not be detected by cohort studies whose participants were recruited several years ago, and which therefore do not include men now in their early adult years. But in any event, young gay men's perceptions of the risks of unsafe sex are likely to be influenced by a number of specific factors, including the particular pressures society places upon them and their different temporal perspective on the epidemic, which, in contrast to older gay men, may have preceded the development of their gay identity. For these reasons, health educators must recognize that their work with gay men should include components targeting younger men; they therefore need to identify, understand and respond to specific factors which may disproportionately affect those individuals.

In doing so, it is important to remember Peter Scott's advice that 'Occam's razor needs to be applied to much of the discourse of "relapse" which may have a rather more immediate and obvious cause: the absence of continuing education activities'.[57] As argued earlier, gay men (of any age) who have become 'newly sexual' in recent years are unlikely to have experienced the community-level safer sex campaigns among gay men in the 1980s. Young gay men are particularly unlikely to have received meaningful sex education at school, where the 1986 Education Act requires teachers and sex educators 'to have due regard to moral considerations and the value of family life'. And as the Stonewall Group has pointed out:

If there was ever any doubt about what was meant by 'moral considerations' or 'family life', it was cleared up by Section 28 of the Local Government Act 1988, which prohibits local authorities from doing anything to 'promote homosexuality' or from teaching 'the acceptability of homosexuality as a pretend family relationship' in schools. This legislation can and does constrain schools in the provision of information on homosexuality. Because there have been no test cases on section 28 as yet, most local authority legal advisors tend to err on the side of extreme caution, frequently aggravated by homophobia.[58]

All these restrictions are clearly intended as forms of protection for supposedly heterosexual or asexual children, against corruption into homosexuality. They are categorically not designed to work in the interests of teenagers who are or will be sexually attracted to their own sex, whose existence, if it is acknowledged at all, is only admitted into this philosophy as the dread consequence of the failure adequately to police the sex education classroom. There is certainly no place for the provision of education that may work for the health and well-being of gay teenagers, such as appropriate information on safer sex.

Faced with this near-impossible situation, well-meaning teachers have been forced to compromise by trying to teach children inclusively about 'penetrative sex' with 'partners' of unstated gender. However, this too is likely to be of little help to those relatively confident gay teenagers who may be most at risk because they may be the most likely to venture early onto the gay scene or find sexual partners elsewhere: some young gay men contacted by the London MESMAC project have described how they ignored school sex education (including HIV education) in its entirety because it failed to acknowledge *explicitly* the existence of their sexuality.[59]

For young men participating in MESMAC and similar youth projects around the UK, HIV is only one problem among many. Gay teenagers have reported being so concerned with the business of coming out to family and friends, which often involves the conscious rejection of much of what one has been taught or has come to take for granted during one's upbringing, that AIDS may seem at best an appalling spectre which has been manipulated to form yet another disincentive to open and happy homosexuality. Certainly the view that '[t]he profound consequences of HIV infection might have been expected to suppress the expression of a homosexual lifestyle in younger men' has been expressed even by some doctors,[60] as well as the more predictable right-wing 'pro-family' groups. AIDS educators working with young gay men have therefore found that they may have to address the entire range of issues such as coming out, developing friendships and relationships, the age of consent, living arrangements, money and employment and so on, if they are to help those young men achieve an empowered response to HIV.

Young gay men in the UK are particularly discriminated against by the age of homosexual consent, which was set at 21 in the 1967 Sexual Offences Act. In the eyes of the law, therefore, sexually active gay men do not exist until they are over 21. This frequently leads to timidity on the part of health educators, who fear that providing advice on safer sex to under-age men may be maliciously interpreted as encouraging or condoning illegal sexual activity. Thus in 1992 the Health Education Authority felt a 'need to point out' the age of consent on safer sex fact cards for gay men that were not even specifically intended for or distributed to younger men; by appearing to endorse the discriminatory age of consent, this message is likely only to have alienated the sympathy and goodwill of under-age men in particular. Despite this legislation, there is no doubt that many young gay men start their sexual careers at a relatively early age. Of 111 men aged under 21 at the time at which they were enrolled in the Project SIGMA cohort, more than 50 per cent had had their first sexual experience by age 16, and over 90 per cent by 18.[61]

Young people are often characterized by social science and lay commentary as possessing 'heightened feelings of invulnerability'[62] or being 'too young to care'[63] about health risks such as HIV. This is an unhelpfully imprecise concept, which tells us little about the decision-making process which affects, at least in part, whether an individual participates in unsafe sex on a given occasion. A number of studies have aimed to identify more precisely the ways in which young gay men's perceptions of risk or specific rationalizations for practising unsafe sex may differ from those of older men. Rather than revealing the recklessness in all sexual encounters which is implied by the crude 'invulnerability' model, these studies typically indicate that young gay men may perceive the chances of acquiring HIV from unprotected anal sex with other young men to be significantly lower than from older men, or may be more likely to make assumptions about the likelihood of their partner being infected with HIV on the basis of appearances.[64] The long average delay between HIV infection and the development of HIV-related symptoms or AIDS means that relatively recent HIV infections among younger gay men are likely to go unnoticed, particularly in countries like Britain where only quite a small proportion of gay men have taken the HIV antibody test. It also means that the human face of the epidemic among gay men, as constructed in particular by the media, is that of a disease which overwhelmingly affects older men. Hence Hays and colleagues found that:

> in focus groups we conducted with young gay men in the San Francisco Bay area, young men expressed a stereotypical view of gay men who were likely to have AIDS as 'older men with moustaches who go to leather bars' ... Heightening awareness of young gay men that HIV infection does exist among their peers is critical.[65]

The importance of shared (gay) identity in promoting a sense of peer support in the uptake and practice of safer sex has been highlighted earlier in this book. To the extent that gay identity and culture may have been remoulded during the 1980s to incorporate an acknowledgement of risk from HIV and an expectation that safer sex will be practised, encouraging the development of a confident gay identity among younger men who are sexually attracted to their own gender will itself be a form of safer sex education.[66] Conversely, obstacles to the development of gay identity, such as the discriminatory age of consent in Britain, must be seen as placing young gay men at increased risk of HIV. However, if the norms within gay culture or subcultures are not supportive, or are even discouraging of safer sex, involvement in the gay community would be expected to have a negative effect on the practice of safer sex. This has indeed been demonstrated by research in American West Coast cities outside the main gay population centres: among young gay men aged between 18 and 27, those who had come out to their family, friends and acquaintances and had a high percentage of friends who were themselves gay were significantly more likely to practise unprotected anal sex, suggesting that 'the norms of the young gay subculture may actually foster HIV risk-taking'.[67]

This research emphasizes the importance of maintaining prevention programmes within the gay communities and developing innovative initiatives that can mobilize peer norms in support of safer sex. But it also provides a salutary reminder of the complexity of the identities and communities formed around same-sex desire. As Keith Alcorn has highlighted:

> In reality the lesbian and gay community has always been a network of communities, primarily split between a political community which pursues an ideal of political power and representation, and the communities of the night, which encompass the genuine diversity which political activists seek to represent. These range from the nightclubs to all the privatised activities through which lesbians and gay men meet together. They provide not only a means of meeting new partners, but also of belonging to a group in which sexuality is the common factor.[68]

Safer sex educators therefore need to be alert to the evolving social, sexual and political environments and subcultures that lie beneath the monolithic concept of 'the gay community', if their work is to be genuinely responsive to emerging needs.

Men in relationships

As Robin Hardy has pointed out:

> What has been commonly obscured in this epidemic is that two guys jerking off at urinals or one guy holding another's dick through a glory hole is risk free – at least in viral terms. It's when you want to take someone home that things start to get tricky. Inexorably in the bedroom you approach the

gray areas. Along with all the standard relationship issues, the threat of AIDS adds an enormously complex burden, from lovers who unconsciously test each other's commitment by forgetting the rubbers to those who, enamored with the notion of casting their lots together, simply throw them away.[69]

Although this point should not be oversimplified, it is broadly true to say that sexual encounters in more-or-less public places such as toilets and parks are more likely to be subject to the pressures of time and physical space than those in the bedroom; consequently, the sex is also more likely to consist of oral and manual acts, such as sucking and wanking. Similarly, it seems probable that anal sex in such public settings will have become less common since the advent of HIV made it advisable to have condoms to hand.

However, there is a much more significant distinction to be made between sex with casual partners (regardless of location) and with regular partners. As described earlier, gay men in regular (and especially monogamous) relationships, have consistently been identified as being more likely to practise unprotected anal sex than men with casual partners. This has at least two important consequences. First, it means that it is virtually impossible to reach a proper interpretation of data on gay men's sexual behaviour which fails to take account of the participants' relationship status, and, ideally, the HIV antibody status of participants who have chosen to take the test. Second, it becomes imperative for health educators to understand the motivation behind unprotected sex in relationships, and to consider flexible and imaginative responses to help those men minimize their chances of giving or getting HIV.

Graham Hart and colleagues have expressed prudent concern about the varying definitions of unsafe sex which are used in the burgeoning literature on 'relapse'.[70] Some studies consider the practice of anal sex *per se* to be unsafe, regardless of condom use;[71] others assess the riskiness of anal sex without a condom on the basis of whether the participants are in a regular relationship or not;[72] still others require condoms to be used regardless of relationship status if the sex is to be considered safer.[73] Such inconsistencies not only make it all the harder to generalize between studies; they also indicate that individual studies may be failing to recognize the range of strategies used by gay men to reduce the risk of HIV transmission. As Hart points out:

> It is clear that not all forms of unprotected anal sex carry risk for HIV infection. This is most apparent for those men who are in monogamous relationships and who are aware of their own and their partner's HIV negative antibody status. In the absence of other infections or ill health, there is no reason why these men should not have 'unsafe' sex.[74]

In other words, it is important to draw a distinction between unprotected anal sex and unsafe sex. Historically, safer sex advice has reflected an unconscious assumption that gay men – or at least gay men at risk from HIV – are not in relationships; prevention campaigns specifically targeting couples have only been initiated relatively recently, in the wake of 'relapse' publicity.[75] Pragmatically, that has meant that gay men have been advised to assume that there is a very real risk that their sexual partners may be HIV-positive, and so to use condoms for all instances of anal sex.

Such a strategy is likely to have become less and less effective as increasing numbers of gay men have taken the HIV antibody test. Men who find that they are HIV-positive may decide that they wish to have unprotected anal sex with other HIV-positive men, despite the growing evidence that infection with other STDs and/or reinfection with HIV may accelerate the progression of HIV disease. Likewise, men who have tested negative may seek to persuade their partners that condom use is unnecessary, particularly if they are unaware that HIV can be transmitted from the passive to the active partner during unprotected anal sex. It is also probable that the effect of these factors will be most pronounced among men in relationships, in which the partners are most likely to communicate about their knowledge or beliefs concerning their own and each other's antibody status, and to take decisions about sex based on mutual trust.

What is more, it is impossible to reach an understanding of gay men's participation in unprotected sex without an appreciation of the emotional, historical and symbolic importance of anal sex to gay men. Connell and colleagues have described how:

Anal intercourse, as it happens, is not just a risky element in a sexual repertoire. It is a practice that has had major historical significance in the social construction of men's homosexuality. It was specifically targeted by religious and criminal sanctions against 'the abominable crime of buggery' and has remained central to hostile stereotypes of homosexual men. Accordingly it became a major issue in attempts at law reform and in the Gay Liberation movement's claims for sexual freedom ... It is a practice which carries a heavy load of social meaning. For gay men it is likely to symbolise oppression and freedom even for those who do not find it a significant part of sexual pleasure.[76]

Moreover, a number of surveys have revealed that for many men, anal sex remains the most pleasurable sexual activity. Among Connell's sample of Australian gay and bisexual men, 'unprotected anal intercourse is the top ranked practice in an appraisal of the "most physically satisfying" among 16 sexual practices, and comes a close third as "most emotionally satisfying"'.[77] In the Project SIGMA cohort, however, a larger proportion of men considered masturbation to orgasm and oral sex to orgasm to be sexually arousing than the 72.5 per cent who were turned on by active anal sex to orgasm, or the 61.7 per cent who found passive anal sex appealing. Anal sex using a condom was considered less arousing.[78]

More specifically, sex with transfer of semen can have important meanings for gay men. As Annick Prieur discovered in interviews with Norwegian gay men, 'Accepting semen has been an important value in the gay culture, a way of showing devotion and belonging'.[79] By contrast, safer sex may seem unacceptably clinical or dispassionate, particularly to men in relationships. One of Prieur's respondents asked 'What's the point with a condom? The whole point is that it should go inside you, otherwise you haven't given him all of yourself'.[80]

This perspective on the meanings of sex to gay men, which must inevitably influence the acceptability of the modifications required to prevent HIV transmission, is absent from purely quantitative survey research, which only measures the extent to which gay men have changed their sexual behaviour because of the AIDS epidemic. However, it is of fundamental importance in understanding the relatively high incidence of unprotected anal sex among men in relationships. For example, Martin Levine and Karolynn Siegel found that a number of gay men in New York 'participated in unprotected intercourse to demonstrate their emotional feelings for their partners who were usually their lovers or boyfriends'. In couples where one or both partners were seropositive, an additional altruistic motive was sometimes described; one seropositive man reported having receptive anal sex without a condom with his infected lover 'because he wanted to show the lover that he was going to be loved and nurtured and all', and to ensure that the lover 'did not feel like a pariah'.[81]

Health educators must therefore choose their response to this phenomenon with care. First, they must consider the possibility that for some gay men, practising unprotected anal sex within a relationship is a conscious risk-reduction strategy.[82] The likely effectiveness of that strategy in large part depends on whether the partners both know their HIV antibody status to be negative, and whether any sex which takes place outside the relationship is limited to safer sex activities, to avoid introducing HIV into the relationship.[83] Such a level of sophistication is perhaps most likely in countries such as Australia and the United States, where for some years HIV antibody testing has been encouraged by gay community organizations; however, at least one American study has found that 'men in primary relationships who have unprotected anal sex with steady partners do not tend to enhance safety via knowledge of partners' serostatus'.[84] In Britain, research data also suggest that only a proportion of men who have unprotected sex within their relationships are doing so on the informed basis of having used testing 'as part of the courtship'.[85] Nevertheless, Project SIGMA's data show an increase in the proportion of men who have a regular partner, but no parallel increase in monogamy; these men appear to have 'added a regular partner to their previous sexual lifestyles rather than replaced a number of casual partners with one regular'.[86] If this reflects an ill-advised decision to use relationships as a means to have unprotected anal sex, in the mistaken belief that simply knowing and trusting one's partner can protect against HIV, health educators have two distinct options for intervention: to encourage condom use, or to encourage both partners to take the HIV antibody test.

The latter course is likely to be the more effective for those men who may have entered relationships because they are not prepared to give up anal sex, but have a strong aversion to condoms. Equally, recommending antibody testing may be the most effective HIV prevention advice for many men in committed (if not necessarily monogamous) partnerships who have in essence decided that they are willing to run the risk of infection by having unprotected sex within their relationship. As described earlier, even during that period in the 1980s when gay men adopted safer sex in unprecedented numbers, relatively few changes were seen among men in relationships. If health educators place all their eggs in the basket of encouraging condom use, they are likely to fail the needs of those men for whom fucking without a condom is the most intimate expression of powerful and important human emotions.

Why did relapse theory take off?

Both of the British research teams which have spoken out in criticism of 'relapse' theory have argued that its emergence is related to the de-gaying of AIDS. Graham Hart and colleagues point out that the concept of relapse was introduced in the context of the budget deficit crisis in the USA in the late 1980s and the subsequent danger that health education programmes for gay men might be axed if their work appeared entirely to be done; hence:

> it has been necessary for workers in the field to put in the strongest terms the present and continuing risks that gay men face in relationship to unprotected anal intercourse, and to press the case for the need for interventions which ensure not only that behaviour change takes place, but that this is maintained.[87]

Project SIGMA's researchers agree that:

> It is no accident that relapse emerges as a problem in the AIDS literature as funding for AIDS prevention work is becoming scarcer, and particularly as the process of the 'de-

gaying' of AIDS gathers pace ... If relapse is accepted [by funding decision-makers], we face the chilling likelihood that funds will not be forthcoming because we are irresponsible, feckless and deserve all we get. Such a prospect should, with Hamlet, give us pause 'and [make] us rather bear those ills we have/ than fly to others that we know not of.'[88]

This reasonable fear must be expressed carefully. There can be no real doubt that the notion of 'relapse' does not adequately describe or explain the continuing occurrence of unprotected anal sex among gay and bisexual men, and that it should be rejected. However, the suggested alternative of '[bearing] those ills we have' is equally unacceptable if it means abandoning those gay men whose very real and definable health education needs have been shamefully neglected during the years in which AIDS has been de-gayed.

As reviewed at the beginning of this chapter, there is clear evidence of continuing unprotected anal sex among gay and bisexual men, and strong indicators of increasing HIV transmission. Researchers from the Communicable Disease Surveillance Centre have drawn attention to the fact that '[a]s the prevalence of HIV-1 infection among homosexual men has risen, so the risk of exposure to HIV-1 with each "unsafe" sexual encounter will have increased';[89] thus even a constant, *stable* level of unsafe sex over a number of years will nevertheless result in a steady *increase* in new infections. Although it may be unrealistic to expect 100 per cent success in prevention,[90] it is surely more dangerous to adopt a complacent approach which accepts a given incidence of unsafe sex as being inevitable.

One of the more insidious properties of the terminology of 'relapse' and 'slippage' is the implication of blame which it contains, in that responsibility for 'relapsing' or 'slipping' is placed firmly on the individual. The proponents of 'relapse' theory seem to have understood little of this objection to the notion. For example, researchers from San Francisco who were among the first to introduce the concept gave a paper at the VI International Conference on AIDS in which they acknowledged the distinction between men who intend to have safer sex but on occasions practise unprotected anal sex and those men in relationships who consciously choose not to use condoms; however, by giving the written summary of their presentation the extraordinary title 'Will the real relapsers please stand up?', they clearly betrayed the sense of a judgement of *fault*, as though requiring an admission of *guilt*, which is inherent in the term.[91]

Taking responsibility

In a presentation at the VI International Conference on AIDS in San Francisco in 1990, a group of Californian researchers described men who had been HIV-negative when recruited to a cohort study in 1985, but who had seroconverted by 1989, as 'prevention failures'.[92] This label is certainly imperfect, in that it could be understood to imply that these men were pathologically incapable of responding to prevention interventions. But the great strength of the term 'prevention failures' is that it makes explicit the relationship between HIV prevention activities and their outcomes in gay men's sexual behaviour. In other words, it reflects the fact that it is impossible to understand gay men's practice of unsafe sex without considering the extent to which gay men have (or have not) been provided with information on and support in adopting safer sex.

By a bitter irony, the greatest success stories of gay men's uptake of safer sex took place almost exclusively in the lean years of the 1980s, when safer sex was promoted by underfunded, gay-community-based organizations, as well as gay men acting as 'barefoot' educators, through informal gay community networks. In the years of 'normalization' which have followed since 1986, the monies available for AIDS education have increased immeasurably, but the work has largely become the domain of professionals working to a heterosexualized agenda within statutory agencies, and initiatives to help gay men sustain the changes to their sexual behaviour and to introduce safer sex to emerging gay generations have been almost entirely neglected.[93] After more than five years of the de-gaying of the epidemic, it is in many regards surprising that more gay men are not practising unsafe sex in the 1990s.

A more constructive approach to the issues collapsed into the phenomenon of relapse would first recognize that there is no inherent quality in gay men that leads them automatically to practise safer sex, but that the adoption and sustaining of safer behaviours is the direct result of successful interventions. The nature of these interventions is discussed in more detail elsewhere in this book; however, it is worth recalling that while some of these may be identified as formal education campaigns, others may be more elusive, such as the influence of peer norms, but nevertheless susceptible to influence by AIDS educators. From this perspective, gay men's practice of unsafe sex is best understood not from the individualistic perspective of 'relapse' theory, but by an attention to the actions – or inactions – of AIDS educators. Any 'relapse' which has occurred has, ironically, been on the part of those charged with responsibility for HIV prevention, who have largely neglected their duties to gay men during the AIDS crisis.

Notes

1.   Peter Davies and Project SIGMA, 'On relapse: recidivism or rational response?', in *AIDS: Rights, Risk and Reason* (eds P. Aggleton, P. Davies and G. Hart). Falmer Press, London, 1992.
2.   *Ibid.*
3.   H. H. Handsfield *et al.*, 'Trends in gonorrhea in homosexually active men – King County, Washington, 1989', *MMWR*, 38(44): 762–4 (1989).
4.   J. A. R. van den Hoek *et al.*, 'Increase in unsafe homosexual behaviour' (letter), *The Lancet*, 336: 179–80 (1990).
5.   John B. F. de Wit *et al.* 'Safe sexual practices not reliably maintained by homosexual men' (letter), *AJPH*, 82(4): 615–16 (1992).
6.   J. R. L. Forsyth *et al.*, 'Resurgent gonorrhoea in homosexual men' (letter), *The Lancet*, 336: 878 (1990).
7.   V. C. Riley, 'Resurgent gonorrhoea in homosexual men' (letter), *The Lancet*, 337: 183 (1991).
8.   M. A. Waugh, 'Resurgent gonorrhoea in homosexual men' (letter), *The Lancet*, 337: 375 (1991).
9.   A. E. Singaratnam *et al.*, 'Preventing the spread of HIV infection' (letter), *BMJ*, 302: 469 (1991).
10. D. R. Tomlinson *et al.*, 'Does rectal gonorrhoea reflect unsafe sex?' (letter), *The Lancet*, 337: 501–2 (1991); P. D. French *et al.*, 'Preventing the spread of HIV infection' (letter), *BMJ*, 302: 962 (1991).
11. Adrian Renton *et al.*, 'Preventing the spread of HIV infection' (letter), *BMJ*, 302: 1207–8 (1991).
12. 'Sexually transmitted diseases: increasing incidence of gonorrhoea and syphilis in homosexual men in Edinburgh', *Weekly Epidemiological Record*, 21, 24 May 1991; based on *Communicable Dis-*

eases and Environmental Health in Scotland Weekly Report, 25(91/04). Communicable Diseases (Scotland) Unit, Glasgow, 1991.

13. Ron Stall *et al.*, 'Relapse from safer sex: the AIDS Behavioral Research Project', *VI International Conference on AIDS*, San Francisco, abstract Th.C.108 (1990); 'Relapse from safer sex: the next challenge for AIDS prevention efforts', *J. AIDS*, 3: 1181–7 (1990).

14. Maria L. Ekstrand *et al.*, 'Maintenance of safer sexual behaviors and predictors of risky sex: the San Francisco Men's Health Study', *AJPH*, 80(8): 973–7 (1990).

15. Maria L. Ekstrand *et al.*, 'Will the real relapsers please stand up?', handout to accompany poster presentation, 'Frequent and infrequent relapsers need different AIDS prevention projects', *VIII International Conference on AIDS*, Amsterdam, abstract PoD 5126 (1992).

16. S. Maurice Adib *et al.*, 'Relapse in sexual behavior among homosexual men: a 2-year follow-up from the Chicago MACS/CCS', *AIDS*, 5: 757–60 (1991).

17. Project SIGMA, *Update*, London, March 1992.

18. Davies and Project SIGMA, *op. cit.*

19. A. J. Hunt *et al.*, 'Changes in sexual behaviour in a large cohort of homosexual men in England and Wales, 1988–9', *BMJ*, 302: 505–6 (1991).

20. Davies and Project SIGMA, *op. cit.*, 1992.

21. A. J. Hunt *et al.*, 'HIV infection in a cohort of homosexual and bisexual men', *BMJ*, 305: 561–2 (1992).

22. Project SIGMA, *op. cit.*

23. Ray Fitzpatrick *et al.*, 'Social psychological factors that may predict high risk sexual behaviour in gay men', *Health Education Journal*, 50(2): 63–6 (1991); Graham Hart *et al.*, '"Relapse" to unsafe sexual behaviour among gay men: a critique of recent behavioural HIV/AIDS research', *Sociology of Health and Illness*, 14(2): 216–32 (1992).

24. B. G. Evans *et al.*, 'Sexually transmitted diseases and HIV-1 infection among homosexual men in England and Wales', *BMJ*, 306: 426–8 (1993); 'Sexually transmitted diseases and HIV infection among homosexual men' (letter), *BMJ*, 306: 792 (1993). See also the discussion of these statistics in Edward King, 'HIV alarm' and 'Biting the bullet', *The Pink Paper*, 258, 3 January 1993; 'Young gay men need "special emphasis" as unsafe sex increases', *Gay Times*, January 1993; 'Sexually transmitted diseases and HIV infection among homosexual men' (letter), *BMJ*, 306: 792 (1993).

25. Dr Barry Evans, CDSC, personal communication, December 1992.

26. Hart, *op. cit.*

27. *Ibid.*; Davies and Project SIGMA, *op. cit.*; Peter M. Davies, 'Safer

sex maintenance among gay men: are we moving in the right direction?' *AIDS*, 7: 279–80 (1993).

28. Hart, *op. cit.*

29. For example, see Maria L. Ekstrand, 'Safer sex maintenance among gay men: are we making any progress?', *AIDS*, 6: 875–7 (1992).

30. See Ellen Herman, 'Getting to serenity: do addiction programs sap our political vitality?', *OUT/LOOK*, 1(2): 10–18 (1988); Adam Carr, 'Love is a drug maybe?', *Outrage*, pp. 32–5, September 1990; Michael Szymanski, 'Sexual compulsion', *Genre*, pp. 36ff, June–July 1992. I am grateful to Simon Watney for drawing these to my attention. Robert Barret, 'Reducing unsafe sexual practices of HIV seropositive gay men: education, counselling and the twelve steps', *IV International Conference on AIDS*, Stockholm, abstract 6530 (1988) is the earliest example of the addiction model of unsafe sex of which I am aware.

31. Davies and Project SIGMA, *op. cit.*

32. See, for example, Leon McKusick *et al.*, 'Reported changes in the sexual behavior of men at risk for AIDS, San Francisco, 1982–84 – the AIDS Behavioral Research Project', *Public Health Reports*, 100(6): 622–9 (1985), reporting evidence for this phenomenon as early as 1983; Ronald O. Valdiserri *et al.*, 'Variables influencing condom use in a cohort of gay and bisexual men', *AJPH*, 78(7): 801–5 (1988).

33. Richard Turner, 'Young gay men: the next wave?', *Sydney Star Observer*, 22 February 1991.

34. Brian A. Evans *et al.*, 'Trends in sexual behaviour and risk factors for HIV infection among homosexual men, 1984–7', *BMJ*, 298: 215–18 (1989). The occurrence of changes in gay men's sexual behaviour *prior* to government campaigns is discussed in Chapter 2.

35. Michael Rooney and Peter Scott, 'Working where the risks are', in *Working Where the Risks Are* (eds B. Evans, S. Sandberg and S. Watson). Health Education Authority, London, 1992.

36. Tony Newton, 'MINISTER FOR AIDS', *News of the World*, 16 November 1986.

37. Robin Hardy, 'Risky business: confronting unsafe sex', *Village Voice*, pp. 35–8, 26 June 1990.

38. See Chapter 5.

39. See the discussion of antibody testing in Chapter 2.

40. Privileged communication.

41. Cindy Patton, *Inventing AIDS*, p. 44. Routledge, London, 1991.

42. Terrence Higgins Trust, *Safer Sex – Keep It Up!*, set of six posters, 1988.

43. This misguided approach to HIV prevention is set out in detail in James J. Goedert, 'Sounding board: what is safe sex?', *NEJM*, 316(21): 1339–1441 (1987).

44. Simon Watney, 'Emergent sexual identities', in *AIDS: The Second Decade* (eds P. Aggleton, P. Davies and G. Hart). Falmer Press, London, 1993.

45. See, for example, the Health Education Authority's 1989 gay press advertisements, 'They used to say masturbation was bad for you. Now it could save your life' and 'If you think safer sex sounds dull, reading this might change your position'. Both adverts implicitly advise gay men to switch from anal sex to non-penetrative options, because 'Even if you do use a condom [for anal sex] it won't make it completely safe'.

46. See, for example, the London Lesbian and Gay Switchboard poster 'SUCK', also placed in the gay press as an advertisement during 1989.

47. Ernest de Vroome *et al.*, 'Overestimating the risk of a low-risk sexual technique increases or decreases behavioral risk, depending on mediating factors', and handout, 'Overestimating the risk of orogenital sex may increase unsafe anogenital sex', *VIII International Conference on AIDS*, Amsterdam, abstract PoD 5125 (1992). See also the discussion of oral sex in Chapter 3.

48. MeSMAC Manchester Enterprises Ltd, 'Fucking Alternatives', leaflet, 1991.

49. San Francisco AIDS Foundation, 'An important message for gay and bisexual men ...', undated poster, *c*. 1990–91.

50. Chris Mihill, 'New Aids fear as young gays shift away from condoms', *The Guardian*, 26 January 1991.

51. Jason Bennetto, 'Number of VD cases soars as Aids advice for safe sex ignored', *Independent on Sunday*, 4 October 1990.

52. Jack O'Sullivan, 'Young homosexuals "giving up safe sex in setback on AIDS"', *The Independent*, 20 April 1990.

53. 'Young gay men spurn safe sex', *General Practitioner*, 26 January 1991.

54. Imogen Edwards-Jones, 'Old enough to know he could die, but too young to care', *The Independent*, 3 November 1992.

55. Ian Warwick and Peter Aggleton, '"Adolescents", young people and AIDS research', in *AIDS: Individual, Cultural and Policy Dimensions* (eds P. Aggleton, P. Davies and G. Hart), Falmer Press, London, 1990.

56. See P. M. Davies *et al.*, 'The sexual behaviour of young gay men in England and Wales', *AIDS Care*, 4(3): 259–72 (1992).

57. Peter Scott, 'How the health education industry has failed gay men', *VI Social Aspects of AIDS* conference, London, May 1992.

58. Stonewall Group, 'Briefing note: homosexuality and sex education in schools', London, November 1991.

59. Jamie Taylor, London MESMAC, personal communication, 1992.

60. Evans, *op. cit.*

61. Davies, 'The sexual behaviour of young gay men'.

62. Robert B. Hays *et al.*, 'High HIV risk-taking among young gay men', *AIDS*, 4: 901–7 (1990).

63. Edwards-Jones, *op. cit.*

64. See, for example, Hays, *op. cit.*; Ron S. Gold *et al.*, 'Situational factors and thought processes associated with unprotected intercourse in young gay men', *AIDS*, 6: 1021–30 (1992).

65. Hays, *op. cit.*

66. See Simon Watney, 'Safer sex as community practice', in *AIDS: Individual, Cultural and Policy Dimensions* (eds P. Aggleton, P. Davies and G. Hart), Falmer Press, London, 1990.

67. Robert B. Hays *et al.*, 'Understanding the high rates of HIV risk-taking among young gay and bisexual men: the Young Men's Study', *VII International Conference on AIDS*, Florence, abstract FC722 (1991); 'Changes in peer norms and sexual enjoyment predict changes in sexual risk-taking among young gay men', *VIII International Conference on AIDS*, Amsterdam, abstract PoD 5183 (1992).

68. Keith Alcorn, 'Communities of the night', *Capital Gay*, 18 September 1992.

69. Hardy, *op. cit.*

70. Hart, *op. cit.*

71. See, for example, A. J. Hunt *et al.*, 'Changes in sexual behaviour in a cohort of homosexual men in England and Wales, 1988–1989', *BMJ*, 302: 505–6 (1991).

72. See, for example, Ron Stall, *op. cit.*; K. R. O'Reilly *et al.*, 'Relapse from safer sex among homosexual men: evidence from four cohorts in the AIDS community demonstration projects', *VI International Conference on AIDS*, San Francisco, abstract FC717 (1990).

73. See, for example, Adib, *op. cit.*

74. Hart, *op. cit.*

75. Examples of such campaigns include the leaflet and posters produced in 1991 by the AIDS Council of New South Wales (ACON) in Australia, using the slogan 'That feeling doesn't stop HIV. Safe sex does', or the Terrence Higgins Trust's *Tales of Gay Sex* photo-story leaflet, 'Hot love safe love', plus accompanying safer sex story booklet, produced in 1991–92.

76. R. W. Connell *et al.*, 'Danger and context: unsafe anal sexual practice among homosexual and bisexual men in the AIDS crisis', *Australian and New Zealand Journal of Sociology*, 26(2): 187–208 (1990).

77. *Ibid.*

78. P. M. Davies *et al.*, *Longitudinal Study of the Sexual Behaviour of Homosexual Males under the Impact of AIDS: A Final Report to the Department of Health*. Project SIGMA, London, 1990.

79. Annick Prieur, 'Norwegian gay men: reasons for continued prac-

tice of unsafe sex', *AIDS Education and Prevention*, **2**(2): 109–15 (1990).

80. *Ibid.*

81. Martin P. Levine and Karolynn Siegel, 'Unprotected sex: understanding gay men's participation', in *The Social Context of AIDS* (eds J. Huber and B. E. Schneider), pp. 47–71. Sage Publications, London, 1992.

82. See Edward King, 'Having unsafe sex safely', *The Pink Paper*, 197, 19 October 1991.

83. Such strategies are described in F. C. I. Hickson *et al.*, 'Maintenance of open gay relationships: some strategies for protection against HIV', *AIDS Care*, **4**(4): 409–19 (1992).

84. David McKirnan *et al.*, 'Primary relationships confer risk for HIV exposure among gay men', *VII International Conference on AIDS*, Florence, abstract MD 4049 (1991).

85. Ford Hickson *et al.*, 'Sexual exclusivity, non-exclusivity and HIV', in *AIDS: The Second Decade* (eds P. Aggleton, P. Davies and G. Hart). Falmer Press, London, 1993; Jill Dawson *et al.*, 'The HIV test and sexual behaviour in a sample of homosexually active men', *Social Science and Medicine*, **32**: 683–8 (1991).

86. Andrew J. Hunt and Project SIGMA, *Gay Men and Changes in Sexual Behaviour*, Project SIGMA Working Paper no. 29, London.

87. Hart, *op. cit.*

88. Davies and Project SIGMA, *op. cit.*

89. Evans, *op. cit.*

90. See W. Cates *et al.*, 'AIDS and absolutism: the demand for perfection in prevention', *NEJM*, **327**(7): 492–4 (1992).

91. Ekstrand, 'Will the real relapsers please stand up?'

92. B. C. Willoughby *et al.*, 'Characteristics of recent seroconverters in a cohort of homosexual men: who are the prevention failures?', *VI International Conference on AIDS*, San Francisco, abstract FC45 (1990).

93. See Edward King, Michael Rooney and Peter Scott, *HIV Prevention for Gay Men: A Survey of Initiatives in the UK*. North-West Thames Regional Health Authority, London, 1992.

Chapter five

The De-gaying of AIDS

AIDS IS A GAY DISEASE! There. I said it. And I
believe it. If I hear one more time that AIDS is not a
gay disease, I shall vomit. AIDS is a gay disease because
a lot of gay men get AIDS.

● *Michael Callen*[1]

This epidemic is unique in so far as prevention has
been prevented, rather than transmission. Resources
and education campaigns have been remorselessly
targeted at those at least risk of contracting HIV, as if
the priority of preventing an epidemic among
heterosexuals had been established at the expense of
halting the epidemics that are actually raging
throughout the developed world.

● *Simon Watney*[2]

SINCE the mid-1980s, AIDS has been systematically de-
gayed. 'De-gaying' is the term used to describe the denial or down-
playing of the involvement of gay men in the HIV epidemic, even
when gay men continue to constitute the group most severely affected, and when the lesbian and gay community continues to play a
pioneering role in non-governmental (and sometimes governmental) responses, such as the development of policy or the provision of
services to people living with HIV.

In some respects, the de-gaying of AIDS occurred in an

unplanned, unconscious way; in others, it reflected institutionalized cowardice and cant. However, in most cases de-gaying was a deliberate strategy, implemented in good faith and with good intentions from a particular moment in the AIDS epidemics of the United States and Great Britain, as an emerging international consensus stressed the potential danger of an explosion of HIV infection among the (heterosexual) population at large. With the benefit of hindsight, however, one can only conclude that the de-homosexualization of AIDS has led directly to the marginalization of gay men's unparalleled experience and contributions to fighting the epidemic, and has ultimately exacerbated the harmful effects of the epidemic on those who are most at risk.

The evolution of prevention policies

Commentators and analysts have formulated a number of different periodizations of the AIDS epidemic, in which various stages of the epidemic are characterized by evolving policy responses. For the social historian Jeffrey Weeks, 1981–82 was a period of 'dawning crisis', when researchers and gay men alike stumbled towards an understanding of and resistance to the epidemic, while government merely showed indifference. Weeks characterizes 1982–85 both by media and popular hysteria and by the development of organized self-help responses, particularly from within the lesbian and gay communities. Finally, from 1985 to 1989, he argues that policies reflected 'crisis management', with the death of Rock Hudson in October 1985 contributing to public and government concern about the 'generalisation of risk' – 'a fear that AIDS might infiltrate the so-called general population'. During this period AIDS organizations tended to grow fast in size and ambition:

> In part, this involved a professionalization of the self-help groupings themselves, as public funds flowed into them, and demands on their services increased ... At the same time, a different sort of professionalism began to emerge which

actively distanced itself from the lesbian and gay community as AIDS became seen as a universal problem.[3]

Virginia Berridge and Philip Strong specify three policy phases which are different from, but complementary to, those of Weeks. This analysis argues that during 1981–86, a 'policy community' was gradually constructed, with significant involvement both of gay groups and of clinical and scientific experts. During a brief period of 'wartime emergency' in 1986–87, AIDS emerged as a political priority, with some sections of society 'put on almost a wartime footing to meet what was regarded as a national emergency'. This has been followed by a period of 'normalization' from 1987/88 to the present, in which: 'AIDS and the reaction to it are becoming part of the normal policy and institutional processes. The threat of immediate epidemic spread has receded; and the threat of widespread heterosexual infection no longer seems imminent.'[4]

A further account by Anthony Vass, based on an analysis of media coverage of the epidemic in Britain, argues that the key moment of transition was in early 1985. From this point, in the crudely simplistic eyes of the newspapers:

> AIDS no longer confined itself to sexually promiscuous homosexuals; or 'innocent' victims, like haemophiliacs; or intravenous drug addicts. AIDS could now be passed on to children, unborn babies, prostitutes, 'normal' heterosexuals, men and women, young and old. Nobody could be complacent, or feel safe.[5]

In response to public and medical concern, the government acted by allocating £4 million to blood-screening facilities and by introducing statutory regulations as an extension to the Public Health (Control of Diseases) Act 1984 to detain in hospital people with AIDS whom the courts decide are a threat to others. Sir Donald Acheson, Chief Medical Officer to the Health Department, declared that the epidemic was 'the biggest health problem since World War Two'.[6]

These various analyses share the view that from 1985/86 onwards, concern about the 'generalisation of risk' described by Weeks figured prominently in the policies of both government and non-governmental AIDS organizations. Having previously been viewed with various degrees of indifference or malicious glee by the populace, by the media and by public health agencies, AIDS now became a concrete concern because of the new impression that it threatened not just gay men, drug users or deeply unfortunate 'normal' people such as recipients of blood products, but (hetero-sexual) society at large.

Why was AIDS de-gayed?

It is important to understand the ways in which responses to AIDS changed in the mid-1980s if the reasons for the de-gaying of the epidemic are to be fully appreciated. As Weeks describes it:

> In Britain there had been virtually no government response until 1984. Only then was there intervention to prevent the further contamination of the blood supply (and by impli-cation, prevent the spread of AIDS to 'the innocent'). In 1985, the government took powers compulsorily to detain in hospital people who were perceived as likely to ignore medical advice and were at risk of spreading the disease. Both these measures were dictated by a fear that AIDS might infiltrate the so-called general population. But in 1985 only £135,000 was set aside by the government for education and prevention. By the end of 1986, with the dramatic adoption of a new policy in November of that year, this had leapt a hundredfold.[7]

In other words, until late 1986 the epidemic was perceived as a threat to society at large *only from without*. Strategies intended to prevent the spread of the epidemic aimed to place various kinds of barrier between those infected with HIV, on the one hand, and a wider community perceived as currently untouched. This approach should be seen in contrast with later education strategies adopted by government, such as the Health Education Authority advertise-ments using the slogan 'AIDS: you're as safe as you want to be'. Here, AIDS has become the enemy *within*, against which individual action is necessary, rather than the policing of borders.

The British government's new policy to educate the public about AIDS was announced in Parliament by Norman Fowler, Secretary of State for Social Services, on 20 November 1986. The policy acknowledged that:

> there was a difficult balance to be struck. At present the infection was virtually confined to the few, relatively small, high risk groups. In this country there had been 565 cases of which 284 had died, however it was estimated that there were 30,000 carriers, of whom 25 to 30 per cent and possibly more, would contract the disease and die. So unless all took action, it would spread more widely into the heterosexual population. That meant striking a balance between warning everyone of the risks, while not causing unnecessary panic.[8]

As the 'Don't die of ignorance' television and poster campaign was launched in January 1987, Fowler held a press conference at which he warned that 4000 deaths from AIDS were predicted in Britain over the next three years alone.[9] 'Aids was still confined largely to particular groups such as homosexuals and drug misusers, but it could spread more widely into the general population, as it had in Africa, unless people changed their behaviour and took the necessary precautions'.[10]

Weeks argues that the 'key precipitating event' in this generalization of risk was the publication of the US Surgeon-General C. Everett Koop's report on AIDS on 22 October 1986. Koop was far from being a liberal: he was a Reagan appointee with a track record as a prominent anti-abortion campaigner. But the *Surgeon General's Report on Acquired Immune Deficiency Syndrome*, described by Randy Shilts as 'a watershed event in the history of the epidemic',[11] warned that:

> Heterosexual transmission is expected to account for an increasing proportion of those who become infected with the AIDS virus in the future. The country must face this epidemic as a unified society ... AIDS is a life-threatening disease and a major public health issue ... It is the responsi-

bility of every citizen to be informed about AIDS and to exercise the appropriate preventive measures.[12]

It should be stressed that the new urgency in AIDS policy was primarily based on an intention to prevent a heterosexual AIDS epidemic, rather than to respond to the existing epidemic among the 'few, relatively small, high risk groups'. As *The Guardian*'s medical correspondent Andrew Veitch pointed out, 'The Government has recognised that while it missed the chance to protect homosexuals, and the 1,000 haemophiliacs who have been infected by contaminated blood products from the US, it can help the rest of us to protect ourselves'.[13] In summing up a seminar on 'Future trends in AIDS' organized by the Department of Health and Social Security in London in March 1987, Professor Healy of the London School of Hygiene and Tropical Medicine described:

> three epidemics in progress with loose links between them ... The main epidemic, numerically speaking, is in male homosexuals ... Next comes the epidemic, linked to the first, in intravenous drug abusers ... Thirdly, we have the epidemic that frightens us all, that in the heterosexual population. The numbers potentially involved are far greater, and here we seem to know almost nothing. Nobody, as I understand it, can tell me whether or not such an epidemic exists or not at the present time. Some heterosexual people are becoming seropositive or manifesting the disease, but whether or not there are enough to maintain an epidemic seems quite uncertain. One main objective of public health policy should presumably be to prevent this epidemic from happening at all.[14]

The general lack of information over the size and nature of the epidemic among heterosexuals was highlighted by later epidemiological reports. The 1988 report on *Short-term Prediction of HIV Infection and AIDS in England and Wales*, known as the Cox Report after its principal author, concluded that 'The predictions in this report are subject to considerable uncertainty arising in part from natural biological variability but more particularly from the absence of or limitations on relevant data'; however, it suggested that 'some 6,000 to 17,000 heterosexual adults might now be infected indicating a significant potential source of infection for other heterosexual adults.'[15] In 1990 the Day Report was published, updating Cox's predictions. Again, it concluded that 'major uncertainty exists in the direction the epidemic is taking among those infected by injecting drug use and through heterosexual contact', and it modified downwards the estimated number of infected heterosexuals at the end of 1988, to within the range of 750 to 3750.[16]

It is not the purpose of this summary to argue that the limited available information on the impact of HIV on heterosexuals should have inhibited government and non-governmental organizations from alerting the population at large to the potential threat, and to the wisdom of safer sex. As Dr Anne Johnson of London's Middlesex Hospital pointed out at a Symposium on current and future spread of HIV in the UK in November 1989:

> there are still many unknowns as to the potential for future spread. At a public health level, I believe that we have a responsibility to track the level of HIV in the population over time with valid scientific methods; but to sit and wait to see whether further spread occurs is not a viable option. We have a responsibility to the public to inform and to educate about the extent and potential extent of the spread of the virus within the population, and this information must include saying where uncertainty lies. This involves the dissemination of accurate and understandable information to the general population *as well as imaginative programmes directed to those who may currently be at highest risk of infection.*[17] (emphasis added)

The problem was that, rather than reflecting this balance, education initiatives were almost entirely diverted to alerting heterosexuals, while interventions for those at highest risk of infection were almost entirely neglected. Indeed, some argued that it was necessary to play down the existing and worsening epidemic among gay men in order to reinforce warnings about the predicted epidemic among heterosexuals; in discussions at the Symposium:

The view was expressed that health education about HIV should concentrate more on what people actually do rather than on their sexual orientation or membership of any risk group. This presented problems in the targeting of health education programmes, but concentration on 'risk groups' carried the danger that the general population would fail to comprehend the relevance to themselves of messages about the risks of HIV infection.[18]

A significant factor which affected the new approach to AIDS in the late 1980s was extrapolation from the AIDS epidemics unfolding in other countries. Simon Watney has cautioned that AIDS is not experienced homogeneously throughout the world; rather, the global phenomenon of AIDS is 'a complex sequence of unfolding and overlapping epidemics, affecting different population groups, relative to different modes of transmission, and differing degrees of access to health education, clean needles, drug treatments, and general standards of health care and social service provision'.[19] Nevertheless, comparisons between the British and the American epidemics figure quite prominently in epidemiologists' discussions of the likely future experience in the UK.[20]

At the 1989 Symposium, Dr Anne Johnson noted that the early evidence of the rapid spread of HIV among gay men in America had allowed voluntary groups in the UK to initiate education campaigns which, as discussed in Chapters 1 and 2, helped prevent the development of a similarly devastating epidemic among British gay men.[21] The lesson that epidemiologists and policy-makers appear to have learned from this was that the indications of significant heterosexual transmission in other parts of the world were a warning of the possibility of a similar, heterosexual epidemic in the UK. Social historians Virginia Berridge and Philip Strong agree that 'Lessons from abroad – in particular the danger of heterosexual spread of the disease – also weighed heavily. Dispatches from the British ambassador in Kinshasa had drawn attention to the rapid heterosexual spread in Zaire and the possibility that Britain might share the same fate'.[22] In the Commons debate on AIDS in November 1986, Norman Fowler stated that 'Unless we all act to protect ourselves it will not be long before we find the numbers infected rising as high here as in other countries'.[23]

Berridge has argued that the media also had a significant influence on the policy process in three interrelated ways: first, playing a key role in alerting the gay community, especially through articles in the gay press; secondly, being used symbiotically by the emerging 'policy community' of gay men, clinicians and scientists to stress the potential threat to the whole population, in the hope of spurring the government into constructive action; and thirdly, to define and reinforce the issues for politicians:

> The period of high-level government reaction over the disease in late 1986 was preceded by a spate of media presentations on the threat of AIDS ... It is said that government ministers at the Department of Health were stimulated by these programmes into seeing AIDS as an urgent issue which merited a government response. Certainly the programmes were reacting on a very media-conscious government, one which was sensitive to what was in the press and especially what it saw on television.[24]

Compared with the press coverage of the early 1980s, which Berridge has described as 'the classic period of "gay plague" presentation', in 1983–85 'the focus within the press shifted to encompass the possibility of heterosexual transmission', with considerable interest in both the safety of the blood supply and the view that the disease might have originated in Africa.[25] Thus during 1985,

> Just as interest by reporters had begun to grow in the area of AIDS, so the *selection* and *presentation* of news started shifting emphasis, from a simplistic, but highly 'newsworthy', view that AIDS is a 'gay plague', to a more threatening and comprehensive – and equally 'newsworthy' – realisation that AIDS could strike at anybody and anywhere.[26]

Events such as the first death of a British baby from AIDS in May 1985, for example, merited prominent coverage in all the national newspapers. New predictions of the likely impact of the epidemic on heterosexuals were reported extensively. The First International Conference on AIDS in April resulted in reports that 'The spread of the deadly AIDS epidemic to heterosexuals in Western industrial countries is inescapable'.[27] The Chief Medical Officer, Sir Donald

Acheson, sent medical advice on AIDS to all doctors, and was quoted as saying that 'Although only 159 cases have been reported, AIDS will undoubtedly become substantially more frequent in the immediate future and cases will occur more widely throughout the country'.[28] As the media reconstructed AIDS as a 'newsworthy' threat to everyone, so anxiety and concern about the epidemic increased among the population at large.

Likewise, Cindy Patton has identified the American media as playing a significant role in leading public opinion and concern about the implications of AIDS for the population at large:

> A significant perceptual shift, at least in the mass media, occured [*sic*] in 1985 with the death of Rock Hudson. The virtual media blackout which had permitted only a handful of sensational or highly specialized medical articles to be published ended as the public began to perceive that 'hetero-sexuals' – the term that referred not to drug users, who were desexualized by the epidemiologic categories, but to other, 'ordinary' heterosexuals – could acquire, indeed had been acquiring HIV. Suddenly, a constituency in the position to *demand* a government response was asking for 'the facts' about AIDS.[29]

By the end of 1985, the British public's thirst for information on AIDS had become intense: a recorded telephone help-line established by the College of Health in December received well over 20,000 calls from the public in the space of just one week.[30] It was against this background that the government launched the 'Don't aid AIDS' information campaign, which ran throughout 1986, and was expanded at the end of the year with the 'Don't die of ignorance' campaign.

The presentation of official statistics

In Britain, data on positive HIV antibody test results and AIDS diagnoses are sent voluntarily and confidentially to the Public Health Laboratory Service (PHLS) Communicable Disease Surveillance Centre (CDSC) or to the Communicable Disease (Scotland) Unit (CD(S)U) by clinicians and laboratory microbiologists. Since 1987, the Department of Health has then given out up-to-date AIDS statistics by press release each month, and more detailed figures for both HIV infection and AIDS each quarter. A more thorough analysis is prepared by the PHLS in the form of *AIDS/ HIV Quarterly Surveillance Tables*, which are circulated primarily to public health officials involved in AIDS.

While the PHLS' role is purely *professional*, the Department of Health press releases usually contain several pages of editorial comment, sometimes including a direct response to the statistics from an appropriate government figure. In this way the Department of Health is able to direct attention to the areas which most concern it, and to present a *political* perspective on the data. These press releases and the media coverage they generate have proved to be a highly effective way of emphasizing the small but growing number of cases of HIV transmission through heterosexual sex, at the direct expense of appropriate attention to the very much greater and increasing number of cases among gay men.

The Department of Health's editorializing mostly consists of useful explanations of important considerations in the interpretation of the figures. For example, the press releases highlight the likelihood that AIDS diagnoses are somewhat under-reported, and that individuals who have elected to take the HIV antibody test are probably only a minority of those currently infected with HIV. However, the comments on the current incidence of HIV in particular risk groups betray something of the relative importance attached to each of these discrete 'mini-epidemics'. For example, between 1988 and 1990 the quarterly press releases commented that the HIV statistics 'show [the epidemic's] spread outside the homosexual and bisexual groups',[31] when during this same period 70–72 per cent of positive HIV antibody tests were attributed to sexual intercourse between men.[32] Likewise, while no comment is made on the fact that during the quarter March–June 1988, 191 gay or bisexual men tested HIV-positive, 28 new infections by heterosexual transmission elicit the concerned observation that:

> the number of heterosexual infections is growing ... the potential for HIV infection spreading into and becoming

established in the general low-risk population is therefore steadily increasing. Evidence from other countries underscores the potential importance of heterosexual spread, and the government's campaign aimed at educating the general population, particularly the young and sexually active, about the continuing danager [*sic*] of HIV infection, forms another essential part of the strategy for the prevention of spread of HIV in this country.[33]

In October 1990 this standard press release form was changed. Now the editorial comment was broken down under just five headings: 'AIDS cases'; 'AIDS in heterosexuals'; 'Region'; 'HIV antibody positive persons'; and 'HIV in heterosexuals'.[34] Bizarrely, all the information about incidence in particular risk groups was now presented under the 'AIDS in heterosexuals' or 'HIV in heterosexuals' headings, including any comments on incidence among gay men. This was at least an honest way of presenting the Department's obvious view that the only interest in the statistics was the extent to which they reflected heterosexual transmission. Thus the section 'AIDS in heterosexuals' contained 21 lines on the 117 new AIDS cases during the previous 3 months which were attributed to heterosexual HIV transmission, while in the same section the 886 new cases among gay or bisexual men merited only 26 words. And again, under the heading 'HIV in heterosexuals', the 407 new positive tests among heterosexuals during the previous year are highlighted as a 57 per cent increase, while newly detected infections among gay or bisexual men are referred to only as a 41 per cent increase, with the actual number, 866, omitted entirely from the press release.[35]

As Simon Watney has pointed out:

it is routine in Britain to find wholly misleading analogies being made in the Press, and elsewhere, between percentage increases in HIV or AIDS cases among heterosexuals, and the overall cumulative statistics, with the false implication that HIV is being more widely transmitted amongst heterosexuals than amongst gay men or drug users. It now seems that an earlier ideological tendency to deny *any* risk to heterosexuals has been replaced by a regular tendency to *over-state* risk from unprotected vaginal intercourse.[36]

Much of the responsibility for this tendency doubtless lies with the Department of Health and its press releases. The statistics for 1990 offer a typical case study. In January 1991, newspaper reports of the latest British statistics carried headlines such as 'AIDS virus infection by normal sex rises',[37] 'AIDS risk growing for girls',[38] 'AIDS spread greatest in heterosexual community'[39] and 'MUMS-TO-BE IN NEW AIDS STUNNER'.[40] Most of these reports quoted the Department of Health's press release saying that 'Cases of AIDS among heterosexuals are still increasing faster than in any other group', and only 2 out of the 8 stories even mentioned the latest totals among gay men.

The statistics contained in the press release did indeed reveal continuing HIV transmission among heterosexuals: during 1990 the total number of persons infected through heterosexual inter-course rose by 61 per cent from 766 to 1237, and cases of AIDS in people infected by this route increased by 98 per cent from 135 to 268. The press release also pointed out that '[AIDS] cases in women have increased rapidly during 1990, by 78 per cent from 114 to 203'. The editorial notes contained only one sentence on AIDS in gay or bisexual men, which stated that 'The number of these cases rose much more slowly during 1990, by 42 per cent from 2326 to 3295'. As if in fear that this sentence might distract editors' attention from the heterosexual statistics, the press release quickly added, still under the heading 'AIDS in Homosexual or Bisexual Men':

> Worldwide, the main route of spread is vaginal intercourse. WHO [the World Health Organization] recently forecast that up to 10 million children could be infected by their mothers by the end of the century. The Government's campaign aimed at educating the general population, par-ticularly the young and sexually active, about the continuing danger is an essential component of the strategy for the prevention of spread of HIV in this country.[41]

Given this emphasis, it is hardly surprising that the press reports focused so disproportionately on heterosexual transmission. A closer look at the figures would have revealed that the total for women with AIDS included those infected through drug use or blood or tissue transfer such as transfusions, and that AIDS cases among women infected through heterosexual sex had in fact increased from 52 to 97 cases, accounting for less than half of the total number of women with AIDS. A more reasonable summary of the breakdown of people with AIDS would have reported that no less than 80 per cent of cases reported by the end of 1990 were among gay or bisexual men; 70 per cent of people known to be HIV-positive were gay or bisexual men, with 1411 testing positive in 1990. This means that in the space of just one year, a far greater number of gay men tested HIV-positive than the total number of male or female persons infected through heterosexual sex throughout the entire British epidemic. Yet the editorial notes on HIV statistics focused exclusively on the 471 new reports of heterosexual transmission and made not a mention of continuing transmission among gay men. In this way, the Department of Health's presentation of the statistics has helped to set an agenda in which the evidence of small-scale but increasing heterosexual transmission is allowed totally to obscure the continuing reality of the British epidemic and its disproportionate impact upon gay and bisexual men.

Likewise, in May 1991 the Junior Health Minister Virginia Bottomley announced the first results from the Medical Research Council's programme of anonymized HIV surveys, in which tests were performed on blood taken for other purposes from about 44,000 people who attended 27 selected antenatal clinics or 6 genitourinary medicine clinics.[42] Prevalence among pregnant women ranged from zero in some places to about 1 in 200 in one inner London clinic; at the STD clinics in London, prevalence among heterosexual women was 1 in 500 and among heterosexual men 1 in 100. Among gay or bisexual men at clinics, prevalence was no less than 1 in 5. 'These results', said Mrs Bottomley, '... provide valuable information to help us target our response to the epidemic and show the extent to which HIV is a problem in London'.[43] Yet in virtually all the ensuing press attention, Mrs Bottomley and her colleagues, such as the Chief Medical Officer Sir Donald Acheson, focused solely on the heterosexual statistics, saying nothing about the shockingly high levels of infection among gay men. Thus the quote from Sir Donald provided in the official press release claimed that 'The results of these surveys … reinforce our earlier messages that HIV and AIDS is increasing in the heterosexual population and is a problem that faces us all.' He went on to summarize safer sex advice as 'Avoid casual sex and try to stick to one faithful partner' – advice which is likely only to increase the risk of infection for a gay man with perhaps a 20 per cent chance of choosing an infected partner.

The specific profile of HIV infection in Scotland is frequently held up as an example of an epidemic which has evolved to the extent that it now predominantly affects heterosexuals. As part of the UK, Scotland is seen as offering a compelling example of the imminent threat to the nation as a whole. Statistics published in September 1992 were reported in *The Independent* newspaper under the headline 'Heterosexual intercourse "commonest HIV source"', blurring any distinction between Scotland and the rest of the UK, while the story itself argued that 'Although the figures refer only to Scotland, they will cause considerable concern in relation to future UK studies of HIV infection'.[44]

These figures showed that in the first 6 months of 1992, a larger proportion of newly detected cases of HIV infection were attributable to heterosexual transmission than any other route. However, the real picture is somewhat more complicated. First, the actual number of heterosexuals taking the HIV antibody test has increased faster than the number of gay and bisexual men or drug users.[45] This means that even if prevalence within all risk groups had remained absolutely stable, the proportion of cases seen among heterosexuals would nevertheless increase. The most recent figures reveal that, compared with 1990, the number of non-drug-using heterosexuals who took the test increased by 44 per cent in 1991, while the proportion who tested HIV-positive actually decreased from 0.7 per cent in 1990 to 0.5 per cent in 1991.[46] Once again, however, these very low prevalence rates are allowed to overshadow those among gay and bisexual men. In 1991, a gay man taking the HIV antibody test in Scotland was 10 times more likely to be infected than a non-drug-using heterosexual.

It is generally believed that the Scottish epidemic continues mostly to affect injecting drug users, and indeed, a cumulative total of 57 per cent of cases of HIV infection in Scotland have been among drug users. However, the introduction of needle-exchange schemes in the mid-1980s appears to have had a dramatic impact on new infections in this population, to such a degree that the proportion of cases among drug users has fallen from 80 per cent in the years up to 1985, to 18 per cent in 1992. By contrast, throughout the 1980s gay and bisexual men constituted a growing proportion of positive test results, rising from 18 per cent by the end of 1985 to 41 per cent in 1990.[47]

Carelessness with the HIV/AIDS statistics can thus lead to entirely mistaken conclusions about the current epidemic. For example, in February 1992 the highly regarded *AIDS Newsletter* published by the Bureau of Hygiene and Tropical Diseases in London reported that during 1991 'the greatest increase in [AIDS] cases was recorded in the transmission category sexual intercourse between men and women (up 66.2% from 266 to 442).'[48] The clear implication is that the 176 new cases of AIDS among heterosexuals in 1991 represented the largest increase in any transmission category. In reality, the same set of statistics revealed that 959 gay or bisexual men had been diagnosed with AIDS during the same 12 months – over 5 times as many as among heterosexuals. It is through mistakes such as this that inaccurate perceptions of the current shape of the epidemic are formed, with serious consequences for the establishment of prevention priorities.

Public education campaigns

As the new concern about AIDS was more precisely a concern about the potential dangers to heterosexuals, rather than the continuing problem among gay men, the Department of Health and Social Security's (DHSS) public health education campaign which began in Britain in March 1986, was designed entirely for a heterosexual audience. The initial 'Don't aid AIDS' campaign featured a series of full-page advertisements signed by the four Chief Medical Officers to the Health Departments of the United Kingdom. The aim was clear: to persuade heterosexuals that AIDS was not 'just' a disease affecting gay men. The advertisements were also placed in gay publications, such as *Capital Gay* newspaper, as though the government believed that the information needs of gay men, who had by then been living at the epicentre of the epidemic for a number of years, were identical to those of heterosexuals brought up on a diet of tabloid AIDS misinformation. This resulted in messages which were frankly contradictory to a gay readership, such as advice that 'Using a sheath reduces the risk of AIDS and other diseases', immediately followed by the warning 'Rectal sex involves the highest risk *and should be avoided*'. Indeed, the campaign seemed determined to play down the impact of the epidemic on gay men, who were mentioned only in the insultingly dismissive observation that 'Up until now, AIDS has been confined mainly to small groups of people', and in the question 'Does AIDS only affect homosexuals?', to which the full answer, in capitals, is the single word 'NO'.[49] These advertisements were to be 'widely criticised for poor presentation and lack of public impact'.[50]

Other advertisements in the 'Don't aid AIDS' series appeared at the end of 1986. One published in the 'youth press' between December 1986 and February 1987 asked 'HOW GAY DO YOU HAVE TO BE TO CATCH AIDS?'. Rather than attempting to get accurate and helpful information to gay teenagers before they started having sex, this poster addressed itself exclusively to straight boys, warning them vaguely that 'the higher you rate your pulling power with women, the more danger you could be in'. The advertisements' approach remained, as Simon Watney put it, 'clearly anti-sex, drawing on an assumed rhetoric concerning "promiscuity" as the supposed "cause" of AIDS, in order to terrify people into monogamy'.[51] It was therefore entirely in character for the Department of Health to condemn as 'very irresponsible' a motion debated at the annual conference of the National Union of Students in December 1986, which correctly pointed out that 'Promiscuous behaviour alone cannot and does not spread AIDS. It is the practices involved not the number of partners which is relevant'.[52]

At the same time, the now infamous 'Don't die of ignorance' newspaper, television and billboard advertisements appeared. As Watney observed:

The worst poster of all coyly offers the question, 'AIDS: HOW MUCH BIGGER DOES IT HAVE TO GET BEFORE

YOU TAKE NOTICE?'. The question however which we should all be asking six years into this epidemic is how large did it have to get before they took any notice? ... Millions of pounds have been spent on a crude loud-hailing exercise which directs itself to nobody in particular, and least of all to those most urgently in need of positive, supportive health education. That is why the didactic call not 'to die in ignorance' is so insufferable, coming from a government which has efficiently kept gay men in ignorance about AIDS throughout the 1980s.[53]

And if there remained any doubt that official concern rested almost exclusively with the predicted threat to heterosexuals rather than the very real and present threat to gay men, it should have been dispersed by the comments of junior health minister Edwina Currie, reported in *The Sun* in February 1987, that 'attention given to homosexual deaths hid the spread of AIDS among heterosexuals'.[54]

On 10 March 1987, Norman Fowler told the House of Commons during Question Time that the advertising in the next stage of the AIDS publicity campaign would at last target gay men and drug users.[55] In December 1985, when the first advertisements were being planned, and when the second round were being developed in April 1986, the Terrence Higgins Trust called for the specific targeting of safer sex advice to gay men.[56] As recounted later in this chapter, these advertisements were not to appear until 1989. In some ways, of course, this may have been a good thing, as there is little evidence that the government had any appreciation of the sex-positive nature and methods of the successful gay-community-based safer sex campaigns of the preceding years, as discussed in Chapters 2 and 3. When officials had anything to say to the members of high risk groups, their advice tended to be insultingly naive and ill-informed; for example, in September 1985 the new Health Minister Barney Hayhoe, speaking on television, 'said everyone in high risk groups should be encouraged to confine their sexual activities to monogamous or very stable relationships ... the best defence would be to cut out casual sex of any kind'.[57] It was people like Barney Hayhoe who should have been taking advice from gay men, rather than the other way round.

On 1 April 1987 the independent Health Education Council,

which had been 'one of the few statutory bodies outside teaching hospitals to challenge government negligence over AIDS',[58] was reformed as the Health Education Authority (HEA) and given a specific remit for, among other campaigns, public education on the epidemic.[59] The HEA was given increased responsibilities and budget and promised 'sturdy independence' by Secretary of State Norman Fowler;[60] however, it soon became clear that this was incompatible with the 'clear line of accountability to ministers and Parliament'[61] which was also imposed. By October 1988 HEA staff had come into conflict with the Department of Health over the use of television adverts; staff were quoted as believing that 'independence is a myth. We no longer have any misconceptions about that'.[62] In respect of community-based work, in 1989 the HEA was instructed by Health Minister David Mellor to 'work fully within government policies'; by this stage the Authority had already been ordered to use more euphemistic language in its gay press advertising.[63]

From the start, gay men had grounds to view the HEA with suspicion: in March 1987 Ann Burdus, the incoming Deputy Chair of the HEA with responsibility for its AIDS campaigns, attacked the 'lunatic antics' of gay activists in a Radio 4 interview, prompting *Capital Gay* newspaper to wonder:

> what lunatic behaviour she had in mind – whether it was the gay community's initiative in establishing the Terrence Higgins Trust, the health education campaign mounted by the gay press or the widespread regional network of AIDS advice lines set up by London Lesbian and Gay Switchboard, local switchboards and Friend branches.[64]

With only two exceptions to date, advertisements placed in the mainstream press have eschewed the opportunity to communicate with gay or bisexual men who do not read the gay press, and have continued to ignore or downplay the impact of the epidemic upon gay men. As part of the 1988/89 'AIDS: You're as safe as you want to be' advertisement series, one poster made the campaign's indifference to those most affected by the epidemic quite explicit, asking 'IF AIDS ONLY AFFECTS 0.002% OF THE POPULATION WHY IS THIS ADVERTISEMENT APPEARING IN EVERY

NATIONAL DAILY NEWSPAPER?', and explaining 'while it may still only affect a few people, its spread is something that now concerns us all'. In response to the campaign launched by the Health Education Authority in February 1989, *Evening Standard* reporter Annalena McAfee asked 'Is the AIDS advertising so frightened of being thought anti-gay, that it is directed at the wrong target?', but got the answer 'No, says the Health Education Authority: heterosexual young men are now most at risk'.[65] The 1990 'Experts speak about HIV and AIDS' series of television and press advertisements was 'aimed at reminding the general public how HIV is spreading in the UK',[66] yet its focus remained strictly on heterosexuals, rather than gay men. One press advertisement featured Sir Donald Acheson, Chief Medical Officer at the Department of Health, saying *'It may not seem very serious now* but if we don't act it could have a disastrous effect on the future of our children and our grandchildren' (emphasis added).[67]

With hindsight, it is clear that the de-gaying of public health education campaigns has had considerable harmful consequences for the sustenance of safer sex among gay men. From 1986 onwards, public, government and media attention were firmly fixed upon the threatened heterosexual explosion of HIV infection. Although newspapers like the *Sunday Times* and the *Daily Mail*, and far-right groups such as Family and Youth Concern and the Conservative Family Campaign, continued to question the likelihood of the epidemic affecting 'low-risk' heterosexuals and to insist that AIDS was a disease of homosexuals, drug users and others who indulged in 'deviant' behaviour, this did not reflect any genuine concern for or interest in the epidemic that nearly everyone agreed *did* exist.[68] HIV workers followed the lead set by the Department of Health and prominent epidemiologists, and put their energy and resources into supporting the 'Everyone is at risk' approach. Likewise, strategies were drawn upon and budgets were allocated, targeting prevention funds to groups such as young people, women and professionals, who were assumed to be uniformly heterosexual. The need for specific, targeted interventions for men who identified proudly and openly as gay went unmet.

From 1987 onwards, prevention initiatives for gay men were hardly ever discussed, let alone funded. Occasionally gay men's safer sex achievements in the 1980s would be held up as an example of a successful response to HIV; so, for instance, Minister of State for Health Virginia Bottomley observed in 1989 that 'the gay community has set a good example in changing its behaviour'.[69] But ironically, as gay men became the role models for behaviour change, their own ongoing needs for education and support were largely ignored. One consequence has been the perception that gay men are in no greater need of education and support than the rest of the general population – or even at less need. The over-riding impression is that the epidemic has somehow lifted up and moved on, taking away any significant risk to gay men, when in reality it has merely expanded, with gay men still right in the epicentre, still most at risk.[70]

Worse, there are some indications that this mistaken message has also been picked up by many gay men themselves. In 1991, when the Terrence Higgins Trust undertook an informal evaluation of an educational campaign by conducting a survey of men in gay pubs and clubs, a significant proportion of respondents argued that the Trust should be prioritizing heterosexuals instead. In 1992, a District HIV Prevention Coordinator in south-east England approached a local gay group for help in developing an educational campaign, only to be told that gay men did not want to be targeted, and that the money should be spent on heterosexuals who were now the most at risk. One can only speculate on the extent to which such views are accompanied by a sense of decreased personal vulnerability, and consequently an increased risk of unsafe sex.

Gay men and de-gaying

An AIDS education resource published in 1992 includes a role-playing game in which various characters debate the setting up of an AIDS advice and counselling service. Various characters are given stereotypical briefs: a businessman opposed to his taxes being spent on HIV services; a local resident worried about damage to the character of the neighbourhood; a mother who objects to children with HIV being allowed into schools, and so on. One of the thirteen characters runs a local gay rights society. Is he there to argue for the needs of gay men as those most affected by the epidemic, or perhaps to offer advice on the achievements of other gay men in establishing AIDS service organizations, or maybe even to speak out against homophobic bigotry? Not at all. By this stage, gay men were widely perceived as the prime movers in attempts to play down the impact of the epidemic upon their community, and this gay character's brief therefore states 'It is a fact that the highest incidence of AIDS is amongst male homosexuals and drug misusers. *How will you argue against this?*' (emphasis added).[71]

One of the more painful truths about the de-gaying of AIDS is that many gay men involved in AIDS work actively participated in a process which seems with hindsight to have been immensely damaging to gay men's interests. Gay men came to be seen not as the pioneers of AIDS education and services, but as deceitful apologists arguing against clear facts. How did this extraordinary change come about?

As has been noted, by the mid-1980s gay community organizations in major cities such as London, New York, San Francisco and Sydney had extensive experience in providing AIDS-related education and services. For a limited period, this experience, and the evidence for the unprecedented success of grass-roots safer sex campaigns among gay men, commanded considerable respect. In the UK in particular, a strong working relationship evolved between the Terrence Higgins Trust and the Department of Health. As substantial government funding for AIDS prevention and services became available, the voluntary sector evolved to take advantage of that funding.

In practice, this meant that community-based organizations in many cases became informal social services agencies, and in so doing, adopted many of the institutional norms of statutory bodies. Although there remained considerable disagreements over AIDS policies between government agencies and community-based organizations, '[t]he AIDS groups grew closer in sensibility to their partner government agencies, even while they fought over issues like mandatory testing, discrimination and control of research'.[72] This transition did not take place without dissent; to Larry Kramer, one of the founders of Gay Men's Health Crisis (GMHC) in New York, the changes in that organization represented a shift in priorities away from protecting the living towards an unacceptable conservatism:

I cannot for the life of me understand how the organization I helped to form has become such a bastion of conservatism and such a bureaucratic mess. The bigger you get, the more cowardly you become; the more money you receive, the more self-satisfied you are ... You and your huge assortment of caretakers perform miraculous tasks helping the dying to die ... I think it must now come as a big surprise to you and your Board of Directors that Gay Men's Health Crisis was not founded to help those who are ill. It was founded to protect the living, to help the living go on living, to help those who are still healthy to stay healthy, to help gay men stay alive. Mercifully, there are still far more of us who are yet alive ... Yes, GMHC was founded to fight, to spread information to gay men, and to fight for them. It was *not* founded, believe it or not, to provide Patient Services of any sort. This came later – and it has come to dominate you. It has provided you with the excuse to be cowards. It has provided you with a cover so that you can say, anytime something controversial requires attention: 'We are too busy taking care of patients.'[73]

Tony Whitehead has voiced related concerns about the 'well-intentioned but perhaps misguided complicity between charity and the statutory sector' in the UK. Speaking in 1988, he argued that 'Instead of simply behaving like so many good little Florence Nightingales, developing our own educational and support services within the gay community, we AIDS activists should have fought for such services within the statutory sector'.[74] In practice, community-based AIDS organizations accepted the government's agenda as they accepted the government's money, and according to Cindy Patton, 'helped degay AIDS by asserting that their group served anyone with AIDS and were not "gay" political or social organizations'.[75]

As AIDS organizations began to offer services to an increasingly diverse clientele, although still very much dominated by the disproportionate impact of the epidemic upon gay men, the pressure to play down any explicit commitment to the needs of gay men increased. But this has been the case not only in service organizations, but also in the case of AIDS activist groups such as ACT UP.

Although ACT UP groups around the world describe themselves as 'non-partisan' – in contrast to popular perceptions of them as the latest manifestation of radical gay liberation – one might reasonably expect them to respond to the epidemiological realities of the local epidemics. Instead, as Robin Hardy has bitterly argued:

> ACT UP's failure to ground its politics in the identity of 98 per cent of its members has diverted it from goals which are critical to gay men. As ACT UP embraces the politics of inclusion, it cuts itself off from the community which has provided the core of its tactics, theory, membership and funding ... Implicit in ACT UP's brand of coalition politics is an assumption that homosexuals must subordinate their gay/lesbian identity to attract other communities to the ranks of AIDS activism. No one has stopped to ask what attention to the political agendas of other minorities might be costing the gay community. Or if it's even working.[76]

In an extreme example of this myopia, a gay man speaking at an ACT UP World AIDS Day rally in London in 1990 argued that gay men were responsible for the alleged lack of specialist services for women with HIV in Britain. In effect, he was arguing that the AIDS organizations originally formed to look after gay men's interests – at a time when it was clear that nobody else would – had not been de-gayed *enough*. Yet by 1990 the British voluntary sector had already been heterosexualized to the extent that not a single designated agency specializing in meeting the specific education or service needs of gay men existed anywhere in the country. It was almost as though some (especially leftist) gay men *required* the epidemic to conform to a pre-existing 'equal opportunities' politics, which was unable to adjust to the reality in which supposedly privileged, white, middle-class gay men have formed the majority of those affected.

Another highly significant reason why some gay men helped to de-gay AIDS was to prevent an upsurge of homophobic discrimination and violence founded on the view that homosexuality was now not merely distasteful, but also the root cause of a deadly transmissible disease. In November 1986 it was reported that:

Cabinet ministers are alarmed that growing public awareness of the threat of AIDS could provoke a backlash against
homosexuals and widespread 'queer-bashing'. They also
fear that if homosexuals are attacked and forced underground some bisexuals may resort to 'revenge sex' in which
they knowingly spread the disease. Ministers accept that
they must do all they can to keep 'gays' as part of the
community and seek their co-operation. The backlash risk
will rise as more AIDS victims are reported and more people
realise there is no cure.[77]

If Cabinet ministers were alarmed, so were gay men. As if to
prove the point, two days after these concerns were published, the
far-right pressure group the Conservative Family Campaign 'called
on the Government to isolate all AIDS victims and to make homosexual acts between consenting adults a criminal offence'.[78] Only
one month later Lord Halsbury introduced a private member's bill
into the House of Lords to 'prohibit any council helping the promotion of homosexuality as an acceptable family relationship,
including teaching such a view in maintained schools'; one of the
justifications given for this measure, which was dropped, but resur-
rected in the Commons the following year as the now infamous
Clause 28 of the Local Government Bill, was that gay men acted as
'reservoirs' for venereal disease.[79] In November 1985 a group of
Conservative MPs claiming the support of 'one or two very influential people' had lobbied the government to close down all Britain's
gay pubs or clubs as a measure 'to stop this killer disease AIDS from
spreading'.[80] And meanwhile in California, activists were mobiliz-
ing to defeat Lyndon Larouche's proposals to make AIDS a notifi-
able disease, registering all people with AIDS and excluding them
from 'sensitive' jobs.

Gay men were thus justifiably alarmed by the effect of the
epidemic on public attitudes to homosexuality; as Simon Watney
has argued, the presence of AIDS among gay men, drug users and
black communities 'is generally perceived not as accidental but as a
symbolic extension of some imagined inner being, manifesting itself
as disease'.[81] For over half of the 269 people interviewed by Antony
Vass in mid-1985, AIDS was:

punishment at its best ... shades of that punishment [ranged] from exclusion and the occasional wish to inflict direct personal injury on those sufferers, to expecting sufferers to wear a label, a badge or bear some other visible mark which exposes their 'crime' of AIDS and warns 'normal' people to keep their distance.[82]

The government strategy of emphasizing the universality of the threat posed by AIDS was therefore one which many gay men gladly embraced. Whether or not it succeeded in averting the discrimination and blame which many gay men feared is highly debatable; it is difficult to know whether an incident of violence or the latest rant from extremist religious or political groups is motivated and/or exacerbated by AIDS, or simply a manifestation of the prejudice against homosexuality which has existed for centuries, and which they would have possessed irrespective of the epidemic. Paradoxically, however, it is clear that in some instances the message that AIDS endangered everyone was seen as a positive *incentive* for clamping down on homosexuality. Thus in 1984 the American Family Association, seeking signatures for a petition to the Surgeon General, wrote to its supporters:

Dear Family Member,
Since AIDS is transmitted primarily by perverse homosexuals your name on my national petition to quarantine all homosexual establishments is crucial to your family's health and security ... If you want your family's health and security protected, these AIDS-carrying homosexuals must be quarantined immediately ... These disease-carrying deviants wander the streets unconcerned, possibly making you their next victims. What else can you expect from sex-crazed degenerates but selfishness?[83]

In this way, 'the threat of a heterosexual epidemic is a double-edged sword'.[84] As an American gay activist who believes that threat is 'nothing more than hype with absolutely no support from the medical and sociological data' argued:

In California, where I live, we've seen that the myth of

heterosexual AIDS has an upside (it increased funding) but also a downside: We spent millions defeating two statewide propositions that would have established mandatory testing, quarantine and other draconian measures.[85]

From 1987 onwards, resistance to AIDS education for the whole population coalesced around two theories: the de-gaying of AIDS was either a connivance between a moralistic government and a misguided gay movement, or it was a 'homosexual conspiracy' by a powerful 'gay lobby' intent on hiding the truth about the disease. These views spanned a strikingly diverse political spectrum, from the Revolutionary Communist Party to far-right pressure groups such as Family and Youth Concern. Advocates of the re-gaying of AIDS, who wish to contest the harmful professionalization and heterosexualization of the epidemic, thus find themselves in the awkward position not only of seeming to criticize the actions taken largely in good faith by gay men, but also of appearing to side with those who number among the clearest opponents of lesbian and gay well-being. For this reason, Chapter 6 is devoted to a detailed examination of the areas in which the critique of the de-gaying of AIDS presented in this book differs from the views of those who consider 'heterosexual AIDS' to be a 'myth'.

Statutory sector work for gay men

Mass-media campaigns for the general population represented only one facet of the state response to AIDS, which began in earnest in 1986. On a local level, state funds were allocated to District and Regional Health Authorities throughout Britain, to enable them to undertake tailored, community-based education and information initiatives for their local populations. Many gay men who had gained their knowledge and expertise in HIV prevention through paid or unpaid work in the voluntary sector or organizations such as Lesbian and Gay Switchboard now moved on to take up posts in the statutory sector.

In a sense, statutory organizations have not been de-gayed, but only because their health education strategies never focused on gay men in the first place. In part their agenda was defined by the specific directions emanating from the Department of Health; in addition, they established their priorities at the time when it was widely perceived that safer sex education for gay men had been successfully completed, and national advertising campaigns were pushing the message that 'Everyone is at risk'.

The first signs of the statutory sector's failure to address the ongoing needs of gay men were evident in early 1987, when the Surrey and South West London Gay Organisations (SAGO) network conducted a survey of prevention and care services provided by 7 district health authorities in the South West Thames Region.[86] Five of the districts stocked leaflets for local distribution; however, 'most were aimed at the general public ... Only one leaflet was specifically designed for gay men'.[87] Only one district had established contact with local gay groups, a fact described as 'a serious gap in their strategic planning'.[88] However, the true extent of the neglect was not revealed until the publication of the report *HIV Prevention for Gay Men: A Survey of Initiatives in the UK* in July 1992, which revealed that out of a sample of 226 agencies with a remit for HIV prevention, virtually all of which were in the statutory sector, only one-third had ever targeted gay men at all, and less than 4 per cent had offered local gay men a substantial package of safer sex promotional activities.[89] This survey is described in more detail in Chapter 7.

Not only has the statutory sector failed to meet its responsibility to support the needs of gay men during the HIV epidemic; it has also contributed to the de-gaying of the voluntary sector. Many of the gay men who have taken paid employment in the statutory sector had previously been involved in safer sex education activities for gay men in the voluntary sector or gay groups; as they were commandeered to work to the heterosexualized agenda of the statutory sector, community-based groups faced a growing dearth of both enthusiasm and expertise in HIV prevention for those most at risk. Thus in 1991 Peter Scott described the 'danger [in] the recruitment (or burnout) of an earlier generation of community development activists into institutional public health structures that threaten to isolate them from their original communities and to leave those communities without significant continuing community education'.[90]

The Health Education Authority: a case study

The Health Education Authority's 'men who have sex with men' project was initiated in 1988. Its objectives were four-fold:

- To reduce the incidence of HIV transmission by ensuring access to information and education which will facilitate personal behaviour change for men both within and outside formal groupings of gay or bisexual men;
- to develop a model of health education that can be disseminated throughout the country to enable and encourage gay and bisexual men to re-evaluate their sexual behaviour in respect of low, medium and high risk of HIV infection;
- to promote awareness of the issues surrounding HIV/AIDS amongst men who have casual or intermittent sexual contact with other men;
- to develop an appropriate health education message for men who have sexual relations with other men in special settings.[91]

Initial advertising and promotional materials were developed; pre-testing research, however, 'indicated that these were likely to be low in impact'. The Authority paused, and commissioned two reviews of safer sex educational materials[92] and safer sex workshops.[93]

Subsequently, new advertising was developed, and placed in lesbian and gay community publications from February until September 1989. The adverts featured photographs by Herb Ritts, with the messages 'If you think safer sex sounds dull, reading this might change your position' and 'They used to say masturbation was bad for you. Now it could save your life'. From September 1989 to spring 1990 two advertisements featuring photography by

Jean Baptiste Mondino were published, this time using the slogan 'They don't have safer sex just because it's safer'. During this period a line-art advertisement encouraging gay men to be sexually imaginative, and three advertisements featuring 'safer sex situation' shots by the press photographer Caroline Mardon and the caption 'Choose safer sex', were also printed.

The next 6-month advertising phase began in July 1990. The Mondino advertisements were placed in a number of non-gay specific magazines, such as *Arena*, *Time Out* and *The Face*, while two new advertisements ran in the gay press, one targeting 'new entrants to the scene' using the slogan 'He's into safer sex so why not give him a hand', and another 'aimed at ensuring that those in relationships continue safer sex practices' with the message 'If your sex life is unprotected so too is your relationship'.

Another advertisement was aimed at 'covert bisexual men'. It featured a close-up photograph of a male hand wearing a wedding ring holding another male hand, and the slogan 'If a married man has an affair, it may not be with a woman'. This was originally published in music, style and listings magazines in spring 1990, supported by a freephone help-line service, and was repeated in a wider range of publications, including *TV Times*, *Angling Times*, *Custom Car* and *BBC Wildlife* magazines, between July and October 1991.

A new advertising campaign began in August 1992. Advertisements providing advice on the choice of condoms and lubricants and proper condom use appeared in the gay press, and a photographic concept aimed at breaking down feelings of immortality or invulnerability among younger gay men was placed in music and style magazines. For the first time, these advertisements carried not only the National AIDS Helpline number, but also those of the Terrence Higgins Trust and London Lesbian and Gay Switchboard.

The other major strand of HEA work for gay or bisexual men was the Men Who Have Sex With Men: Action in the Community (MESMAC) project. This was a community development initiative developed on the basis of Peter Gordon's review of safer sex workshops,[94] and based at four project sites reflecting a range of working situations. Newcastle Social Services hosted a project site targeting men in both urban and rural settings; Leicester Black HIV/AIDS Forum housed the Leicester Black MESMAC Project;

the Terrence Higgins Trust provided a base for the London project focusing on younger gay men; and Leeds AIDS Advice agreed to host the site looking specifically at the needs of men in a large city. MESMAC had two aims:

- To establish local community initiatives with men who have sex with men, which will explore felt needs in relation to safer sex and work towards meeting these needs;
- To produce a training package to equip a core team of facilitators to develop this work as a general resource for safer sex work with men who have sex with men in various localities in England.[95]

Thorough evaluation of both the processes of MESMAC work and the outcomes of the project was given high priority. During the first phase of activity, between March 1990 and December 1991, the MESMAC projects undertook 49 different initiatives involving some 2700 gay and bisexual men, while in 1992 more than this number of individuals were contacted at just one of the four sites. Despite the project's 'men who have sex with men' terminology, which is discussed later, the vast majority of men involved in MESMAC activities identified as gay or bisexual.[96]

All this sounds like a most impressive body of work, and in a number of regards it is. Few other countries have seen such a programme undertaken specifically for gay or bisexual men, and bearing the government's official stamp. But nevertheless, by 1992 the HEA had become the object of some derision in the lesbian and gay press, and its 'men who have sex with men' project Advisory Group had resigned *en masse*. This striking lack of support from the community had its roots in a number of concrete difficulties.

First, it is important to remember that the first government advertisement for gay men appeared in February 1989, by which time over 5200 gay men had already tested positive and many thousands more were no doubt also infected, and the mass behaviour changes of the early to mid-1980s were already suffering the effects of subsequent neglect. Prior to 1989, government monies had been given to the Terrence Higgins Trust as a form of 'backdoor' funding for gay safer sex campaigns, whose importance the government recognized – indeed, the Chief Medical Officer Sir Donald Acheson met with activists as early as 1983 to express support for the Trust's initial activities in the gay community[97] – but which were far too politically sensitive for it to be undertaken openly itself. After 1988, the Trust received no funding through the HEA for the educational work it undertook with gay men.[98]

As an official agency with government backing, the HEA believed that it could speak to gay men with authority and impartiality. However, this potential advantage was accompanied by a host of disadvantages. There was no theoretical or historical reason to believe that gay men would respond more favourably to the voice of officialdom than to messages clearly originating from within the gay community. The advantage of community 'ownership' of educational interventions was implicitly acknowledged in the establishment of the MESMAC projects, three of which were sited in local voluntary organizations, and which used the grass-roots community-development approach to explore the self-perceived needs of gay or bisexual men and equip individuals and groups to meet those needs themselves. Advertisements, however, always face the risk that they will be rejected as unwelcome impositions from above, and this may have been particularly true of ones bearing the logo of a statutory agency such as the HEA, as opposed to a community group.

The HEA's accountability to the Department of Health also proved to be inhibitory. In the absence of hard scientific research on effective wording for use in communicating with gay men, the Department of Health vetoed the common-sense approach of addressing the audience in the everyday language used by that audience. Thus the first edition of the Authority's leaflet 'Safer sex for gay men' employed the most tortured terminology, such as the description of fingering as 'digital intercourse', which subsequent evaluation established to have been greeted with hilarity by gay men.[99] Advertisements routinely recommended practices such as 'body rubbing', 'massage' and 'mutual masturbation', with other, more creative non-penetrative options such as sadomasochistic sex or bondage omitted in favour of a blushing suggestion to 'use your imagination'. In 1991 the Department of Health requested that a 'reminder' of the discriminatory age of consent be added to the HEA's safer sex fact cards for gay men,[100] and again disputed the use of explicit language such as 'fuck' in a gay men's safer sex leaflet,[101] despite the fact that HEA research indicated that this was the terminology used and preferred by the target audience.[102] However, these facts may be less surprising in view of the government's description of its HIV prevention initiatives as 'an equal opportunities strategy aimed at providing appropriate and adequate services sensitive to the needs of the communities regardless of age, sex, class or race'.[103] Sexual orientation is notable by its absence.

Within the HEA's HIV and Sexual Health programme, just as within most other agencies undertaking HIV prevention activities, there was a striking imbalance between the pressing need for initiatives targeting gay or bisexual men and the relative funding and priority allocated to such initiatives. At the launch of the gay press campaign in February 1989, Nick Partridge of the Terrence Higgins Trust attacked the initiative as a 'wasted opportunity', pointing out that it had been allocated only 3 per cent of the £10 million annual AIDS education budget.[104] At the time of writing, the HEA employs at least 15 staff in HIV/AIDS-related posts, yet only one of these posts is concerned specifically with the projects for 'men who have sex with men'. In other words, less than 7 per cent of HIV staff time is devoted to gay men, when about 70 per cent of people who have been infected in Britain are gay men.[105] Furthermore, a report in the national lesbian and gay weekly newspaper *The Pink Paper* alleged that HEA funding for campaigns targeting gay men was actually reduced from £1.7 million in 1990/91 – only 18 per cent of the overall AIDS budget of £9.3 million – to a low of £700,000 in 1991/92.[106]

In February 1992, the Advisory Group to the HEA's 'men who have sex with men' programme resigned 'in protest at the Authority's failure to act upon their advice in the development of safer sex campaigns for gay men'.[107] In a letter to the HEA's chair, Sir Donald Maitland, members of the group reported that their 'detailed and, occasionally, very critical comments and advice on strategy and planning have had no discernable influence' and that:

> as a result there is growing and serious concern among some members of the Group about the theory and methodology underlying the HEA's approach to work in this area, doubt about the effectiveness of the work and concern that claims

for effectiveness are being made in the absence of [reliable evidence].[108]

In summary, the HEA's ability to provide useful and effective health education campaigns for gay or bisexual men was hampered by a number of entirely avoidable factors. The Advisory Group, which included 'internationally acknowledged experts on HIV education and prevention work amongst gay men',[109] found that they were unable to influence strategy or campaign development largely because 'despite a genuine willingness on the part of programme staff to be influenced, the organisational framework within which strategic and planning decisions are taken by the HEA are not, in practice, amenable to influence by "grassroots" representation on an internal Advisory Group'.[110]

Similarly, the Authority's accountability to the Department of Health, and its obligation to act in accordance with the policies of a government not renowned for its concern with the well-being of gay men, seriously inhibited its ability to gain gay men's trust and acceptance for its messages. It was for this reason that in 1987 the Bow Group had proposed that:

> the best way forward is for the Health Education Authority to run no campaigns itself but to fund and support the efforts of organisations like the Terrence Higgins Trust, whose campaigns are notable for an occasional obscenity and a general effectiveness that a more august body is unlikely to be able to match.[111]

Likewise, in May 1987 the Commons Social Services Committee recommended that 'if the Government wishes to target information at the gay community, the Terrence Higgins Trust would be the most effective agent through which to provide the bulk of the targeted information to the whole country'.[112] Both these eminently sensible pieces of advice were ignored.

More recently there have been very positive developments in the HEA's work with gay and bisexual men, particularly in the field development division, which provides advice, assistance and consultancy to local prevention service providers. New materials have at last started to employ the terminology used by gay men themselves, and the now-completed MESMAC projects have clearly undertaken valuable community development work in the field. It is unfortunate, however, that these positive developments have only taken place after some years of difficulties. History now shows that the government's decision that the HEA itself should be the provider of education campaigns, rather than commissioning them from agencies with strong gay community ties, both undercut the effectiveness of the campaigns, and at the same time contributed to the 'de-gaying' of those agencies.

'Men who have sex with men' versus gay men[113]

By the late 1980s, very little educational work for gay men was being undertaken in either the voluntary or the statutory sectors, the emphasis having shifted either to the general public at large, or to discrete subpopulations such as young people or women, all of whom are usually assumed to be entirely heterosexual.[114] When sex between men was addressed as a risk activity by AIDS educators, it was increasingly likely that its practitioners would be described as 'men who have sex with men' rather than 'gay men' or 'gay and bisexual men'. While there appear to have been a number of well-intentioned motives for the adoption of 'men who have sex with men' terminology (MWHSWM), in practice the term reflected a rather subtle form of de-gaying.

The term 'MWHSWM' was embraced particularly enthusiastically by statutory sector authorities involved in HIV prevention work, such as the Health Education Authority in its MESMAC project described earlier, and numerous smaller, local initiatives. In some local government bureaucracies, the very idea of promoting safer gay sex encountered a number of obstacles: political sensitivities and a concern to avoid controversy, especially in relation to the notion of promoting homosexuality; the mistaken view that gay men were no longer particularly at risk from HIV; and in some cases, the straightforward, prejudiced view that the health of gay men was of little importance. In these circumstances, the use of MWHSWM terminology offered 'a way of getting resources which might otherwise have been felt to have been unavailable for ex-plicitly gay and bisexual work'.[115]

The terminology was also intended to focus attention on the disjunctions between behaviour and identity. At a time when there was a common misapprehension that safer sex campaigns among men who self-identified as gay had been successfully completed, the next priority in preventing homosexual transmission of HIV seemed to be among 'hard-to-reach' men who occasionally had sex with other men, but who did not consider themselves to be gay.

Unfortunately, 'MWHSWM' can be a profoundly alienating term for men who are confident and proud in their gay or bisexual identity. For gay men, the term 'gay' is something we choose to use to describe ourselves and our sense of shared identity and interests with other gay men. By contrast, 'MWHSWM' is not a term of self-identification, but rather a pseudo-scientific classification applied *by* others *to* homosexually active men, and thereby creating and perpetuating a gulf between the 'professional' educator and the 'subject'. Health education messages based on MWHSWM termin-ology are thus likely to meet with quite avoidable resistance from gay men, simply because they clearly originate outside the com-munity and are imposed upon it, rather than being generated from within.

The inappropriateness of 'MWHSWM' in work for confi-dent gay men means that its use in health education appears to prioritize the needs of heterosexually identified 'men who have sex with men' above or instead of those of gay men. Not only is work with homosexually active men accorded at best a low priority in the overall scheme of HIV prevention initiatives; even where MWHSWM are targeted, the needs of those most at risk – namely, 'out' gay men on the commercial scene – are neglected. To this extent, use of the term 'MWHSWM' frequently characterizes work which remains complacent or indifferent to the ongoing needs of gay men at the core of their communities.[116]

Moreover, the use of 'MWHSWM' may ironically also ob-scure a proper recognition of and effective response to the needs of those men who do not identify as gay. In the first place, this is because research has shown that men who do have a strong gay identity are more likely to be able to adopt and sustain the practice of safer sex.[117] A valid aim of HIV education would therefore be to help so-called 'men who have sex with men' to develop a confident gay identity. Instead, 'MWHSWM' focuses exclusively and mechanistically on their sexual activity, and thence simply labels them with a term around which they are highly unlikely to mobilize.

The term also 'gives the misleading impression that this is a homogenous group with the same needs, obstacles and potential',[118] when in reality gay men, bisexual men and heterosexual men who sometimes have sex with other men may well have dramatically different needs. In particular, the term 'bisexual men' draws attention to the fact that these men may have sex with both men and women, in a way that MWHSWM does not.

Additionally, as Peter Scott has pointed out, the MWHSWM terminology may prevent what is likely to be the most cost-effective and efficient form of safer sex peer education, by alienating gay men:

> It is important to understand that even those MWHSWM who identify themselves as heterosexual will, in practice, have sexual encounters with confident gay and bisexual men. The advantage of a clear focus upon gay and bisexual men [as opposed to the MWHSWM model] is that they are themselves relatively easy to reach ... whilst at the same time they are most capable of reaching the hardest to reach, by dint of having sexual and social encounters with them. There is no evidence to suggest that anyone else can influence these men 'on the margins' any more effectively.[119]

The voluntary sector

The de-gaying of AIDS was not a phenomenon unique to the statutory sector, nor was it a process entirely imposed by people who did not identify as gay. For reasons discussed earlier, many gay men working in the AIDS field encouraged the view that AIDS was an 'equal opportunities virus' and played down both its disproportionate impact on gay men and the pre-eminent role played by gay men in organized responses to the epidemic. Voluntary agencies, most of them originally founded by and for gay men, were themselves extensively de-gayed.

Eric Rofes, who worked on AIDS issues throughout the 1980s as the head of the Boston Lesbian and Gay Political Alliance, as the executive director of the Los Angeles Gay and Lesbian Community Services Center and as executive director of the Shanti Project in San Francisco, has documented the broad nature of the changes in very many AIDS service organizations during the latter half of the decade. He argued that in about 1985:

> a key decision was made by AIDS leaders to put forward the message that 'AIDS is not a gay disease'. The intent of this strategy apparently was to win increased public support and funding, and to alert all sectors of the population about AIDS prevention. Since that time many AIDS groups have downplayed gay and lesbian participation, denied that they are 'gay organisations', and attempted to appeal to the 'general public' by expunging gay references and sanitizing gay culture. At other times AIDS groups do acknowledge our bases in the gay and lesbian community, particularly when seeking support for fundraising events or trying to draw in new volunteers. This schizophrenia on the part of AIDS organisations sets off movement activists who have struggled for years to bring gay and lesbian issues out of the closet.[120]

Rofes noted that lesbians and gay men involved in the AIDS field have from the start had to contend with homophobic disregard and indifference from the traditional systems and institutions of mainstream society; the de-gaying of AIDS organizations, however, meant that this now had to be confronted in community-based AIDS projects, including those founded by gay men. In response:

> AIDS service providers often find these concerns petty or obsessive ... Everyone knows gay men get AIDS. Why does the community need recognition and acknowledgement? If our own aim is to serve people with AIDS, aren't we justified if we can win increased funding and provide better services by de-emphasizing our gay participation? When they hear

this argument, activists rooted in the gay and lesbian movement wonder whether AIDS workers wear blinders. Have
they no memory of years spent meeting with public officials,
journalists, religious leaders, educators and lawyers to force
them simply to say the words 'gay' and 'lesbian'? Are they
unaware that we still struggle to force publications to allow
individuals to be identified as gay, phone directories to
include specifically gay and lesbian listings, and obituary
writers to name lovers as lovers, rather than as 'friends' or
'companions'? De-gaying AIDS might bring more funding,
but isn't the cost too high?[121]

Rofes described how many community activists have reacted
to de-gaying with 'a profound sense of betrayal'. That betrayal may
be felt all the more keenly because of the unique role that community-based organizations (CBOs) are able to play in undertaking
HIV prevention activities for marginalized groups. Governments
throughout the world have preferred to fund CBOs to produce
safer sex campaigns for gay men rather than do the job directly
themselves, due to either the political reason of the sensitive and
often controversial nature of such work or the pragmatic reason
that education works best when it is perceived as coming from
peers within a community, rather than being imposed by authorities outside that community. A key reason for statutory organizations' neglect of prevention campaigns for gay men appears to
have been their perception that this work was already being done
by CBOs.[122] Ironically, those CBOs may also be attacked for what
prevention work they do undertake for gay men, or simply because
they are perceived as homosexual propagandist groups. This leaves
gay men in the worst of all possible worlds: on the one hand, gay
organizations ignore the epidemic for fear of signalling that it is a
'gay disease', and on the other hand, CBOs, which everyone
assumes to be looking after gay men's interests and needs during
the HIV crisis, are in reality more concerned with distancing themselves from gay men.

It should perhaps be stressed that the de-gaying of AIDS
organizations did not as a rule extend to their direct client services,
such as counselling, buddying and legal and welfare rights advice.
Since most of these services are intended for all people with HIV, it

is hardly surprising that in countries where the epidemic disproportionately affects gay men, the vast majority of clients are gay
men. A better measure of specific concern for the interests of gay
men in this area of AIDS organizations' work might be the degree
to which gay-sensitization or anti-homophobia training is provided
to service providers, whether staff or volunteers, rather than the
demographics of the client population. However, although anti-
sexism and anti-racism training are – quite properly – often
provided to service providers, specific sensitivity training on homosexuality and gay identity, which should be of equal importance, is
virtually unheard of. This extraordinary oversight is persisting even
as the proportion of the staff of generalist organizations who are
themselves gay steadily declines.

The Terrence Higgins Trust: a case study

The de-gaying of a gay-founded AIDS organization can be
quite thoroughly documented in the example of the Terrence Higgins Trust in London. The purpose of focusing on the Trust here is
not to single it out as a particularly culpable organization, since the
neglect of safer sex education for gay men in the latter 1980s
occurred in both statutory and voluntary agencies throughout the
UK and much of the rest of the industrialized world; indeed, in
many respects the Trust is one of the *least* reprehensible of agencies,
in that both in the mid-1980s and in the early 1990s it has provided
undeniably important prevention services for gay and bisexual
men. However, the Trust is the organization with which I am most
familiar, and for which the most documentation is available.

The Trust was founded in 1982 by friends of Terry Higgins,
one of the first British gay men to die with AIDS. Following the
screening of the *Horizon* television documentary 'Killer in the Village' in 1983, the Trust was re-established with an influx of volunteers from London Gay Switchboard, who continued to swell the
Trust's volunteer base throughout the early years. By the end of
1983 the Trust had produced its first leaflets, and its telephone
help-line opened on St Valentine's Day in 1984.[123] In September

1985 the organization received its first government grant of £35,000, to fund the help-line and the production of new leaflets.[124]

During the mid-1980s the Trust produced an impressive body of educational work for gay men. It produced its first advice for gay men, in conjunction with the Gay Medical Association, in autumn 1983. The leaflet 'More facts for gay men' was first published in late 1984; over a 2-month period, some 20,000 leaflets were distributed, largely through STD clinics.[125] 'More facts for gay men' was revised and reissued in April 1985. In late 1985 the Trust launched a campaign to popularize the safety-pin as a symbol to be worn by people who might not want to talk about AIDS, but were interested in having only safer sex;[126] safety-pins subsequently appeared on a series of fliers entitled 'Safer sex – don't dream it ... do it!' featuring a photograph borrowed from an Australian safer sex poster and advice on using condoms. Also in 1985 the Trust was 'giving away T-shirts with "Terrence Higgins Trust Volunteer" emblazoned across the chest, on condition that they are worn in gay venues and that the wearers, who are specially trained, will promise to answer questions on safer sex or HTLV-3 infection'.[127] In 1986 the popular 'Sex ...' leaflet, providing updated safer sex advice in straightforward language, with erotic drawings and cartoons, was published. Advertisements and articles in the gay press and soft-porn magazines such as *Vulcan* and *Him* told gay men how they could obtain the leaflets through the post. Throughout this period the Trust arranged a series of two-and-a-half-hour open discussions, with titles such as 'Safer sex ... an acceptable alternative?', to provide gay men with a forum in which to discuss and come to terms with the new realities with other gay men. Other 'roadshow' events aimed to promote safer sex by talking face to face and giving away condoms, posters and leaflets.[128] Even materials produced for the population at large, such as the leaflet issued in conjunction with Thames Television in October 1986, at this time explained in straightforward and factual terms that 'While anyone *could* be infected, only people in [high risk] groups are liable to have been exposed to the infection'.[129] If anything, this leaflet went further than most in stressing the very limited spread of the epidemic and differentiating between providing information to 'the public' and to those 'at risk'; in a foreword,

Professor Michael Adler said bluntly that 'AIDS has been blown out of all proportion by the media. It is a rare disease ... It is very important that the public realise that they are not at risk'.[130]

Tony Whitehead, chair of the Steering Committee and the Board of Directors of the Trust between 1983 and 1988, has suggested that 'much of the changes observed in [the sexual behaviour of] gay men in 1986 and 1987 can be attributed to the early work of [London Lesbian and Gay] Switchboard, Terrence Higgins Trust, the Gay Medical Association and the gay press'.[131] Whitehead argued that the Trust's early work was so successful for a number of reasons which were all intrinsically rooted in the gay community:

1. We were a gay male organisation. We were not perceiving abstract threats to other people. We were faced with very real risks to ourselves and the people we cared about.

2. We lacked professional skills. On the one hand there were some harmful consequences but on the other hand we didn't know about consultation, pilot runs or evaluation. We simply sat down and did the work.

3. As gay men, most of us had been activists, we were familiar with each other and we knew people involved in other gay organisations and the gay press. This was a great advantage.

4. Our approach was informed by our awareness of the gay political scene and our concepts about ethics. We wanted to empower gay men and not proscribe lists of do's or don'ts. The resultant work was strong on empowerment and relatively sex positive.[132]

By 1986 the Terrence Higgins Trust had achieved a prominent place among the various policy lobbies operating on the national level. It remained 'the only central source of education, comfort and indeed hope for many either suffering with or concerned about AIDS'.[133] It had firm contacts with Sir Donald Acheson, the Chief Medical Officer, and was represented on a 'social issues' advisory group to the Department of Health. It enjoyed good communications with doctors at the Communicable Diseases

Surveillance Centre (CDSC). As Whitehead has described, the Trust was subject to enormous demands:

> We were called upon by the medical community for medical information, for information about the care of people with AIDS. We were also called upon to meet the needs of the other parts of society and develop wide-reaching responses to diverse needs for information on prevention and other kinds of support.[134]

All this put the Trust in a relatively powerful position. However, the agenda that united all the strands of the emergent 'gay/medical/scientific policy community' at this time was 'a stress on the need for urgent action and for public education to highlight the heterosexual nature of the disease rather than the "gay plague" angle of the popular press'.[135] According to Zoë Schramm-Evans, 'the price of [the Trust's] power was a high one – the public and sometimes private denial of the gay essence of the Trust'.[136]

Schramm-Evans goes as far as crediting the Terrence Higgins Trust with inspiring the government approach which resulted in the 1986 advertising campaign run by the Department of Health and Social Security – that 'everyone' was at risk. Moreover, she argues that 'few people in the Trust who had any knowledge of the political epidemiology [sic] of AIDS believed that it would ever spread significantly into the heterosexual population' and that its public face was entirely designed to protect the gay community at a time of very considerable public and political opprobrium. These rather extreme conclusions are disputed by others involved with the Trust at the time.[137] Indeed, tensions between the Trust and the government were becoming increasingly clear, as Tony Whitehead denounced as 'an insult' the lack of funding for the Trust or other 'gay community based organisations' in the package of measures announced by the Social Services Secretary in November 1985, and called for the implementation of a public education campaign targeting gay men and drug users in advance of that planned for the general public.[138] The Trust was not consulted in the planning of the 'Don't die of ignorance' campaign and, like London Lesbian and Gay Switchboard, it was not warned that the number of its telephone help-line, which had only four lines, was to be listed in the leaflet sent to 23 million households in January 1987; consequently new lines had to be installed as up to 400 callers per minute jammed the local exchange.[139] What is more, it was highly unlikely that the Thatcher government, of all governments, would form policy on the basis of the views of an organization founded by and publicly identified with gay men. Rather, the Trust's was just one voice in a powerful consensus which included leading epidemiologists and clinicians, as reflected in publications such as the Cox Report of 1988, which predicted that between 2500 and 12,000 new cases of AIDS would be diagnosed in 1992 (the true figure turned out to be 1492).

Substantial internal changes took place in the Terrence Higgins Trust during the second half of the 1980s. According to Whitehead, 'In the early 1980s THT spent about 80% of its health education budget on gay men, by 1986 that was about 8% ... New priorities emerged. "We must fulfil all public needs, be seen as responsible recipients of Government funds etc".'[140] Those government funds, which had stabilized at just short of half a million pounds per year by the end of the decade, allowed the Trust to grow, employing more staff, expanding its services to people with HIV, moving to new premises, producing a wider range of leaflets, helping other local AIDS groups to establish themselves, and so on. But in this process the Trust may have sacrificed many of the qualities which it originally possessed as a gay-community-based and -identified organization, from which its ability to work effectively with gay men was derived. As Adam Carr has argued, 'no organization can effectively influence and lead the gay community if it is not firmly based, and seen to be firmly based, in that community'.[141]

Whitehead, in common with others, has described how 'during the first years of the Trust's existence the radicals held power. As they left, burnt out or died, then the balance of power shifted towards conservatives'.[142] Meurig Horton, a long-time volunteer at the Trust, has described a growing sense of division and tension between rank-and-file health education activists, who were keen to see the Trust maintain frank, sex-positive safer sex campaigns for gay men, and directors, managers and staff whose view of the organization was rooted in the framework of conventional charities such as Age Concern.[143] As the Trust became increasingly institutionalized, and as the growing demand for its direct services to people living with HIV meant that it was becoming more and more similar to statutory social service agencies, its desire to be perceived as 'respectable' also grew. According to Horton, by the late 1980s the Terrence Higgins Trust was a 'timid organisation full of conservative queers';[144] Simon Watney, after attending a Trust directors' meeting in 1987 'virtually to *beg* for funds for gay men's health education',[145] angrily parodied it as:

> full of middle-aged Thatcherite queers taking two hours to decide whether they should give another AIDS help-line £200 or £300. A camp, Fifties, Kenneth Williams voice: 'We don't want the Government to think we're just a bunch of screaming queens, *do* we?' ... Trying to please everyone – the National Health Service, the DHSS [Department of Health and Social Security], the DES [Department of Education and Science], the Government, all political parties, gays, non-gays ... Helping people die, with no idea how they might have lived, no idea what I'm talking about now, reading this page with blind incomprehension and shaking their heads: 'We can't change the world dearrr, *can* we?'[146]

As early as 1984 there were accusations from others that 'the Terrence Higgins Trust was overly identified with the gay community'.[147] In 1987 the Trust featured prominently in a *Sunday Telegraph* article which asked 'Is there a gay conspiracy?',[148] and from the late 1980s it was the subject of a series of attacks by far-right groups such as Family and Youth Concern and the Conservative Family Campaign, which reprinted and quoted from a number of the Trust's earlier publications for gay men.[149] Faced with such criticism, there were real fears that government funding would be withdrawn, and that the survival of the organization was genuinely in doubt.[150] Such attacks thus simply reinforced the conviction of those conservative gay men within the organization that any frank association between homosexuality and the Trust could only damage the organization, and prevent the provision of effective services to people with HIV and AIDS.

This left the Trust with a schizophrenic attitude to its origins within the gay community. In an interview in 1991 the Trust's (then) Chief Executive Naomi Wayne declared 'I don't think this organisation has to excuse where it came from', while at the same time claiming that 'AIDS is not a gay or even a male problem ... As long as AIDS is ghettoised as gay, it will not be taken seriously'.[151] According to one of its counsellors, interviewed by a newspaper in 1992, the organization had been 'tarnished by the gay label'.[152] Just as the de-gayed view of the epidemic saw AIDS as initially a gay problem which had now moved on to affect everyone else (rather than having simply expanded but with gay men still right at the epicentre), so the Trust appeared to view itself as an initially gay organization which had now turned into something else entirely. So, for example, it routinely objected to being described as a gay organization, as opposed to an AIDS organization. This is a message whose only purpose can be to reassure heterosexuals about the 'respectability' of the Trust. To gay men, it is an unwelcoming message suggesting denial and disregard.

During the period from 1987 to 1991, in which the effects of the de-gaying of AIDS were most widespread and apparent, the Terrence Higgins Trust undertook virtually no new activities targeting gay men. The main exception was a set of six posters bearing black-and-white homoerotic photos and the slogan 'Safer sex – keep it up!', which were translated from Dutch originals in December 1988; however, these were viewed as a low-cost crisis intervention measure by health education volunteers.[153] The only other new publication for gay men was one of the six posters entitled 'Get set for safer sex', produced in 1990, which carried a photograph of two androgynous-looking men kissing, and the slogan 'No risk in a kiss'. While the Trust's direct services had expanded to meet a growing demand from people living with HIV and AIDS, there remained only one health education post; since the organization now viewed itself as a generalist AIDS organization, rather than one concentrating particularly on gay men, that worker's time was spent on projects for other population groups which the Trust had not previously targeted. According to a later manager of education and information at the Trust, 'there is no doubt that during this time work with gay men suffered'.[154]

Nevertheless, there are indications that the Department of

Health still believed that the Trust's history placed it in a strong position to undertake safer sex activities which would be well received by gay and bisexual men. Tony Whitehead recalls that the Department was always perfectly clear that it wanted to maintain some distance between its money and the most explicit gay safer sex education, but that this did not mean that the money could not be spent on much-needed gay men's campaigns.[155] If anything, the government seems to have become less shy about its willingness to support the Trust's safer sex initiatives for gay men; for example, in a November 1988 press release, the Department of Health explained that its grant of £400,000 for the forthcoming financial year was 'intended in particular to help develop the Trust's health education work with drug users and with homosexual and bisexual men', as well as other services.[156] This was only 3 months before the first Health Education Authority advertisements were published in the gay press, and suggests that the Department considered the Trust would continue to have an important role to play in the spectrum of HIV prevention services for gay men. In the event, however, the only Terrence Higgins Trust expenditure on novel gay safer sex activities during 1989–90 appears to have been the pre-trialling of a draft booklet, which was eventually to inform the development of the 'Tales of gay sex' campaign in 1991.

In late 1990 the Trust's health education team was at last expanded, and its first staff post responsible specifically for work with gay men was appointed.[157] New resources such as the 'Tales of gay sex' photostory leaflets, the leaflet 'Safer sex for gay men' and the groundbreaking video *The Gay Man's Guide to Safer Sex* were produced. In 1992 the Trust's Gay Men's Health Education Group collaborated with the National AIDS Manual, North-West Thames Regional Health Authority and Gay Men Fighting AIDS to produce a critical report documenting the extent of the de-gaying of statutory AIDS prevention services throughout the UK.[158] While this recommitment to the interests of gay men was of course welcome, it remains regrettable that similar efforts were not sustained during the late 1980s. Commenting on the effects of the de-gaying of AIDS, Tony Whitehead concluded, 'I think on the one hand where the Terrence Higgins Trust accepts so much credit, they must also accept some responsibility for where things have gone wrong'.[159]

The international phenomenon

While this chapter has focused mainly on the de-gaying of AIDS in Britain, it is important to recognize that it is a continuing international phenomenon. This was starkly demonstrated at the II European Conference on Homosexuality and HIV in Amsterdam in February 1992, the follow-up to the 1990 *Re-gaying AIDS* conference in Copenhagen, which is discussed in Chapter 7. Delegates from community-based AIDS groups in Germany and Britain were horrified at the 'criminal' neglect of the single most important issue of the second decade of the epidemic – 'namely, the utter mismatch between the continuing, demonstrable epidemiological levels of risk facing gay men, and the ludicrously small resources available to us'.[160] Simon Watney observed that:

> In the name of a conference on 'Homosexuality and HIV' it seemed that relations between lesbians and gay men frequently had a higher priority than the AIDS crisis ... A powerful and perhaps central strand of northern European post-Gay Liberation lesbian and gay politics is hopelessly unable to acknowledge, let alone confront the true scale of the catastrophe that already surrounds us.[161]

Watney presented a catalogue of 'massive homophobia, prejudice and plain stupidity' which was hindering education and prevention work for gay men throughout Europe. In Germany, Deutsche AIDS-Hilfe had been a beacon of hope during the period of the de-gaying of AIDS service organizations: it identified its role as working on a community level with the major risk groups of gay men, drug users and sex workers.[162] By 1992, however, its pioneering safer sex campaigns for gay men were having to be produced entirely with non-government money, due to official disapproval of earlier, sexually explicit materials produced with state funding, and the whole organization was being threatened with severe financial cuts. Watney described how:

> Two planned campaigns from the Stop AIDS organisation in Switzerland have been scrapped as a result of right-wing

pressure on the government, and older education material has been censored. The new conservative government in Sweden continues the previous Social Democratic policy of regarding HIV antibody testing as if it were a form of primary HIV prevention rather than a means of access to treatment and care. Moreover, the Swedish government continues to support a new institution, Noah's Ark, which it set up and lavishly supports as a direct rival to the RFSL, the country's main lesbian and gay organisation with long-standing gay-affirmative policies and experience in HIV/AIDS work. Swedish bath-houses have long since been shut down, whilst across the border in Norway they remain open, with lube and condoms and education materials available to all clients. Meanwhile in Holland the bath-houses are also open, but with little evidence of education materials or condoms, largely as a consequence of the Dutch government's HIV education policies, which until [1991] simply told gay men: 'Don't Fuck'. Hardly a helpful message.[163]

Australia's response to AIDS is rightly praised by many in the field for its sensitive behavioural research on gay men and safer sex and the strong support of government for community-based organizing, which have resulted in some of the best gay safer sex campaigns in the world.[164] As in most Western countries, the earliest activity came from the gay community. Following a statement from the Australian Red Cross in mid-1983 recommending that gay and bisexual men refrain from donating blood, the AIDS Action Committee in Sydney, which formed the basis of the later AIDS Council of New South Wales (ACON), was established. The Victorian AIDS Action Committee (VAAC) was established in July 1983, following a public meeting called by the ALSO Foundation, Melbourne's main gay welfare organization,[165] and other AIDS Councils also had their roots in existing gay movements. At the same time a Working Party on AIDS was formed within the National Health and Medical Research Council (NHMRC). Thus '[f]rom the outset community-based groups and sections of the medical professions were established as key interest groups in AIDS policy-making',[166] and gay community organizations secured representation on key policy groups, such as the 1985–88 National

Advisory Committee (NACAIDS), and its replacement, the Australian National Council on AIDS (ANCA).

Operating on a federal level, the Australian Commonwealth required state governments to provide funding for community-based organizations. The individual AIDS Councils in each state were represented on a federal level by AFAO – the Australian Federation of AIDS Organizations. However, the federal system also allowed individual states to adopt different policies; so, for example, homosexuality is covered under anti-discrimination laws in South Australia and New South Wales, but is illegal in Tasmania and only relatively recently decriminalized in Western Australia and Queensland.

Dennis Altman has described how '[t]he strength of the AIDS Councils, as recognised and state-funded providers of services, education and advocacy, reflects three aspects of Australian political culture: federalism, the pre-existence of a gay movement, and support, at least from the Labor Party, for community health initiatives'.[167] The Community Health Program laid down the principle that 'services should be developed in consultation with, and, where appropriate, with the involvement of the community to be served',[168] allowing state support for the establishment of a Gay Men's Community Health Centre in Victoria. By 1987, Australia's response to the epidemic was described by the World Health Organization as 'a model of how to act aggressively and in a coordinated fashion to address the many issues involved'.[169]

Pioneering collaborative social science research on the extent and corollaries of gay men's adoption of safer sex has taken place between Macquarie University, the University of Sydney and ACON; its findings about the importance of attachment to an organized gay community and its safer sex education programmes, discussed in Chapter 3, have been of great international importance. The AIDS Councils have produced pioneering safer sex campaigns, including specific materials addressing the needs of young gay men and men in relationships, and interventions designed to strengthen a gay safer sex culture.[170]

Despite all this, Australia has not entirely avoided the problems associated with de-gaying. The first major government campaign began in April 1987, and since then, observed Martyn Goddard, 'the main aim of Federal education campaigns has not been to reduce homosexual transmission ... [but] to convince the population at large that everyone was at risk – which many experts believed then, but which has turned out not to be the case'. It was only belatedly recognized that in Australia 'HIV remains almost entirely a gay men's epidemic'; in 1992 'Federal authorities finally decided to concentrate their efforts, for the first time, on homosexual and bisexual men'.[171] Articles in the gay press have also expressed concern that:

> professionalization (which is not the same as professionalism) is a serious danger to the future of AIDS Councils as community-based and community-controlled organizations, whose unique ability to respond to AIDS in the gay community rests in the sense (and reality) of ownership of the organizations by gay community volunteers.[172]

In late 1990, Adam Carr warned that 'gay men working in AIDS need to have a good, hard think about our relationship with the rest of the AIDS industry'. By arguing that 'AIDS is not a gay disease', gay men were perceived as attempting to obscure the reality of the epidemic, in order to 'take the political heat off ourselves', while at the same time 'simply playing into the hands of those who want to divert AIDS funding away from programs in the gay community and toward their own constituencies'.[173]

The Australian example thus illustrates both the achievements of grass-roots safer sex activism, undertaken with the active support of government, and the tensions that have emerged as perceptions of and responses to the epidemic have developed and changed over time.

History rewritten

Cindy Patton has described an 'amnesia surrounding the history of activism between 1981 and 1985'.[174] The events of those years were critical in the history of the epidemic: they encompassed the emergence of the epidemic, the invention of safer sex, the growth of community responses and the unprecedentedly successful behaviour changes among gay men. Yet according to Patton's analysis, the growing involvement of state agencies and the creeping professionalization and bureaucratization of community-based organizations have resulted in a revised version of that history, in which the nature of early organizing is forgotten and the significance of gay AIDS activism is consciously or unconsciously played down.

This is not simply a case of petulantly demanding acknowledgement, or fretting unduly about the historical record when there remain countless urgent tasks in the present. Rather, as Michael Helquist pointed out in the American gay monthly *The Advocate* in 1987:

> We have been doing more than burying our dead these last five years; the gay community has learned important lessons that are crucial to AIDS prevention in this country and elsewhere. Our experience includes confronting denial and dealing with its many manifestations; facing the societal taboos and fears about illness, death and dying; and recognising the importance of making changes in sexual behavior – since sex is too important to avoid altogether. The issue here is not so much one of giving credit where credit is due, but rather one of taking advantage of all the skills, knowledge and information available to prevent more people – whether gay or straight – from becoming infected with a lethal virus.[175]

De-gayed accounts of the history of HIV prevention are being presented in books and articles all the time, and at each repetition of the myths, reality becomes harder to assert. In the newly invented 'history', the relatively small size of the British epidemic is usually attributed to government interventions of some kind. In some cases the credit is given to state health education activities: a good example is the Health Education Authority's description of 'STD/HIV prevention in the United Kingdom', which was contributed to the papers of the Second International Workshop on Preventing the Transmission of HIV and other STDs, of which one of the aims was 'to share information and experience, and review progress in [HIV] prevention'.[176] Here, the Department of Health and the Health Education Authority's activities since 1986, whose success has been at best dubious, take up a full page, while the pioneering campaigns by gay men and the organizations which they established are barely mentioned in just three short sentences – and even then they are only vaguely credited to 'local community organisations'. It was left to Peter Davies of Project SIGMA to point out that:

> Today, at the start of the second decade of AIDS, these [lesbian and gay community] efforts are being systematically excluded from official histories of AIDS. Histories typically begin with a description of state responses, while in the memory of many of us who were involved in the early years of AIDS such responses were the 'end of the beginning' of AIDS. Throughout northern Europe, certainly, cases of AIDS began to appear in the very early 1980s, typically 1981–2, gay community organisations emerge soon afterwards and state responses do not begin until about 1985/86. It is not only an offence against history that such a distortion should be allowed, but an insult to the memories of those who fought against and, in many cases died because of state indifference in the early years.[177]

Yet the changes within those gay community organizations since the 1980s have been such that even groups such as the Terrence Higgins Trust now endorse false histories, such as the bizarre notion that the government's policy on HIV antibody testing had a significant role in controlling the epidemic. Antibody testing only became widely available in 1985, long after the widespread adoption of safer sex among gay men; moreover, testing has not been shown to increase the likelihood of an individual subsequently practising safer sex.[178] Nevertheless, according to the Terrence Higgins Trust:

> The Governments [*sic*] approach to HIV testing during the first ten years of this epidemic has been helpful and appropriate. The scale of the epidemic in the United Kingdom is far less than in similar European countries such as France because of this measured approach which has been developed in conjunction with experts in the field.[179]

There can be little doubt that the main reason why the HIV epidemic in Britain is so much smaller than that in other European countries, such as France, was the rapid organizing among British gay men which led to the widespread adoption of safer sex, long before a state response emerged. Indeed, in a speech at a conference on prevention work for gay men in Birmingham in March 1992, John Thompson of the Department of Health's AIDS Unit himself pointed out that:

> From 1982 to 1986 any HIV prevention work that occurred was largely done by individuals, voluntary organisations and the gay community itself. It had a fair measure of success, however. This can be seen in the plummeting rates of sexually transmitted diseases and in reported changes in behaviour. This, together with the development of needle exchange schemes, is probably why the overall infection rates are as relatively low in comparison with other countries as they are today.[180]

In France before the epidemic there was relatively little sense of gay identity among homosexuals, relatively few homosexual organizations and only one regular news publication with a relatively small circulation. Keith Alcorn has described Paris as:

> a city where sex is such a private matter, people with AIDS are left to suffer in silence by a gay community that apart from a few dedicated activists and volunteers, doesn't care. 'C'est la vie' is the slogan, fucking with condoms is the practice. The 'community' doesn't care because the French have always sneered at the idea of a gay identity as something to shout about or organize a political movement around.[181]

The gay political instinct described by Tony Whitehead, which inspired the foundation of community-based AIDS organizations in the UK and elsewhere, and which both presupposed and strengthened a sense of shared interest in combatting the epidemic, has been largely absent in France. Worse still, gay organizations in France actually discouraged the development of targeted campaigns for gay men for fear that they would be 'stigmatizing'.[182] In the event, while stigmatism may or may not have been avoided, up to a quarter of a million people in France are now estimated to be HIV-positive, the majority being homosexuals. As Cindy Patton has argued, the successes in controlling the epidemic:

> are derived from gay activists, not from the professionals who came late and reluctantly to the health crisis. If we embrace a revised history in which professionals imagine they conjured safe sex out of formulas and studies, we will become even more dependent on the medical establishment that is so callous towards women's and gay health concerns.[183]

Conclusion

The de-gaying of AIDS was a specific response to a number of distinct factors in the late 1980s. First and foremost, it was generally believed that there was a very real potential for the epidemic to spread rapidly among non-drug-using heterosexuals. This triggered a vast over-reaction in which the present realities of the epidemic were deliberately played down. Rather than maintaining a balance between educational campaigns for the general population and for those currently most at risk, resources were diverted entirely towards heterosexuals. This approach was uncritically embraced by voluntary and statutory bodies throughout the country.

Secondly, gay men were with good reason concerned about the potential for a homophobic backlash, due to perceptions of AIDS as being directly caused by homosexuality or perversion. There were genuine fears that the epidemic would not be taken seriously for as long as it was thought only to affect gay men. With the benefit of hindsight, however, it is now clear that in practice the de-gaying of the epidemic worked to gay men's disadvantage, in that it marginalized their concerns and obstructed the provision of ongoing safer sex campaigns.

This critique of the de-gaying process should not be confused with the contradictory attacks on the heterosexualization of

AIDS from the moral right and the fundamentalist left. The next chapter discusses how these factions ignore gay men's interests during the AIDS epidemic, and in themselves collude in the de-gaying of the epidemic.

Notes

1.   Michael Callen, 'AIDS is a gay disease!', *PWA Coalition Newsline*, 42, March 1989.
2.   Simon Watney, 'Powers of observation: AIDS and the writing of history', in *Practices of Freedom*. Rivers Oram, London, 1993.
3.   Jeffrey Weeks, 'AIDS: the intellectual agenda', in *AIDS: Social Representations, Social Practices* (eds P. Aggleton, G. Hart and P. Davies). Falmer Press, London, 1989.
4.   Virginia Berridge and Philip Strong, 'AIDS policies in the United Kingdom: a preliminary analysis', in *AIDS: The Making of a Chronic Disease* (eds E. Fee and D. M. Fox). University of California Press, Berkeley, CA, 1992.
5.   Antony Vass, *AIDS: A Plague in Us*, p. 44. Venus Academica, St Ives, 1986.
6.   '£4m for AIDS blood checks', *Daily Mail*, 16 March 1985, reported in Vass, *op. cit.*
7.   Weeks, *op. cit.*
8.   '£20m campaign to educate public about AIDS scourge', *The Times*, 22 November 1986.
9.   Thomson Prentice, '4,000 doomed to die of AIDS, Fowler warns', *The Times*, 9 January 1987.
10.   Peter Hildrew, 'Fowler launches TV and cinema AIDS campaign', *The Guardian*, 9 January 1987.
11.   Randy Shilts, *And the Band Played On*, p. 588. Penguin, London, 1988.
12.   C. Everett Koop, *Surgeon General's Report on Acquired Immune Deficiency Syndrome*. US Public Health Service, 1986.
13.   Andrew Veitch, 'How to avoid catching AIDS', *The Guardian*, 21 November 1986.
14.   M. J. R. Healy, 'Summing up', *Future Trends in AIDS*. HMSO, London, 1987.
15.   Department of Health and the Welsh Office, *Short-term Prediction of HIV Infection and AIDS in England and Wales*. HMSO, London, 1988.
16.   Public Health Laboratory Service Working Group, 'Acquired immune deficiency syndrome in England and Wales to end 1993. Projections using data to end September 1989', *Communicable Disease Report*, January 1990.

17. Dr Anne Johnson, 'The epidemiology of HIV in the UK: sexual transmission', in *HIV and AIDS: An Assessment of Current and Future Spread in the UK, Proceedings of the Symposium held on Friday 24th November 1989, Queen Elizabeth II Conference Centre, Westminster, London*. UK Health Departments and Health Education Authority, London, 1989.

18. 'Questions and discussion. 5. Prospects for the UK: following a presentation by Professor Roy Anderson', in *HIV and AIDS*.

19. Simon Watney, 'Taking liberties: an introduction', in *Taking Liberties: AIDS and Cultural Politics* (eds E. Carter and S. Watney). Serpent's Tail, London, 1989.

20. See, for example, Johnson, *op. cit.*, or 'Incidence of new AIDS cases. 3.5 Some non-exponential growth patterns', in Department of Health and the Welsh Office, *op. cit.*

21. Johnson, *op. cit.*

22. Berridge and Strong, *op. cit.* I am grateful to Keith Alcorn for drawing this to my attention.

23. Quoted in Andrew Veitch, 'Anti-Aids publicity gets £10m extra', *The Guardian*, 22 November 1986.

24. Virginia Berridge, 'AIDS, the media and health policy', in *AIDS: Rights, Risk and Reason* (eds P. Aggleton, P. Davies and G. Hart). Falmer Press, London, 1992.

25. Berridge, *op. cit.* See also Vass, *op. cit.*

26. Vass, *op. cit.*

27. C. Doyle, 'AIDS will "erupt" in major cities', *The Observer*, 21 April 1985.

28. Andrew Veitch, 'Symptoms of AIDS', *The Guardian*, 16 May 1985.

29. Cindy Patton, *Inventing AIDS*, p. 18. Routledge, London, 1990.

30. Vass, *op. cit.*

31. See, for example, Department of Health and Social Security, 'Quarterly AIDS figures', press release, 11 July 1988.

32. 'Trend in exposure category distribution (%) of HIV-1 infected persons: reported to 30 June 1992 England Wales and N. Ireland', *Unpublished Quarterly Tables*, 16, June 1992, Table 11, PHLS AIDS Centre – Communicable Disease Surveillance Centre, and Communicable Diseases (Scotland) Unit.

33. Department of Health and Social Security, *op. cit.*, 1988.

34. Department of Health, 'Quarterly AIDS figures', press release, 15 October 1990.

35. I should like to thank Dr Barry Evans of the PHLS for providing me with this figure.

36. Simon Watney, 'Le "fighting spirit" des gays anglais', *Le Journal du SIDA*, **38/39**: 18–22 (1992).

37. Thomson Prentice, 'AIDS virus infection by normal sex rises', *The Times*, London, 22 January 1991.

38.   'AIDS risk growing for girls', *Daily Mirror*, 22 January 1991.
39.   Celia Hall, 'Aids spread greatest in heterosexual community', *The Independent*, 22 January 1991.
40.   Eben Black, 'MUMS-TO-BE IN NEW AIDS STUNNER', *The Sun*, 22 January 1991.
41.   Department of Health, 'Quarterly AIDS figures', press release, 21 January 1991.
42.   I should like to thank Simon Watney for drawing this example to my attention. He discusses it in his article, 'Le "fighting spirit" des gays anglais'.
43.   Department of Health, 'Virginia Bottomley announces first results of anonymised HIV testing', press release, 17 May 1991.
44.   James Cusick, 'Heterosexual intercourse "commonest HIV source"', *The Independent*, 11 September 1992.
45.   Communicable Diseases (Scotland) Unit, 'Monitoring the spread and impact of HIV infection in Scotland', 1982–1991, *AIDS: Scotland*, 7 (1992).
46.   'Trends in exposure category distribution (%) of HIV-1 infected persons: reports to 30 September 1992 Scotland', *Unpublished Quarterly Tables*, 17, September 1992, Table 12, PHLS AIDS Centre – Communicable Disease Surveillance Centre, and Communicable Diseases (Scotland) Unit.
47.   *Ibid.*
48.   'UK statistics: AIDS', *AIDS Newsletter*, 7(2): 2, item 75 (1992).
49.   Department of Health and Social Security, 'Are you at risk from AIDS?', full-page advertisement, *The Guardian*, 17 March 1986; 'AIDS. How to keep yourself safe', full-page advertisement, *Capital Gay*, 11 April 1986.
50.   Berridge and Strong, *op. cit.*
51.   Simon Watney, 'Visual AIDS – advertising ignorance', in *Social Aspects of AIDS* (eds P. Aggleton and H. Homans). Falmer Press, London 1988. Typical advertisement slogans included 'How to stop yourself dying for sex' – the answer was 'Have as few partners as possible' – and 'Now it can cause death as well as life' ('Any contraceptive can prevent a new life from starting. But only a condom can prevent your death').
52.   Andrew Veitch, 'AIDS deaths rise by 18 as cases double', *The Guardian*, 5 December 1986.
53.   Simon Watney, *Policing Desire*, pp. 137–8. Methuen, London, 1987. See also Watney's analysis of the role of government campaigns in inducing exaggerated perceptions of the risk of HIV infection in the population at large: 'People's perceptions of the risk of AIDS and the role of the mass media', *Health Education Journal*, 46(2): 62–5, 1987.
54.   'Currie's handy AIDS tip', *The Sun*, 13 February 1987.

55. 'Homosexuals and drug addicts target of next campaign', *The Guardian*, 11 March 1987.

56. 'Aids response "inadequate" says Terrence Higgins Trust', *Gay Times*, 88, December 1985; 'battles ahead for "safe sex" health campaign', *Gay Times*, 91, April 1986.

57. David McKie, 'Hayhoe advises on Aids', *The Guardian*, 30 September 1985.

58. Zoë Schramm-Evans, 'Responses to AIDS: 1986–1987', in *AIDS: Individual, Cultural and Policy Dimensions* (eds P. Aggleton, P. Davies and G. Hart), p. 226. Falmer Press, London, 1990.

59. 'HEC prepares for its new role within the NHS', *Health Education News*, 62, January–February 1987.

60. *Health Education News*, 62, January–February 1987.

61. Quoted in: '£20m campaign to educate public about AIDS scourge', *The Times*, 22 November 1986.

62. 'Health agency in rift with Whitehall over use of TV', *The Times*, 28 October 1988.

63. Celia Hall, 'Health education body "loses independence"', *The Independent*, 16 May 1989.

64. 'Aids chief attacks gay rights "lunatics"', *Capital Gay*, 8 March 1987.

65. Annalena McAfee, 'Face to face with the new AIDS threat', *Evening Standard*, 21 February 1989.

66. Health Education Authority, 'AIDS campaign – latest phase', press release, 14 February 1990.

67. Health Education Authority, 'Experts', television and press advertisement campaign, 14 February to 31 March 1990.

68. See Chapter 6.

69. Virginia Bottomley, 'Closing address', *HIV and AIDS*, p. 40.

70. Edward King, 'Who's really at risk?', *The Pink Paper*, 217, 15 March 1992.

71. Graham Thomas, *AIDS Education Resource and HIV Simulation Game* (second edition). Daniels Publishing, Cambridge, 1992.

72. Patton, *op. cit.*, p. 19.

73. Larry Kramer, 'An open letter to Richard Dunne', reprinted in *Reports from the Holocaust: The Making of an AIDS Activist*. Penguin, London, 1989.

74. Tony Whitehead, 'The voluntary sector – five years on', in *Taking Liberties – AIDS and Cultural Politics*.

75. Patton, *op. cit.*, p. 118.

76. Robin Hardy, 'Die harder: AIDS activism is abandoning gay men', *Village Voice*, 2 July 1991.

77. John Lewis, 'Fears of anti-"gay" backlash over Aids', *Sunday Telegraph*, 16 November 1986.

78. Reported in Andrew Veitch, 'Aids briefings for opposition spokes-

men stopped by ministers despite Fowler plea', *The Guardian*, 18 November 1986.

79. 'Lords seek ban on schools' promotion of homosexuality', *The Guardian*, 19 December 1986.

80. 'Secret group of MPs say: "CLOSE THE GAY BARS"', *Capital Gay*, 29 November 1985.

81. Watney, *Policing Desire*.

82. Vass, *op. cit.*

83. Quoted by Cindy Patton, 'Illness as weapon', *Gay Community News*, 30 June 1984.

84. Stuart Byron, 'Truth and consequence: puncturing the myth of heterosexual AIDS', *The Advocate*, 27 February 1990.

85. *Ibid.*

86. Ray Amer, *A Survey on AIDS and HIV Prevention*. South West London Gay Organisations, London, 1987.

87. *Ibid.*, p. 14.

88. *Ibid.*, p. 25.

89. Edward King, Michael Rooney and Peter Scott, *HIV Prevention for Gay Men: A Survey of Initiatives in the UK*. North-West Thames Regional Health Authority HIV Project, London, 1992.

90. Peter Scott, 'Community development and the challenges of the HIV crisis', paper presented at *Action for Change – Community Development Approaches for the HIV Crisis* conference, London, July 1991.

91. *Men Who Have Sex with Men: Project Summary (3) September 1989*. Health Education Authority, London, 1989.

92. Lottie Pollak, unpublished report, 1989.

93. Peter Gordon, 'Safer sex education workshops for gay and bisexual men', 1989 (unpublished). Parts of this review were published in *Men Who Have Sex with Men: Action in the Community (MES-MAC) 1st Report*. Health Education Authority, London, 1991.

94. *Ibid.*

95. *Men Who Have Sex with Men: Action in the Community*, 1st Report.

96. Statistics from Alan Prout, 'MESMAC evaluation', speech at *MES-MAC: Community, Contacts and Collective Action*, conference, London, 23 January 1993. The work of the MESMAC sites is documented in a number of reports published by the Health Education Authority in London. They have also compiled a useful *MESMAC DIY Guide* to provide a reference point for workers in the field.

97. Berridge and Strong, *op. cit.*, p. 306.

98. Nick Partridge, chief executive of the Terrence Higgins Trust: comments at press conference, June 1992.

99. Mike Paxton, *AIDS: The Leaflet – 'Safer Sex for Gay Men'*.

Debrief Notes: The Findings from a Qualitative Research Study.
The Research Practice, London, December 1990.

100. Edward King, 'The seven deadly sins of the HEA', *The Pink Paper*, 230, 14 June 1992.

101. Privileged communication.

102. Andrew Saxton, 'HEA says "fuck"', *Capital Gay*, 559, 28 August 1992.

103. 'The government's strategy on HIV and AIDS education', poster. Department of Health, London, 1992.

104. Aileen Ballantyne, 'Gay ads dismay Aids charity', *The Guardian*, 7 February 1989.

105. King, *op. cit.*

106. 'AIDS budget slashed', *The Pink Paper*, 214, 1 March 1992. These figures were printed in the gay press on a number of occasions, and reproduced in publicity material produced by Gay Men Fighting AIDS, without challenge from the HEA. However, their repetition in the June 1992 issue of *Body Positive Newsletter* prompted a letter from Lindsay Neill, manager of the HEA's HIV/AIDS and Sexual Health Programme, to the newsletter editor on 30 July 1992, alleging that the article contained unspecified 'inaccurate information'.

107. Mark Perrow, 'Anatomy of an advertising disaster', *Capital Gay*, 545, 22 May 1992.

108. Jonathan Grimshaw, letter on behalf of HEA Men Who Have Sex With Men Project Advisory Group to Sir Donald Maitland, Health Education Authority chairman, 13 February 1992.

109. 'Gays quit top health authority', *Capital Gay*, 532, p. 9, 21 February 1992.

110. *Ibid.*

111. Corinne Camilleri-Ferrante and Martin Kochanski, *AIDS*, p. 8. The Bow Group, London, 1987.

112. House of Commons, *Problems Associated with AIDS (Third Report from the Social Services Committee)*, Session 1986–87, paragraph 65.

113. Arguments about the MWHSWM terminology are summarized in Peter Scott's 'Beginning HIV prevention work with gay and bisexual men', in *Healthy Alliances in HIV Prevention* (eds B. Evans, S. Sandberg and S. Watson). Health Education Authority, London, 1993.

114. See King, Rooney and Scott, *op. cit.* This is described in detail in Chapter 7.

115. Scott, 'Beginning HIV prevention work'.

116. S. Bartlett *et al.*, in *A Report on the Distribution of Free Condoms and Lubricant in Gay Bars in Newcastle-upon-Tyne* (ed. D. Miller), 11, MESMAC Tyneside, Newcastle-upon-Tyne, 1993.

This describes a specific example of this phenomenon as recognized and rectified by workers on a 'men who have sex with men' project.

117. See Susan Kippax *et al.*, 'The importance of gay community in the prevention of HIV transmission: a study of Australian men who have sex with men', in *AIDS: Rights, Risk and Reason*.

118. Scott, 'Beginning HIV prevention work'.

119. *Ibid.*

120. Eric E. Rofes, 'Gay Lib vs. AIDS: averting civil war in the 1990s', *OUT/LOOK*, 2(4): 8–17 (1990).

121. *Ibid.*

122. This reason was cited by 18 per cent of British statutory health agencies surveyed in King, Rooney and Scott, *op. cit.* In reality, 'we found this generally not to be an accurate picture of local provision'.

123. Described in Berridge and Strong, *op. cit.*

124. Described in Schramm-Evans, *op. cit.*

125. John Eldridge, 'Assessing the gay Durex market' (letter), *Capital Gay*, 25 January 1985.

126. Julian Meldrum, 'Barefoot doctors and safety pins', *Capital Gay*, 8 November 1985.

127. *Ibid.*

128. Peter Weatherburn and Andrew Hunt, *HIV Education: The Effect on the Sexual Behaviour of Gay Men*, Project SIGMA Working Paper Number 30, Project SIGMA, London.

129. Thames Television, 'The facts about A.I.D.S.', leaflet. London, October 1986.

130. *Ibid.*

131. Tony Whitehead, 'Gay men's health promotion – an historical overview', speech at Risks Worth Taking conference, December 1991, précised in *Risks Worth Taking* (ed. Michael Rooney). North-West Thames Regional Health Authority, London, 1992.

132. Whitehead, *op. cit.*

133. Schramm-Evans, *op. cit.*

134. Whitehead, *op. cit.*

135. Berridge and Strong, *op. cit.*

136. Schramm-Evans, *op. cit.*

137. Simon Watney, personal communication. Tony Whitehead confirms that stressing the dangers of a large heterosexual epidemic was both a political necessity *and* a reflection of epidemiological opinion at the time (personal communication, February 1993).

138. 'Aids response "inadequate" says Terrence Higgins Trust'; 'NOT A PENNY! Gay groups ignored in fight against Aids', *Capital Gay*, 6 December 1985.

139. See Tim Clark, 'Safe Sex', *Time Out*, 21–28 January 1987.

140. Whitehead, *op. cit.*

141. Adam Carr, 'World War 3', *Outrage*, January 1990.

142. Whitehead, *op. cit.*
143. Meurig Horton, personal communication, February 1993.
144. *Ibid.*
145. Simon Watney, personal communication, February 1993.
146. Simon Watney, 'Laocoon', *Square Peg*, 15: 26–7 (1987).
147. Julian Meldrum, 'Power points', *Capital Gay*, 14 December 1984.
148. Graham Turner, 'Is there a homosexual conspiracy?', *Sunday Telegraph*, 5 June 1988.
149. Typical of the unsympathetic reporting of the Trust's work generated by this leaflet was William Oddie, 'Sticking to the stated aims', *Daily Telegraph*, p. 19, 7 May 1991.
150. Tony Whitehead, personal communication, February 1993.
151. Quoted in Suzie MacKenzie, 'Rallying to a common cause', *The Guardian*, 6 March 1991.
152. Quoted in Jane Hardy, 'An unusual job for a pensioner', *The Guardian*, 26 February 1992.
153. Meurig Horton, Peter Scott, Simon Watney, personal communications, 1993.
154. Robin Gorna (Manager of Education and Information at the Trust), 'The Terrence Higgins Trust's work with gay men – a historical review', speech at Terrence Higgins Trust press conference, 30 November 1992. Others, however, disagree: according to Nick Partridge (Chief Executive of the Trust), 'The Terrence Higgins Trust is one of the few agencies to have consistently run safer sex campaigns for gay men throughout the epidemic', quoted in 'Terrence Higgins Trust launches new safer sex initiative for World AIDS Day', press release, 30 November 1992.
155. Tony Whitehead, personal communication, February 1993.
156. Department of Health press release, November 1988.
157. I held that post from 1990 until 1992.
158. King, Rooney and Scott, *op. cit.* This is discussed in detail in Chapter 7.
159. Whitehead, *op. cit.*
160. Peter Scott, quoted in Simon Watney, 'The killing fields of Europe', *Outrage*, pp. 44–7, July 1992.
161. *Ibid.*
162. Edward King, 'Embarrassing comparison', *The Pink Paper*, 195, 5 October 1991.
163. Watney, 'The killing fields of Europe'.
164. This section is based extensively on Dennis Altman, 'The most political of diseases', in *AIDS in Australia* (eds E. Timewell, V. Minichiello and D. Plummer), pp. 55–72. Prentice-Hall, Australia, 1992.
165. Adam Carr, 'When we were very young: the early years of the HIV/AIDS epidemic in Victoria', *National AIDS Bulletin* (Australian Federation of AIDS Organisations), pp. 15–17, July 1992.

166. Altman, *op. cit.*, p. 56.
167. *Ibid.*, p. 63.
168. *Ibid.*, p. 64.
169. Quoted in *ibid.*, p. 55.
170. See G. W. Dowsett, 'The sociological context', in *AIDS in Australia*, pp. 87–107.
171. Martyn Goddard, 'The hidden 500', *Sydney Star Observer*, 1992.
172. Adam Carr, 'VAC and ACON on HIV testing', *Outrage*, pp. 54–5, March 1990.
173. Adam Carr, 'Heterosexuals and AIDS: why do we bother?', *Outrage*, pp. 58–9, November 1990. Similar arguments are made by Ross Duffin, 'Homophobia and AIDS', *Journal of the Victorian AIDS Council*, 14: 3, 21 (1990).
174. Patton, *Inventing AIDS*.
175. Michael Helquist, 'Heterosexuals go on alert – but ignore valuable gay experience', *The Advocate*, 14 April 1987.
176. Conference papers, *Promoting Sexual Health: The Second International Workshop on Preventing the Sexual Transmission of HIV and Other STDs*, Robinson College, Cambridge, 24–27 March 1991.
177. Peter Davies, 'Report of working group: men who have sex with men', in *Promoting Sexual Health: Proceedings of the Second International Workshop on Prevention of Sexual Transmission of HIV and Other Sexually Transmitted Diseases, Cambridge, 24–27 March 1991* (ed. H. Curtis). Health Education Authority and British Medical Association (BMA) Foundation for AIDS, London, 1992.
178. See the discussion in Chapter 3.
179. Terrence Higgins Trust, 'AIDS organisations respond to government guidelines on HIV testing and partner notification', undated press release, issued 16 December 1992. It is doubtless significant that the views of the Trust's health education staff were ignored in the writing of the release (personal communication).
180. John Thompson, speech at 'Risks Worth Taking' conference, Birmingham, 4 March 1992.
181. Keith Alcorn, 'InSIGHT: Europride – in the wrong city?', *Capital Gay*, 550, p. 33, 26 June 1992.
182. J. B. Brunet, Director of the Centre Européen pour la Surveillance Epidémiologique du SIDA, reported in the Global AIDS Policy Coalition's *AIDS in the World* (eds J. Mann, D. J. M. Tarantola and T. W. Netter), p. 385. Harvard University Press, Cambridge, MA, 1992.
183. Quoted in Simon Watney, 'Re-gaying Aids', *Gay Times*, March 1990.

Chapter six

Making Myths

Ironically it is often those who are most insistent that
Aids is a homosexual disease who are most critical of
messages aimed at men engaged in homosexual
behaviour.

● *Dennis Altman, 'The most political of diseases', in*
Aids in Australia

THE de-gaying of AIDS has provoked critical responses on
a number of fronts. Some groups objected to HIV prevention
campaigns targeting non-drug-using heterosexuals on moralistic
grounds: to them, AIDS is almost a manifestation of inner corruption and spiritual unhealthiness, and is thus not perceived to
present a threat to 'normal' heterosexuals. This 'Moral' view,
exemplified in Britain by far-right groups such as Family and Youth
Concern or the Conservative Family Campaign, typically argues
that a powerful gay lobby has deliberately exaggerated the extent of
the problem and the likelihood of a significant epidemic among
heterosexuals in order to secure greater funding for research and
care, and to distract attention from the epidemic's root cause of
immorality. Others believe that the importance of AIDS even to gay
and bisexual men has been exaggerated by naive gay men, who
have unwittingly entered into alliance with a government which is
deliberately using public fear of the epidemic to stifle sexual and
other freedoms. To adherents to this crude Marxist creed, AIDS
affects only a tiny minority even of gay men; this form of critique
might be described as fundamentalist in its relentlessly reductive

explanation of every social phenomenon in terms of class oppression and economic determination.

Those whose primary concern is that de-gaying has resulted in a catastrophic neglect of health education for gay and bisexual men have found that they are often wrongly perceived as being in agreement with these unorthodox positions. Much energy has been devoted by both the statutory and voluntary sectors to challenging in particular the view that 'heterosexual AIDS' is a 'myth', a position most strongly argued by the writer Michael Fumento. The misapprehension that the re-gaying of AIDS is simply the latest variant on this theme can thus result in considerable misplaced hostility. This risk has been exacerbated by members of both the Moral and the fundamentalist Marxist camps, who have tried to claim that advocates of re-gaying support their own views. This makes it all the more important that the differences between the critique of the de-gaying of AIDS presented in this book and the opinions of the Moral and the fundamentalist Marxist groups are thoroughly explained.

The heterosexual epidemics

The term 'heterosexual AIDS' has become commonplace in the debates about the evolving epidemic in Britain and elsewhere. The term is inherently misleading, first in its implication that the syndrome has a sexuality all of its own, and secondly in its insinuation that AIDS as it affects heterosexuals is in some way significantly different from AIDS – the tightly defined medical condition – in any other population group. By marking a supposed distinction between 'heterosexual AIDS' and 'non-heterosexual AIDS' it reinforces the notion that HIV infection among heterosexuals is a novel curiosity. In reality, of course, the existence of heterosexuals with AIDS has been reported since the earliest months of the epidemic. By December 1992 there had been a total of 1332 cases of AIDS among heterosexuals, and nearly 6000 heterosexuals had tested HIV-positive.[1]

However, 'heterosexual AIDS' is understood to have a range of different meanings. To the Department of Health, whose regular press releases describing the latest statistics gathered by the Communicable Disease Surveillance Centre (CDSC) and its Scottish counterpart the Communicable Disease (Scotland) Unit (CD(S)U) provide the material on which most media commentary is based, heterosexual AIDS describes all those people with HIV whose sexual preference is heterosexual, regardless of how they became infected with HIV. Tables classifying adult HIV and AIDS statistics by sexual orientation were introduced into the Department of Health's press releases from January 1991, and are intended to 'demonstrate the potential for further HIV-1 transmission in the UK through sexual intercourse between men and women'.[2] This approach can be criticized on account of its deeply pessimistic emphasis on the potential danger that every HIV-infected person will infect others through unprotected sex. It also blurs the very real distinction between the statistical likelihood of infection through heterosexual sex in a country such as Britain, where the prevalence of HIV is extremely low outside recognizable risk groups, and that in the countries described by the World Health Organization as 'pattern II', where heterosexual transmission accounts for the majority of infections.

To those who consider heterosexual AIDS to be a 'myth', however, this is a misleading approach. They define 'heterosexual AIDS' in terms of HIV-positive individuals who have progressed to symptomatic disease, and who became infected with HIV through vaginal intercourse in Britain with someone who was not a member of a recognized risk group. The proponents of this view consider that the best way to monitor the epidemic is, first, by limiting the analysis to cases of AIDS rather than HIV infection, since reporting of AIDS is likely to be more comprehensive and reliable than that of positive HIV antibody test results, or of projections of seroprevalence in the largely untested population. Secondly, they restrict their analysis to the route by which an individual with AIDS became infected with HIV, as opposed to the potential for that person to transmit HIV through unprotected heterosexual sex. Using these criteria, and excluding cases where the mode of infection is undetermined, there had been only 63 cases of heterosexual AIDS in Britain (34 men and 29 women), or 0.9 per cent of the cumulative total number of people with AIDS, by the end of 1992.[3]

However, this view fails to take seriously cases in which individuals have been infected through sex between men and women, when one (or both) is a member of a recognized risk group. It is very often impossible to know whether or not one's sexual partner has ever shared drug-injecting equipment, or, if male, has ever had sex with other men. Gay men have learnt that there is a very significant possibility that any of our sexual partners – or indeed we ourselves – may unknowingly be HIV-positive, and so have adopted the strategy of practising safer sex with everyone, rather than relying on unrealistic attempts to 'choose carefully'. Although today HIV remains largely restricted to high-risk groups such as gay and bisexual men, whose members are clearly the most at risk from unsafe sex, those risk groups are also very much part of society as a whole. At the time of writing, 288 women and 56 men are known to have become infected with HIV through unprotected sex in the UK with partners in risk groups, and a further 1698 have been infected through heterosexual sex with a partner abroad.[4] The only sound educational strategy is therefore to encourage all sexually active people to practise safer sex, especially with new partners.

Any judgement of the extent of the threat posed by HIV to heterosexuals, and consequently, the need for and priority of prevention campaigns for the population at large, will obviously be highly dependent upon the definition of 'heterosexual AIDS' which is used. In the media, these two extremes have vied for supremacy, resulting in contradictory and inconsistent reporting which appears to have done little more than confuse the public. Newspaper reports endorsing the view that AIDS poses 'virtually no risk' to 'the vast majority of the non-promiscuous heterosexual population'[5] have provoked full-scale Health Education Authority multi-media campaigns with the objective of 'emphasising that [HIV] can be and is being transmitted sexually within the heterosexual population'.[6] It is against this backdrop that critics of the de-gaying of AIDS have had to negotiate the difficult task of articulating the needs of gay and bisexual men, while avoiding being used as pawns in the wider debate about heterosexuals.

The myth of heterosexual AIDS

Michael Fumento, a former AIDS analyst for the US Commission on Civil Rights, has emerged as the leading proponent of the view that:

> among the great wide percentage of the nation the media calls 'the general population', that section the media and the public health authorities has tried desperately to terrify, there is no epidemic. AIDS will pick off a person here and there in this group, but the original infected person will be in one of the two groups in which the disease is epidemic. Most heterosexuals will continue to have more to fear from bathtub drowning than from AIDS.[7]

In his book, *The Myth of Heterosexual AIDS*, Fumento presents a strong case that early predictions of a substantial HIV epidemic among non-drug-using heterosexuals have proved, happily, to be inaccurate. Fumento contends that that epidemic has not happened and will not happen, but that this reality remains unrecognized or suppressed by an unstated coalition of powerful vested interests. One such lobby was the 'liberal democratizers', who feared that if AIDS were perceived primarily as a 'gay disease', funding for prevention and treatment research would be blocked and homosexuality would be further stigmatized. This camp was characterized by the rejection of the notion of risk groups and the adoption of slogans such as 'AIDS doesn't discriminate' or 'We're all in this together'.[8]

By contrast, the 'conservative alarmists' considered the threat posed by AIDS was so great that mass testing of either the high-risk groups or the whole population was necessary.[9] Part of their justification was that casual transmission of HIV was actually far more easy than doctors and scientists were admitting; Fumento quotes an interview in which former US presidential candidate Pat Robertson declared: 'If, say, we're in a room with 25 people with AIDS and they're breathing various things into the atmosphere, the chance of somebody catching it has become quite strong.'[10] Fumento notes that '[t]he major thrust of the conservative position on AIDS was to discourage heterosexuals from engaging in illicit relations', by exaggerating the danger of HIV infection to all sexually active people, and insisting that only chastity and monogamous marriage could stem the epidemic. At the same time, and apparently without any sense of contradiction, the conservatives emphasized the intrinsic link between 'unnatural' homosexuality and AIDS, as exemplified by the exhortation by the right-wing columnist and director of media communications in the Reagan White House, Patrick J. Buchanan, to 'Pity the poor homosexuals – they have declared war upon Nature and now Nature is exacting an awful retribution'.[11]

The 'homosexual lobby' also comes in for harsh criticism.[12] Motivated by 'denial, and the need for research funds', homosexuals and their allies are said to have exaggerated the number of people at risk from AIDS by employing inflated estimates of the proportion of the male population which is homosexually active, and responding aggressively to those who argued that AIDS would remain essentially confined to gay men, drug users and their partners. However, Fumento argues that one of the unanticipated consequences of the assertion by gay men that AIDS was destined to hit everyone was that:

> now not only were their sexual practices and life styles in general looked upon with suspicion or outright disgust; but, indeed, they were setting themselves up as the rats and fleas of the new plague. Those already disinclined to homosexuality had a field day – several years of field days.[13]

And finally, Fumento argues that the epidemic has attracted a 'syndrome of those opportunists in the medical fields and their collaborators in the media who put their own interests in fame and spectacular articles ahead of the public's right to know',[14] and documents at length 'an epidemic of media hype'.[15]

The bulk of the book's 400 pages, however, is devoted to a thorough analysis of the epidemiological evidence on the progress of the epidemic. While this is not the place for a detailed review of his convincing arguments, they are well summarized in the words of the *New York Times Book Review*'s discussion of *The Myth of Heterosexual AIDS*:

The arguments, statistics and perceptions that he adduces to support his position appear almost as irrefutable as they are controversial ... [A] few cases, even many cases of heterosexual AIDS, do not an epidemic make, and despite some occasionally spurious logic of his own, Mr. Fumento carefully, persuasively explains why there will be no epidemic. ... But what about Africa? In a chapter entitled just that, Mr. Fumento clearly demonstrates why it is wrong to say that AIDS will spread into the general population in the United States, 'mimicking the course it has taken in Africa.' The epidemiology of the disease on the two continents is just as different as the cultures.[16]

It is unpopular to say it, but Fumento's book is an important and convincing one. When read as a whole, his case – and particularly his analysis of the epidemiology – is very strong indeed. It is therefore all the more unfortunate that Fumento's agenda in publishing *The Myth of Heterosexual AIDS* appear to be highly questionable and, some would say, pernicious. First, Fumento's interpretation of the motives of those whom he considers to have been self-serving, deceitful scaremongers is often unfair. There is no doubt that in a number of instances both liberals and conservatives have found ways of utilizing the epidemic to advance their specific agendas. However, Fumento appears to be unwilling even to admit the possibility that, in most cases, the fears of those who predicted a substantial epidemic among non-drug-using heterosexuals were based either on the word of authority figures such as leading epidemiologists, themselves often working with incomplete and unclear data, or on well-intentioned over-reactions. The only occasion on which Fumento even approaches such a spirit of generosity in his analysis is in his comments on 'the homosexual lobby':

It would seem that if any group had an excuse for exaggerating the threat of AIDS to heterosexuals, it would be the homosexuals. While some homosexuals stridently demanded a cure for AIDS so they could march right back to the bathhouses without fear of infection, many just wanted to live. With some authorities citing infection rates as high as 70 to 90 per cent in some homosexual communities, not

only did many homosexuals simply assume they were seropositive without bothering to get tested, but they assumed
that even if they were not seropositive, probably most of
their friends were. If heterosexual fear was needed to prime
the research pump, then so it would be. However under-
standable this motivation, it does not alter the truth that,
like their heterosexual alarmist counterparts, they were
deceivers nonetheless.[17]

Here, the comments on bathhouses exemplify another regrettable
trait in Fumento's book: his subtle homophobia and his general
lack of any sympathy for those whom he accepts are genuinely at
risk from or already infected with HIV. As the *New York Times* put
it:

by the time he gets round to calling acquired immune deficiency syndrome 'a terrible disease,' on page 331 ... it's
difficult to escape the feeling that he isn't so sure that AIDS
is really such a bad thing. After all, even when he calls it 'a
terrible disease,' he quickly adds – in the same sentence,
much like a man giving a winter weather report – 'the worst
will soon be over'; in the very next sentence, he says, 'There
are many other terrible diseases.' Well, yes. So?[18]

The impact of the epidemic to date is described dismissively as 'a
dud. The deaths of homosexuals and drug users were supposed to
be a mere portent of things to come; instead they would, for the
most part, be all that was'.[19] Fumento's definition of 'heterosexual
AIDS' is close to that described earlier, which discounts heterosexual partners of bisexual men or of drug users as being heterosexual
at all. He highlights American statistics which, like those for
Britain, show that women infected through heterosexual sex are far
more likely to have been the sexual partners of injecting drug users
than of bisexual men, but then quickly changes topic without discussing what option, other than safer sex, is available to a woman
who cannot be certain that her new lover is not and has not been a
drug user.

Throw-away comments make it clear that Fumento views
practising homosexuality as disgusting and unnatural. For

example, he opines that the act of rimming is 'vile',[20] and maintains that 'certain bodily orifices seem to be two-way and others one-way, and if it were questionable where the rectum falls, AIDS has helped decide the issue'; thus he depicts the syndrome as a diagnostic tool for what is natural or unnatural in a manner not dissimilar to Patrick Buchanan's comment, quoted above, which he himself criticizes.[21] Likewise, in his analysis of the relative likelihood of HIV transmission through various forms of sex, Fumento feels obliged to add the revealing 'caveat' that 'no immoral act is made moral by its comparative safety in preventing viral transmission',[22] and later finds himself agreeing that 'the moralists are also absolutely right when they say that condoms can't make sinful sex safe, as in safe for the soul'.[23] He is completely unable to understand why the use of straightforward language, such as 'cock' rather than 'penis', in safer sex materials for gay men is anything more than 'vulgarity' – '[l]ike the little boy who repeats for effect a swear word heard at school'.[24]

Fumento's book must therefore be read cautiously. But nevertheless, his analysis of the ways in which AIDS has been de-homosexualized – whether to manufacture sensational news stories, to help charity fundraising, to make for television dramas that the majority of the audience could relate to, or to improve research funding – is perfectly accurate (even if his views on the motives of the de-gayers are less fair), and his belief that the exaggeration of the risk to heterosexuals has diverted both attention and resources from the real epidemics among high risk groups is undeniably correct. Unfortunately, however, the arguments presented in *The Myth of Heterosexual AIDS* have been seized upon by elements of the media and by right-wing Moral groups whose agenda is far more pernicious than that of Fumento himself.

The legacy of the 'gay plague'

Many writers have described and analysed the media presentation of AIDS in the early 1980s.[25] Virginia Berridge has characterized the years 1981 to 1983 in the UK as 'the classic period of "gay plague" presentation in the press', during which '[t]here was relatively little mainstream press coverage; but cases of gay men with AIDS in the United States nevertheless reinforced the idea of AIDS as a disease of others'.[26] In the period roughly between 1983 and the torrential onset of the British government public information campaign in 1987, press responses were complex and often contradictory; the possibility of the transmission of HIV to heterosexuals was highlighted by concerns over the safety of the blood supply and the risks of overseas travel, yet more often than not such cases were implicitly presented as being newsworthy precisely because they were exceptions to the perceived 'gay plague' rule.[27]

As described in Chapter 5, de-gaying the epidemic became the official policy of the statutory sector, including the Department of Health and, therefore, the agencies dependent upon its funding and goodwill. Yet significant voices in the media have maintained their conviction that AIDS is in some way intrinsically linked to homosexuality or other forms of 'abnormality'. Cindy Patton has described this phenomenon as the 'queer paradigm', by which 'the insistence that AIDS is somehow a mark of perversion transforms infected persons into "queers", regardless of their exposure route'.[28]

To these sections of the mainstream press, the thesis that 'normal' heterosexuals do not get AIDS is highly attractive. It is as though their initial 'gay plague' response to the epidemic has been vindicated by the unfolding history. Consequently, press coverage of the debate over epidemiology has tended to focus on one issue: whether HIV is or is not a significant threat to the majority of heterosexuals. And in that debate, the importance of targeted HIV prevention campaigns for gay and bisexual men has come to be seen simply as a side issue to be exploited by one camp or the other, rather than a fundamental concern for policy-makers and planners.

During the summer of 1992, considerable column inches were devoted to three news events related to AIDS, which between them reveal much about the mainstream media's agenda. In the first, it was reported that an HIV-positive man with haemophilia had infected a number of women through unprotected sex. Initial press coverage was devoted to identifying and pillorying the individual in question. MPs joined with newspaper editors in calling for new legislation to make it a criminal offence deliberately to infect somebody with HIV. Essentially, the tone of the reports was one of panic, since the episode was clear evidence of the wisdom of public education campaigns which advised everyone to practise safer sex in order to avoid giving or getting HIV, and provided a graphic illustration of the interaction of members of high-risk groups with society as a whole.

A few days later, however, it was claimed that the man had practised anal sex with at least three of the four women whom he was said to have infected. The *Sunday Times'* front-page declared that this 'NEW EVIDENCE CASTS DOUBT ON BIRM-INGHAM AIDS SCARE'. As the editor of *Nature* commented, '[t]he implication was that unnatural intercourse was responsible for the Birmingham episode. Really straight heterosexuals might relax'.[29] Indeed, this was to be the tone of virtually all the subsequent reporting; as long as they kept to vaginal sex, heterosexuals were at little or no risk of HIV infection.

In the second episode, Dr David Barlow, a consultant at St Thomas's Hospital in London, revealed in July 1992 that of the 700 people with AIDS who were being treated there, none had been infected through heterosexual intercourse in Britain with a partner who was not a member of a high-risk group. Despite his care in stressing that infection through vaginal intercourse certainly does occur, and that the routine practice of safer sex was essential to prevent further spread of the epidemic beyond the high-risk groups,[30] Barlow's statistics were interpreted by the media as '[p]owerful evidence ... to support the case for re-targeting the anti-AIDS message at "high risk" groups'.[31]

Later that month, the BBC current affairs documentary series *Panorama* produced a programme which again reported that the vast majority of people with HIV were either members of definable risk groups such as gay men and injecting drug users, or were the sexual partners of members of those groups. It therefore argued that prevention campaigns should be targeted at those risk groups, rather than at the population as a whole. Press coverage concluded that '[m]illions of pounds are being wasted on advertisements warning about AIDS',[32] and that 'the only ways straight people can contract [HIV] are from infected transfusions, unnatural sex or via sores'.[33]

Press coverage of these three stories focused on a number of common features. First, it frequently disputed the very possibility of HIV transmission through unprotected vaginal sex, in a triumph of wishful thinking over fact. Although there is clear evidence that there is a greater likelihood of HIV transmission during a single occasion of anal sex compared with vaginal intercourse – one recent study suggested that the relative risk is in the ratio 5.1:1[34] – there is also no doubt that in most cases of HIV transmission during heterosexual sex, the route of infection is vaginal sex.

Secondly, reporting of each case included demands that current safer sex campaigns, which encourage the population at large to practise safer sex, should be discontinued. This would obviously be a misguided move, since in all three episodes the infection of sexual partners of members of risk groups was clearly recognized as a genuine risk – indeed, it formed the very basis of the Birmingham haemophiliac story. This is the reason why it is sensible to encourage safer sex as a universal precaution, whether one is a member of a high-risk group or not. Yet it is striking that the media consistently adopts an 'all-or-nothing' approach to the targeting of health education, by which every penny of HIV prevention funds should be spent on campaigns targeting high-risk groups, if HIV prevention is to be funded at all.

It would therefore be a huge mistake to conclude that editorial views such as that of the *Daily Express*, which declared 'It is downright wrong to continue using the Birmingham case to terrify normal heterosexuals that they are as much in jeopardy as homosexual men – who are infinitely more at risk',[35] indicate that the continuing epidemic among gay men has suddenly become newsworthy, and that we can expect the *Express* to start campaigning alongside the critics of the de-gaying of AIDS for more funds to be spent on safer sex initiatives for gay men. Rather, the editorial went on to state, contradictorily, that 'the homosexual lobby ... is entirely aware of the facts'. The true motive behind media calls for the retargeting of AIDS education appears to be to *prevent* campaigns that highlight the risks to 'normal' heterosexuals. Papers such as the *Daily Express* will no doubt sit smugly by as new infections continue among gay men, content in their belief that 'the gay community has already been warned of the dangers'.[36]

This distinction between the tabloid agenda and that of the advocates of re-gaying AIDS is vital to make. As Dennis Altman has pointed out, '[i]ronically it is often those who are most insistent that AIDS is a homosexual disease who are most critical of messages aimed at men engaged in homosexual behaviour'.[37] While re-gaying certainly does necessitate a re-evaluation of the allocation of prevention resources, its key objection to current practice is that safer sex campaigns for gay men have been almost entirely neglected since the late 1980s. Where there should have been a balance between general population advertising and targeted work for members of the key risk groups, the vast majority of prevention funds have instead been devoted to campaigns for 'low-risk' heterosexuals, *at the expense of* initiatives for those most at risk.

A class of their own[38]

A uniquely eccentric perspective on the epidemiology and prevention of AIDS has come from a number of fundamentalist Marxist writers. All are agreed on one thing – that, as Don Milligan of the Revolutionary Communist Party (RCP) puts it, 'straight people are not actually at risk' from HIV.[39] Beyond this, however, there appears to be no clear party line, and different individuals come up with significantly different views.

Don Milligan and Dr Michael Fitzpatrick set out their theories in a 1987 pamphlet entitled *The Truth about the AIDS Panic*,[40] provoked by the government's 'Don't die of ignorance' advertising campaign. Their basic thesis is 'that AIDS is not a problem for most people, and that its spread among gay men can only be tackled by ending discrimination against homosexuality'.[41] The government is deliberately exaggerating the threat posed by HIV to the general population, they argue, in order to distract from their vulnerability on economic matters; the 'AIDS scare' also fits in perfectly with the state's desire to 'bolster conventional family values and proscribe all departures from these norms',[42] and to 'medicalise the lives of ordinary people'.[43]

Although this particular version of the Marxist critique of AIDS acknowledges that the epidemic is indeed a major issue for gay men, its opinions of safer sex campaigns for gay men are somewhat confused. When interviewed, Milligan has agreed that '[s]afer sex campaigning on the gay scene has saved people from disease and death. I don't have any doubt about that',[44] yet his pamphlet includes a chapter entitled 'The dangers of safe sex'. Here it is argued that:

> The defect of the safe sex campaign as a means of preventing the spread of HIV infection among gay men is that it fails to take into account the dominant feature in the life of homosexuals – the fact that they are oppressed ... For the majority of gay men who are forced to pursue their homosexual encounters furtively, campaigns for safe sex are *useless* ... The climate of guilt, secrecy and fear that surrounds much homosexual activity in Britain creates the conditions in which the AIDS virus can flourish. It is the *oppression of homosexuals* that allows HIV infection to spread among gay men. Hence, the way to stop the spread of AIDS is neither to pretend that it is a threat to heterosexuals, nor to make futile exhortations to gays, but rather to challenge *every* act of discrimination or harassment directed against homosexuals.[45]

Thus in the pamphlet, those life-saving safer sex campaigns are dismissed as 'futile exhortations'. Milligan and Fitzpatrick's opinion that HIV predominantly affects a silent majority of closeted gay men whose sexual encounters with other men are 'episodic and often thoughtless',[46] by which they presumably mean 'cottaging' in public toilets and other public sex environments, is in clear defiance of both common sense and the epidemiological facts. The more furtive and fleeting a sexual encounter, and the greater the risk of discovery in a public place such as a 'cottage', the *less* likely it is that men will place themselves or their partners at risk of HIV infection, because the circumstances will not be conducive to anal sex. Hence, there is no evidence that HIV disproportionately affects bisexual men, a category which would include married men who engage in 'furtive' sex with other men: by December 1992 only 12 per cent of reported AIDS cases had been among men who defined themselves as bisexual rather than gay or homosexual,[47] and there is good reason to assume that many of these may have become infected during unsafe sex with men they met on the 'out' gay scene. And while no one would deny that there are important health grounds for challenging lesbian and gay oppression, in order to encourage gay self-esteem and a concern for the well-being of oneself and other gay men, to prioritize this ongoing, long-term project *in place of* immediate safer sex interventions could only cost lives.

But Milligan and Fitzpatrick are quite explicit about the incompatability of safer sex and the interests of gay men: they believe that 'by endorsing the safe sex campaign, [the gay movement] has given its approval to the continuing suppression of gay rights ... The safe sex campaign is a threat not only to homosexuals, but to the entire working class'.[48] These extraordinary statements seem to be based on a hostility to any form of autonomous lesbian and gay self-organizing, a hostility that has characterized many leftist sects for decades. In 1980, Philip Derbyshire described how, under the strategies of the International Marxist Group: 'While the autonomous movements (feminists, gays, blacks) are granted an importance, they cannot of themselves effect real shifts in power. This is a restatement, in a different key, of the principle that only trotskyists can lead a real revolution.'[49] In other words, for the RCP the 'politically correct' response to AIDS is class struggle, and to this extent the clear successes of autonomous gay safer sex campaigning do indeed represent a very real threat, not so much to gay men and the working class, but to the party dogma.

Other, perhaps less confident advocates of the RCP line are not quite so willing to dismiss the importance of safer sex to gay men. For some months, *Scene Out*, a monthly gay magazine for the north of England, employed an AIDS columnist called Andrew Greenlees. *Scene Out*'s editor acknowledged that '[Greenlees's] political attachments do sometimes take over in the writing of his column', to the extent that an unprecedented coalition of representatives from virtually all the major British HIV agencies, ranging from ACT UP/London to the National AIDS Trust, wrote to *Scene Out* expressing concern at Greenlees's 'very narrow and inaccurate view of important issues'.[50] In large part this 'view' consisted of a rehashing of Milligan and Fitzpatrick's writings, including the myth that 'HIV has remained more or less confined to homosexual encounters precisely because the nature of most homosexual encounters produced by widespread and systematic oppression are often furtive, episodic and unplanned'.[51] But Greenlees did at least admit that 'education and counselling about prevention for [gay men, injecting drug users and their partners] is certainly essential'.[52]

The most extreme of the Marxist positions is that of Susil Gupta, a lecturer in economics at the City of London Polytechnic, and editor of an 'independent Marxist review' called *Analysis*. To Gupta, HIV 'is not an epidemic in any shape or form';[53] instead, it is 'largely a fraud invented and sustained by moral re-armers and a burgeoning AIDS service industry'.[54] While many moralists have argued that the epidemic is unimportant because it predominantly affects 'undesirable' groups such as gay men and drug users, Gupta is virtually the only writer of recent years who has denied even the existence of a problem among gay men. To reach this conclusion, he uses a number of bogus analyses.

First, he compares the total mortality among gay men caused by AIDS between 1981 and 1990 with other causes of death. Since nobody has a clear idea of how many gay men there are in Britain, Gupta uses an estimate of 10 per cent of the male population, and thus produces statistics which purport to reveal that during the first decade of the epidemic, more gay men died of genitourinary problems or complications of the digestive tract than of AIDS. In the first place, it is somewhat distasteful to imply that AIDS is only of significance if it kills 'enough' people, or that the importance of educational measures against a preventable disease such as AIDS needs to be assessed or legitimized in this way. But even on these terms, the flaws in such a simplistic approach are many and obvious. First, and fundamentally, it is entirely unreasonable to assume that gay men consist of a representative cross-section of British males. While the phenomenon of same-sex desire clearly does cross all boundaries of age, race, class and geography, it is important to differentiate between such homosexuals and men who have adopted an 'out' gay identity. It is the latter who created and participated in the commercial gay 'communities' which have existed since the 1970s, and which provided gay men with the opportunities to meet many sexual partners; accordingly, it was largely among these men that HIV rapidly spread in the early 1980s. The relatively youthful history of gay liberation means that older men with homosexual desires are less likely to have adopted positive gay identities, and to have embraced the new freedoms, than younger men. It is specifically among gay men that AIDS has become such a devastating epidemic; to be at all meaningful, there-fore, Gupta's analysis should have distinguished between gay-identified and non-gay-identified homosexual men. By contrast, the sums he presents even include the causes of death of male children in comparison with those of adult gay men with AIDS.

Secondly, recent research suggests that the 10 per cent figure may be a significant over-estimate of the proportion of the adult population which is homosexual. If the true figure were nearer 2 per cent, even by Gupta's method AIDS would be the fourth most common cause of death among all male adults and children, and the leading cause of death among all men aged between 22 and 44. Published research has indeed calculated that HIV disease has be-come the major cause of mortality among males aged between 15 and 44 in parts of London.[55]

As Simon Watney has pointed out, Gupta essentially believes that HIV only presents a risk to 'a supposed minority-within-a-minority [of gay men], whose health is intrinsically bad because of their promiscuous urban lifestyle'.[56] In Gupta's own words:

> *Aids is a disease of ghettos* and it can only be eradicated by eliminating the conditions of oppression that force men and women to live in miserable sexual and social circumstances. While men and women are persecuted, villified [*sic*], con-tinually harassed and ridiculed they will inevitably be forced to put their health at risk. It is not gay 'promiscuity' or a large number of sexual encounters *per se* that has allowed Aids to flourish, but the fact that the small percentage of gays who are not willing to live a closeted or abstemious existence are herded into a tiny ghetto called the 'gay scene'. In such a close community, it is not surprising to find that any communicable disease ... not only spreads rapidly, but establishes a permanent presence ... As long as gays and others continue to live in repressed communities, diseases like Aids will continue to kill them.[57]

This is an intriguing combination of the RCP's dogma on oppression with an almost moralistic objection to the fact that many gay men *choose* to frequent the gay scene, as opposed to being 'herded' onto it, in order to find friendship and social support, as well as sexual partners. Moreover, many studies have shown that informed peer support and the development of social norms on the gay scene that encourage safer sex have been crucial factors in bringing about the behaviour changes which have *prevented* the infection of many more gay men.[58] But, sadly, it is too much to expect Gupta to acknowledge these successes; to him, safer sex is simply 'an informal form of gay quarantine'.[59]

In charge of the conspiracy to mislead and medicalize the British public is 'the AIDS industry'. Gupta's assertion that there are more HIV/AIDS workers than there are people with AIDS has been gleefully seized upon in various parts of the national press as a means simultaneously to belittle the size of the epidemic and to attack the responses to it. The claim appears to be based on a crude calculation using the *National AIDS Manual*'s Directory of HIV/AIDS Services, which includes numerous individuals in local statutory organizations who have been assigned responsibility for HIV services or health promotion as just one element in their work, or who are part-time or volunteer workers, or who work on needle exchanges and other harm-minimization projects funded from drug services budgets rather than from designated AIDS monies.[60] A more telling comparison might have weighed the number of gay men who are diagnosed with AIDS or who test HIV antibody positive each year against the pitifully small number of people funded to carry out targeted gay safer sex campaigns, or the paltry proportion of HIV prevention budgets allocated for that work.

All these Marxist writers belong to the school of thought which is entirely dismissive of the health of those who may unknowingly have sex with members of high risk groups. Just like those in the media who consider 'heterosexual AIDS' to be a 'myth', they are so concerned with making their case – that AIDS is the direct consequence of homophobic oppression or ghettoization – that practical questions, such as giving advice to a woman beginning a sexual relationship with a new partner, are ignored. And in their shockingly casual dismissal of the human tragedy of the epidemic and the vital importance of safer sex especially to those most at risk, the gulf between these distracting irrelevances and the critics of the de-gaying of AIDS could not be greater.

Conclusion

The agenda of re-gaying AIDS should not be confused with those of the most vocal critics of current AIDS policies, whether on the fundamentalist left or the moralistic right. The key difference is that both these camps are concerned predominantly with blocking HIV prevention campaigns targeting the population at large, albeit for radically different reasons. They are not in the least interested in the task prioritized by the critics of the de-gaying of AIDS – namely, ensuring that safer sex initiatives for gay and bisexual men are given the priority and funding which they merit.

Notes

1. Department of Health, *AIDS and HIV-1 Infection in the United Kingdom: Monthly Report*, 27 January 1993.
2. Department of Health, 'Quarterly AIDS figures', press release, 21 January 1991.
3. Calculation based on the total number of men and women with AIDS thought to have been infected through heterosexual intercourse with a partner who was neither a bisexual male, an injecting drug user, a recipient of blood or blood products, a haemophiliac, or from a World Health Organization 'pattern II' country where heterosexual spread of HIV-1 is common, as a percentage of the cumulative total of AIDS cases reported by December 1992, according to figures in the Department of Health's *AIDS and HIV-1 Infection in the United Kingdom*.
4. *Ibid.*
5. 'Pinning down the Aids threat', *Daily Telegraph*, 21 July 1992.
6. *HIV, AIDS and Sexual Health Programme Briefing Pack May 1990*. Health Education Authority, London, 1990.
7. Michael Fumento, *The Myth of Heterosexual AIDS*, p. 33. Basic Books, New York, 1990.
8. *Ibid.*, pp. 148–63.
9. *Ibid.*, pp. 183–201.
10. 'Robertson has his version of AIDS facts', *Washington Post*, p. A12, 20 December 1987, quoted in Fumento, *op. cit.*, p. 188.
11. Patrick J. Buchanan, *New York Post*, 24 May 1983, quoted in Fumento, *op. cit.*, p. 199.
12. Fumento, *op. cit.*, pp. 202–20.
13. *Ibid.*, p. 217.
14. *Ibid.*, p. 257.

15. *Ibid.*, pp. 272–98.
16. David Shaw, 'The epidemic: did the press cry wolf', *New York Times Book Review*, 1990.
17. Fumento, *op. cit.*, pp. 219–20.
18. Fumento, *op. cit.*
19. Shaw, *op. cit.*, p. 14.
20. *Ibid.*, p. 195.
21. *Ibid.*, footnote to p. 50.
22. *Ibid.*, p. 61.
23. *Ibid.*, p. 181.
24. *Ibid.*, p. 8.
25. See Simon Watney, *Policing Desire* (second edition). University of Minnesota Press, Minneapolis, 1989; Virginia Berridge, 'AIDS, the media and health policy', in *AIDS: Rights, Risk and Reason* (eds P. Aggleton, P. Davies and G. Hart). Falmer Press, London, 1992; James Kinsella, *Covering the Plague: AIDS and the American Media*. Rutgers University Press, 1989; Antony Vass, *AIDS – A Plague in Us*. Venus Academica, St Ives, 1986; Rosalie Aroni, 'Looking at the media', in *AIDS in Australia* (eds E. Timewell, V. Minichiello and D. Plummer). Prentice-Hall, Australia, 1992.
26. Berridge, *op. cit.*
27. See Watney, *op. cit.*
28. Cindy Patton, *Inventing AIDS*, pp. 116–18. Routledge, London, 1990.
29. John Maddox, 'Media make AIDS wishes come true', *Nature*, 358: 13 (1992).
30. David Barlow, ' "Normal" sex can still be a risk' (letter), *Evening Standard*, 15 July 1992.
31. Jenny Hope, '700 AIDS patients and all "high-risk" ', *Daily Mail*, 9 July 1992.
32. Clare Dover, 'Wasted AIDS mi££ions', *Daily Express*, 21 July 1992.
33. Garry Bushell, 'Garry's verdict', *The Sun*, 21 July 1992.
34. European Study Group on Heterosexual Transmission of HIV, 'Comparison of female to male and male to female transmission of HIV in 563 stable couples', *BMJ*, 304: 809–13 (1992).
35. 'Opinion: give us right AIDS advice', *Daily Express*, 29 June 1992.
36. Nicholas Buckley, 'Tell us the truth on AIDS, say MPs', *Daily Express*, 29 June 1992.
37. Dennis Altman, 'The most political of diseases' in Timewell, Minichiello and Plummer, *op. cit.*
38. I am grateful to Keith Alcorn for his illuminating comments on this topic.
39. Quoted in: 'Reflections on the AIDS panic', *Living Marxism*, 15, pp. 14–19, January 1990.

40. Dr Michael Fitzpatrick and Don Milligan, *The Truth about the Aids Panic*. Junius Publications, London, 1987.
41. *Ibid.*, p. 2.
42. *Ibid.*, p. 60.
43. Michael Fitzpatrick, quoted in: 'Reflections on the Aids panic'.
44. Quoted in *ibid.*
45. Fitzpatrick and Milligan, *op. cit.*, pp. 34, 36.
46. Don Milligan, quoted in: 'Reflections on the Aids panic'. See also Don Milligan, 'Fighting the epidemic', *Rouge*, 2, pp. 12–14, 1990.
47. Department of Health, *AIDS and HIV-1 Infection in the United Kingdom*.
48. Fitzpatrick and Milligan, *op. cit.*, pp. 53, 64.
49. Philip Derbyshire, 'Sects and sexuality: Trotskyism and the politics of homosexuality', in *Homosexuality: Power and Politics* (ed. Gay Left Collective), pp. 104–15. Allison and Busby, London, 1980.
50. 'HIV and AIDS', *Scene Out*, 18, p. 18, September 1990.
51. Andrew Greenlees, 'AIDS dialogue', *Scene Out*, 18, p. 19, September 1990.
52. Andrew Greenlees, 'AIDS dialogue', *Scene Out*, 13, p. 14, April 1990.
53. Comments at *AIDS: Dissenting Voices* conference, New Cavendish Club, London, 28 November 1992.
54. Susil Gupta, 'The AIDS fraud', *Analysis*, winter 1991–92, 22–44.
55. J. Aldous *et al.*, 'Impact of HIV infection on mortality in young men in a London health authority', *BMJ*, 305: 219–21 (1992).
56. Simon Watney, 'AIDS: dissenting voices', unpublished article.
57. Gupta, *op. cit.*, p. 29.
58. See Chapter 3.
59. Comments at *AIDS: Dissenting Voices* conference, New Cavendish Club, London, 28 November 1992.
60. Keith Alcorn, Assistant Editor, *National AIDS Manual*, personal communication, February 1993.

Chapter seven

Re-gaying AIDS

It's time to wake up and take stock. Ten years on into
this bitter epidemic what have we achieved? The AIDS
crisis is not yet over for gay men – it's actually much
worse than it was in the 1980s.

● *Peter Scott[1]*

THE emergence of an opposition to the de-gaying of AIDS
and a critique of the new institutionalization of responses to the
epidemic has been a long and gradual process. As early as 1986,
Cindy Patton argued that 'the history of resistance to the political
crisis surrounding AIDS is in danger of being lost to a revised
history that counts only the actions and concerns of the professionals who have taken up AIDS as an issue'.[2] In February 1990
the I European Conference on HIV and Homosexuality, held in
Copenhagen, had the subtitle 'Re-gaying HIV'; at a time of increasing complacency about the epidemic's ongoing impact upon gay
men, it stressed that 'it would be a severe mistake to believe that
this crisis is over and to think that every gay man in the western
countries is practising safe sex'.[3] In Britain, as the neglect of ongoing safer sex education for gay men has become increasingly clear,
and an entirely predictable increase in unsafe sex and in new HIV
infections has been documented, advocates of re-gaying AIDS have
coalesced around a new organization, Gay Men Fighting AIDS
(GMFA).

Defining the agenda

Writing in *Radical America*, Cindy Patton was among the first to insist that the experiences and expertise of the gay community in responding to AIDS should be acknowledged and drawn upon in the development of 'new strategies and new lines of resistance'.[4] Her concerns focused on two issues. First, she argued that '[t]he overprofessionalization of safer sex organizing, and the lack of historical insight by professionals' has meant that the achievements of innovative, community-based safer sex strategies, which succeeded because they were couched in terms of risk reduction as a collective community resistance to the epidemic, are no longer recognized. Secondly, widespread use of the HIV antibody test was becoming an increasingly important component in both political and educational responses to the epidemic. Patton argued that 'AIDS is with us as a disease and a social phenomenon, and will not go away no matter how many people take tests'. Instead, resistance to AIDS:

> should be based on understanding how transmission occurs and on taking simple steps to avert it. The message is to expand our concept of sex, to increase the discussion of pleasurable possibilities, and to eroticize measures that reduce transmission of *all* sexually transmitted diseases.[5]

Patton's theme of the importance of learning from and remaining true to the history of gay community organizing was to be reinforced and complemented by the growing recognition of the failure to sustain community-based educational initiatives for gay men. Speaking at the V International Conference on AIDS held in Montreal in June 1989, Ben Shatz of the US AIDS Civil Rights Project criticized the lack of support for gay men's health education, and observed that:

> A common response to my complaint is that there is now little transmission in the gay community or that AIDS is moving out of the homosexual population. I say that AIDS is not moving out of the gay community; it is simply moving

into other communities. Furthermore, don't believe there is little transmission among gay men. Thousands of gays continue to seroconvert annually. If it were the same number of white heterosexual doctors, there would be an uproar.[6]

Likewise, in a plenary speech at the I European Conference on HIV and Homosexuality in 1990, Hans Moerkerk, director of the Health Education Centre of Amsterdam, pointed out that:

> the de-homosexualisation of AIDS was understandable from the point of view that AIDS is not a gay disease, but at the same time gave society a chance to ignore the fact that so many of our friends have become affected by the virus; especially in the situation of most West and Northern European countries it can and may not be denied that gay men constitute the largest group of sufferers. Although we have to fight constantly against gay and lesbian discrimination, and also in relation to AIDS, we have to be alert not to let ourselves be 'praised out of the market' ... Many of our governments, although officially quite open in favour of homosexuality, should like to see the gay and lesbian community continue this kind of de-homosexualisation.[7]

As Simon Watney described it in a report for *Gay Times*, this conference was 'extremely significant and timely, reminding us of the extent to which the role of lesbians and gay men in the development of effective health education, and all other aspects of care provision, tends to be neglected or even deliberately suppressed for misguided strategic reasons'.[8]

Cataloguing the neglect

The failure to maintain gay safer sex initiatives for gay men has for years been all too apparent to some gay men working in the AIDS field in Britain, and in some instances has sparked overtly activist responses. In early 1991 the Birmingham Gay Men's Health Group published 'some interesting facts' in a leaflet of that name, pointing out that:

Less than 1% of the West Midlands Regional Health Authority spending on HIV prevention is used on projects specifically for gay men.

There are health promotion officers throughout Birmingham with responsibility for HIV prevention among black and ethnic minority communities, young people and in schools and youth clubs [but none] with a job description that even mentions gay men.

No health promotion department in the city has spent money on leaflets and posters aimed at gay men and to be used in gay social venues.

The only contribution to HIV prevention work among gay men made by the voluntary AIDS organisations in Birmingham (other than Gay Men's Health Group which gets no funding) is a condom drop in the Nightingale [club] in 1987.

Of all the new HIV diagnoses in the West Midlands in 1990, 63% were gay or bisexual men.[9]

However, it is comparatively recently that the problem has been formally documented with the degree of scientific rigour which seems to be required if policy-makers and budget managers are to be influenced. In late 1991, Peter Scott, editor of the *National AIDS Manual*,[10] calculated that there were no more than 15 to 20 small educational projects with any relevance for gay men anywhere in the country.[11] Scott subsequently organized a formal survey of 226 of the 240 agencies that had responsibility for HIV prevention activities, with the aims of establishing the true level of work once and for all, and of identifying explanatory trends among those organizations which were not working for gay or bisexual men. Varying amounts of staff and volunteer time were donated between the *National AIDS Manual*, the Terrence Higgins Trust Gay Men's Health Education Group, Gay Men Fighting AIDS and North-West Thames Regional Health Authority's (NWTRHA) HIV Project. The anonymized results of the survey were published in July 1992, in the report *HIV Prevention for Gay Men.*[12]

The findings, if not surprising, were shocking nonetheless. Only 77 agencies – a third of the whole sample – had engaged in HIV prevention activities of any kind for gay or bisexual men, at any time during the epidemic. In some cases those activities consisted of little more than producing a photocopied leaflet whose usefulness was never evaluated; these respondents were therefore further classified to identify those which had undertaken 'substantial' work or 'comprehensive' work with gay men, based on the good practice recommendations in a Health Education Authority guide to effective HIV prevention activities for gay men.[13] These definitions erred on the side of generosity: to qualify as 'substantial' activity, a written needs assessment undertaken by any method had to have been prepared, and there needed to be 'commitment of resources to a basic minimum package of measures as evidenced by the employment of a worker (even part time) with a specific remit for HIV prevention work with gay men'.[14] Only 8 agencies met these quite undemanding criteria, leaving 96.5 per cent of the sample which did not provide a substantial package of HIV prevention initiatives for gay men. To qualify as a 'comprehensive' package, agencies also had to have provided at least one education event, such as a roadshow or leaflet distribution, in the gay community; to have provided staff training on prevention work for gay men; and to have produced at least one local health education resource, such as a leaflet, for gay men. Only 3 agencies out of the 226 (1.3 per cent) had provided a package of comprehensive activities by these criteria. The authors considered that these figures revealed:

> a disquieting lack of strategic direction in the response to the epidemic. Only a tiny proportion of those charged with the responsibility for HIV prevention work are actually fulfilling that responsibility in relation to gay and bisexual men who constitute by far the largest group in the population affected by HIV and AIDS.[15]

On the other hand, 149 organizations (66 per cent of the whole sample) reported that they had never engaged in any HIV prevention activities for gay or bisexual men – a finding described by the authors as 'dismaying'.[16] When asked why not, over 40 respondents confessed that they did not know how to contact gay men. This should be recognized as an extraordinary admission coming from professional HIV educators, over ten years into an epidemic which continues disproportionately to affect gay men. An additional 14 agencies reported that there were no gay or bisexual men locally, a belief that in some cases seemed to stem from somewhat uninformed concepts about gay men: for example, one District HIV Prevention Coordinator reported 'we've no homosexual community here; you might try district X – they have a theatre'.[17]

The second most common explanation was given by 32 agencies: while they did undertake educational initiatives, their target audiences did not include gay men. By far the majority of these were instead prioritizing work with heterosexual women; less than a third were targeting injecting drug users, another risk group relatively neglected by health education professionals. There were 25 agencies that believed that gay men's health education would be too controversial or even illegal, and 16 that reported that their managers opposed such work. A further 27 that were under the impression that other local groups – perhaps voluntary organizations or gay groups – were providing educational services to gay or bisexual men. If true, this would be a reasonable argument, since community-based organizations are usually much better placed both to contact gay men and to be received sympathetically by them than are statutory agencies. However, such groups are inevitably underfunded, and none of these respondents was providing financial resources or even non-financial support such as the use of photocopying equipment. Moreover, the nominated organizations usually turned out in practice to be self-help groups or organizations providing valuable care services to people with HIV, including gay men with HIV, rather than prevention initiatives targeting the as yet uninfected.

As discussed in Chapter 3, targeted educational initiatives which are specifically tailored to be effective with a clearly defined population group have the greatest chance of success. As the report pointed out:

> it is well established that generic work alone will not sufficiently address the needs of any of the groups most affected. Moreover, generic resources, by definition, are constrained by the lowest common social and cultural denominators. Consequently they invariably fail to provide appropriate and relevant in-depth information for the par-

ticular needs of gay or bisexual men. In other words, the majority of apparently general population resources are actually heterosexual resources, in so far as they have to adopt heterosexual language, assumptions, and values.[18]

Most of the agencies surveyed were providing targeted campaigns but had omitted gay men, a situation described as 'astonishing' in view of the epidemiological facts.[19] However, 24 respondents reported that they did not target any group – precisely because they were afraid of giving the impression that there were such things as 'risk groups'. A typical response was 'We mustn't target gay men; we target young people and the public'.[20] This and other objections to specific, targeted work for gay men are discussed later in this chapter.

Assessing need

While the survey's results revealed the almost complete lack of gay safer sex education of any kind, a number of key areas of neglect were particularly striking. The most fundamental was the lack of national or local needs assessments. In the absence of a proper needs assessment it is impossible for health educators to know where their limited resources and energies are most needed and can be used most effectively; needs assessment also provides a baseline picture of the target group, enabling educators to assess whether their interventions have been at all helpful, and if so, to what extent. Without such evaluation, effective educational methods may not be recognized as such, and ineffective or even harmful measures may be unjustifiably sustained or repeated.[21]

The professionalization of AIDS in the late 1980s meant that HIV prevention increasingly became the responsibility of professional workers, whose qualifications were more likely to be through formal health promotion training than through familiarity with the culture of gay men or the successful community-based initiatives of the early to mid-1980s. It thus became all the more important that these workers be guided by a reliable national needs assessment, upon which more finely tuned local assessments could be based. This might be considered to have been an obvious task for the Health Education Authority, which sees its responsibilities as including:

> information and research programmes to assess new needs for health education, as well as monitoring the progress of changing public beliefs, attitudes and understanding of certain issues. Only by doing this, is it possible to plan initiatives and make sure the best use is made of public funds.[22]

The HEA is also one of the few national health bodies with the necessary resources to undertake such a needs assessment. While the HEA has produced some valuable qualitative data from surveys in gay bars, it has not taken the logical extra step of a quantitative national assessment.[23]

The NWTRHA survey found that only 9 per cent of the sample had conducted any kind of local needs assessment, 'and some of these were token or perfunctory'.[24] Of the 30 agencies which reported that they were engaged in outreach work with gay men – a term which covered work ranging from impressive community development projects employing a number of workers through to occasional visits to a local gay bar by a Director of Public Health – only 8 had been established on the basis of a needs assessment. This means that while there may appear to be quite a significant level of outreach activity, it is extremely unclear whether those most in need of education or support are the ones being reached, or whether the work is having a significant impact on HIV transmission. Moreover, the report observed that:

> there has been no formal comparative evaluation of the cost-effectiveness of paid-staff outreach as opposed to other HIV prevention activities ... [I]t is arguable that it is more cost-effective to spend money in employing staff to encourage volunteer-based peer education than in sending out isolated detached workers to reach a much smaller number of clients.[25]

It almost goes without saying that there is no point in conducting a needs assessment and then failing to act upon its findings.

The central role of needs assessment in determining the priorities of HIV prevention work means that it is vital for the assessment to be thoroughly and competently performed. In the case of the prevention needs of gay men, it is particularly important not to rely solely on the impressions or advice of local HIV workers, voluntary groups or medical services, since the de-gaying of AIDS has distorted many people's perceptions of the importance and extent of gay men's ongoing requirements. In other words, it is essential that needs assessment is approached with an open mind, and that, as far as possible, the data are obtained directly from local gay men, rather than through mediating individuals or institutions.

Gay Men Fighting AIDS

Simon Watney has described how, by 1992, a number of gay men involved in community-based safer sex education in Britain had developed:

> an accumulated sense of the impossibility of steering such massive institutions [as the Health Education Authority and the Terrence Higgins Trust] back into line with gay men's actual needs ... Torn between the fear of defunding by government agencies and the fear of attracting hostile media attention, these organisations have become timid politically, especially in relation to such 'sensitive' or 'controversial' subjects as gay men's health education. Furthermore, AIDS education has always had a lower priority there than the provision of direct services to people living with HIV and AIDS.[26]

A flurry of significant developments took place during the months in early 1992 in which the report *HIV Prevention for Gay Men* was being researched. In February, the Advisory Group to the Health Education Authority's Men Who Have Sex With Men project officer resigned *en masse* in despair at their inability to influence significantly the direction or content of HEA campaigns.[27] In the same month, a number of British gay safer sex educators attended

the II European Conference on Homosexuality and HIV in Amsterdam, the follow-up event to the 1990 Re-Gaying HIV conference
described earlier. As discussed in Chapter 5, they were unanimously
horrified by what Peter Scott described as the 'criminal' neglect of
'the single most important issue of the second decade of the epidemic: the utter mismatch between the levels of risk facing gay
men, and the ludicrously small resources available to us'.[28] These
two events did, however, have constructive consequences; they
provided the impetus for the formation of the first British AIDS
organization devoted specifically to gay men's needs.

Scott called a meeting and launched the new organization,
Gay Men Fighting AIDS (GMFA), in March 1992. GMFA's aims
were:

> to focus attention on the failure of HIV education to ad-
> equately target gay men; to fight censorship, homophobia
> and other obstacles to effective education and care; to
> campaign for changes in the law that will benefit gay men
> during a life threatening health crisis; to design, advise about
> and provide health education campaigns of the highest pro-
> fessional standard for gay men.[29]

GMFA was to be devoted exclusively to gay men, and was
set up as a not-for-profit limited company rather than a charity, to
minimize restrictions on political lobbying or other potentially controversial activities. Despite the fact that nearly all of the established national and local AIDS organizations were originally
founded by gay men for gay men, the process of generalization and
de-gaying meant that few had significant experience or expertise in
this field, and others were prepared to compromise and sanitize
their gay men's campaigns in the interests of their image in the eyes
of funders or other client groups. As Keith Alcorn put it:

> Gay men in the AIDS field are constantly forced to make
> painful choices between putting gay men's needs second and
> getting funding, or being completely disfunded. Some even
> go along with this in the mistaken belief that this is an equal
> opportunities epidemic, and that they are professionals first

and gay men second. This is not an equal opportunities epidemic.[30]

GMFA's primary intention was to recreate in the 1990s the same kind of community-level educational activities which developed almost spontaneously at the beginning of the epidemic – and which were virtually the only demonstrably successful initiatives that had ever taken place. In part, that involved lobbying and publicity activities to raise awareness, among both gay men and HIV workers, of the increasing need for initiatives to encourage and sustain safer sex behaviour, and of the way in which the gay safer sex culture was being left to atrophy. In addition, GMFA obtained funding for a collaborative project with the Terrence Higgins Trust called Stop AIDS London. Breaking away from professionalized models of HIV education, which relied on formal outreach workers or volunteers acting within strict codes of conduct to make contact with gay men, the project used a 'population diffusion' model, which aimed to make initial contact with as many individuals as possible, but then equip them to act as informal, individual peer educators in the rest of their everyday social and sexual contacts with other gay men. The ultimate objective was to use a diverse range of interventions to help to create a groundswell of explicit grass-roots support for safer sex. 'If the last 100 years of social science have taught us anything', explained Peter Scott, it is that gay men are likely to be most effectively introduced to safer sex and helped to sustain safer sex 'if they are being persuaded by many other individuals they meet all the time'.[31]

The emergence of GMFA provided a focus not only for the increased debate about prevention policies and priorities, but also for the critics of re-gaying AIDS. Controversy centred on a number of issues. First, the terminology of 'high-risk groups', firmly rejected during the 1980s, was again called into question; to the advocates of re-gaying, a high-risk group was precisely what gay men were. Secondly, as the relatively limited impact of the epidemic on non-drug-using heterosexuals became increasingly clear, the distinctions between a British epidemic primarily affecting gay men, and a global epidemic in which heterosexual transmission was the main mode of HIV transmission, became increasingly pronounced. Thirdly, GMFA's commitment to focus exclusively on gay men prompted charges of separatism and misogyny. A further debate focused on the implications of re-gaying AIDS for the resourcing of HIV prevention work; while some argued that a reprioritization of work with gay and bisexual men would damage initiatives for other social constituencies, others feared that by questioning the impact of the epidemic on the population at large, re-gaying could lead to marginalization and disfunding across the spectrum of AIDS care and prevention activities.

High-risk groups versus high-risk behaviours

From about 1986, considerable effort was devoted to contesting the notion that gay men, drug users, prostitutes, Africans or other constituencies were high-risk groups for AIDS. This was for a number of perfectly sensible reasons. First, in the early years of the epidemic there were well-grounded fears of a moralistic backlash, particularly against gay men. Those who saw AIDS as a 'gay plague' spoke of the disease as though it were a natural consequence of gay men's unnatural sexuality. As documented in Chapter 4, the first proposed ban on the so-called 'promotion' of homosexuality was discussed in Parliament at this time; MPs debated the closing down of gay pubs and clubs; the tabloid newspapers consistently presented gay men and 'their' disease as an appalling threat to the rest of society. A consequence of the classification of gay men in their entirety as a high-risk group 'was to reinforce the relationship between the disease and "marginal" members of the population'[32] – a relationship which for AIDS workers was all too similar to the 'gay plague' arguments of the bigots. Discouraging the term was therefore seen as an important strategy in preventing the further stigmatization of the gay population.

Moreover, the risk groups for the disease were perceived to be not only those most affected by the epidemic, but also those who were a risk to *others*. Indeed, the suggestion that the risk groups were 'those whose members were at a greater risk of infection *and* of infecting others'[33] was made explicit from the very first use of the term in relation to AIDS by epidemiologists at the US Centers for Disease Control (CDC),[34] although the CDC also stressed that each high-risk group 'contains many persons who probably have little risk of acquiring AIDS'.[35] To this extent, referring to high-risk groups allowed a certain coyness, whereby embarrassed public health officials could avoid having to discuss the nitty-gritty of anal sex, rimming, fisting and so on. This is why AIDS educators preferred the more precise terminology of 'risk behaviours', since it clearly identified the modes of transmission of HIV as acts over which the individual generally had a high level of personal control, dissipating generalized fears of contagion.

Thirdly, the concept of high-risk groups was being misused to deny the existence of any risk at all to those outside the groups. In other words, the term was effectively reinforcing heterosexual denial. Finally, fears were expressed that labelling all gay men as being at 'high risk' might induce a sense of fatalism and powerlessness among them, damaging health education efforts, when in reality a large majority of gay men (in Britain at least) are as yet uninfected, and can avoid infection by practising safer sex.

In practice, however, the rejection of the terminology of risk groups seems to have achieved few of its objectives, and almost certainly contributed to the neglect of education services for gay men. First, it is far too overly simplistic to suggest that simply acknowledging the existence of high-risk groups for AIDS will inevitably lead to increased violence or 'further discriminatory practices' against those groups.[36] Anti-gay discrimination existed long before AIDS; to assume that bigoted individuals need the epidemic as a justification for their prejudice is to apply an overly rationalistic analysis to a fundamentally *irrational* response. One might reasonably argue that focusing attention on the magnitude of the problem faced by the gay community, and gay men's remarkable if incomplete responses to the epidemic, could only win sympathy and support. In the event, gay men *en masse* have been discriminated against by, for example, the life assurance industry, *despite* the strenuous attempts to suppress the terminology of high-risk groups.

It is, of course, true that identity and behaviour do not coincide precisely, and that it is specific acts that may present a risk of HIV transmission, rather than membership of a social group *per se*. In practice, however, two 'clustering' factors must also be taken into consideration. Sexually transmitted infections are not distributed evenly throughout the population of sexually active individuals, but tend to cluster among those who are most sexually active, or their partners. Thus, while everyone may be 'at risk' of an infection, in that they are biologically susceptible to it, everyone does not have an equal probability of encountering the infection. The true risk to which an individual is exposed through unsafe sex or needle sharing depends on the likelihood that his or her partner is infected with HIV. In other words, while anyone having unsafe sex risks getting HIV, and the consequences of HIV infection are so serious that it is therefore sensible to advise everyone to practise safer sex, the risk of infection is nevertheless very much greater for a gay man having unsafe sex than for a heterosexual.[37] Thus, as Simon Watney has observed, 'the rejection of the concept of "risk groups" in favor of "risk behaviors" encouraged the development of a euphemistic, generalised AIDS education that floated the lie that everyone was at *equal* risk of HIV transmission'.[38]

Particular behavioural characteristics also tend to cluster in accordance with group membership. So, for example, sharing needles to inject drugs is a behaviour which is largely limited to people who, by merit of their drug use, can quite reasonably be described as drug users. To this extent, referring to risk behaviours is often merely a veiled way of describing risk groups. For example, Michael Fumento quotes the following extract from a cable television programme which sets out to dismiss the existence of high-risk groups, but nevertheless ends up defining them:

> Let's get rid of that word 'high-risk group' because it's a misnomer. All kinds of people engage in high-risk *behavior* and so let's talk about the behavior. And those we consider to be practising high-risk behavior are homosexual men, bisexual men, IV-drug abusers and heterosexual people who have multiple partners or who have sex habits which would get them into contact with other people who have high-risk behavior.[39]

To this extent, the British epidemic to this day has almost exclusively affected members of epidemiologically definable social groups: gay and bisexual men; recipients of infected blood products; injecting drug users; and the sexual partners of members of these groups. Acknowledging the existence of these groups is a prerequisite for properly targeted educational interventions. Furthermore, when health educators are working with limited budgets it becomes essential for their work to be prioritized, so that the most effective use is made of valuable time and resources. Establishing a sense of where the greatest need exists, and so where the greatest educational efforts should be focused, is the fundamental purpose of this 'needs assessment' process. This necessitates a recognition of and an appropriate response to the fact that everyone is *not* equally at risk from HIV.

Similar misunderstandings can be seen to have resulted from over-reactions to the description of AIDS as a 'gay plague' or a 'gay disease'. It is perfectly proper to point out that AIDS is not in any way caused by homosexuality and has no innate ability to identify and target gay men selectively. However, as long-time AIDS survivor Michael Callen has argued, 'It should be possible to get out the message that non-gay people can get AIDS without having to deny or downplay the fact that the overwhelming majority of people with AIDS are gay ... AIDS *is* a gay disease because a lot of gay men get AIDS.'[40]

The global versus the local

Re-gaying AIDS means focusing on and responding to the particular specificities of the epidemic in those countries, such as Australia, Britain, Canada and, to a lesser extent, the USA, where gay men continue to be the worst affected group. The local patterns of infections in those countries remain in stark contrast to the global generality, in which HIV is primarily transmitted through heterosexual sex. The editors of the *AIDS in the World* survey point out that in reality, '[t]he global HIV/AIDS epidemic is composed of thousands of epidemics – both separate and interdependent – occurring in communities literally around the world ... Adjacent countries, districts and even villages may have quite different HIV/AIDS histories and current profiles'.[41] As described in Chapter 5, in the mid-1980s reports of considerable heterosexual transmission in developing countries and the emerging consensus that HIV would not remain restricted to high-risk groups in the industrialized world both contributed to the neglect of the epidemic among gay men. Critics of re-gaying have continued to draw attention to the global dimensions of the AIDS epidemic, rather than acknowledging the huge differences between individual epidemics in different parts of the world.

Consider, for example, the response to an editorial in *The Independent* newspaper in December 1992. Entitled 'Realism about AIDS', this very sensible piece pointed out that 'the more alarmist predictions of an explosion have not come to pass', and called on educators to 'differentiate more clearly between high-risk and low-risk groups. The former should be told that they are at particular risk, the latter should be told, frankly, that the danger they run is very small indeed – but that it is real and growing.'[42] In a letter of response, Christopher Spence, Director of the AIDS centre London Lighthouse, denounced the article for:

> irresponsibly perpetuat[ing] the myth of 'high-risk groups' and, correspondingly, of the low risk of HIV infection among sexually active heterosexual people in this country ... Globally, the World Health Organisation reminds us that at the present rate, we shall be dealing with 30–100 million people with HIV/AIDS at the end of the century ... The overwhelming majority of these infections will continue to be the result of heterosexual intercourse.[43]

In practice, however, the vast majority of HIV transmission taking place *in Britain* continues to be among gay men. As Simon Watney has argued, 'It is all very well ... to refer to the global epidemic, but most of us only live on one part of the planet. Whilst we clearly need to get resources to developing countries, it never fails to amaze me how such arguments are used as if they justified the wholesale neglect of differing local needs in the developed world.'[44] Commenting on the tendency to use the global perspective to ignore the local realities, Jonathan Mann, former head of the WHO's Global Program on AIDS and editor of *AIDS in the World*, has noted that, unfortunately, 'any set of data can be misapplied'.[45]

Separatism versus specificity

An unexpected criticism of GMFA has been the charge of separatism – that, as an organization specifically devoted to the interests of gay men, it is 'ducking the issues which link the struggle for gay men's rights to those of women, drug users, Black people and children living with HIV/AIDS'.[46] This was the cornerstone of an article in the newsletter of Mainliners, a drugs and HIV agency, which argued that:

> no steps forward can be taken until all of us – whatever our community of interest, our sexuality, gender, race, HIV status or nationality – unite as workers and world citizens to fight exploitation, censorship, oppression and the system which puts profit before health every time.[47]

This rhetoric betrays the ideological basis of the argument, which derives from a particular leftist class politics similar to that of the Revolutionary Communist Party, discussed in Chapter 6.

The emergence of a new specialist organization after several years in which community AIDS organizations had largely striven to cast off from their roots and remould themselves as generalist institutions was bound to be a shock to the system. However, a curious discrimination is going on here. It would be unthinkable to attack an organization such as Positively Women, the major national organization for women with HIV and AIDS in Britain, because it does not provide services for men; or to criticize the Black HIV/AIDS Network, which provides advocacy for and train-ing services on the needs of black and ethnic minority people affec-ted by HIV, for not working with white people. These organiz-ations are properly recognized as being not separatist, but *specialist.* That it should be considered appropriate to denounce the only existing agency dedicated specifically to the needs of those who make up nearly two-thirds of people with HIV in Britain, and over three-quarters of people with AIDS, is a damning indication of the extent to which gay men's interests appear to have become expendable since the late 1980s.

There has been more than one instance like this, in which the process of dehomosexualization of AIDS has gone so far that gay men, or more specifically white, middle-class gay men, have actually become the bogeymen of the epidemic. This view typically imagines that white, middle-class gay men set up AIDS organizations to look after their own, to the exclusion of others affected by the epidemic. Certainly many AIDS organizations were initially established by gay men to provide care and education which was clearly not forthcoming from state institutions. However, as described in Chapter 5, the commonest pattern has been for those groups gradually to evolve into generalist organizations and actively distance themselves from their roots, in order to appear 'respectable' and so secure statutory funding.

Paradoxically, in their 1989–90 *Annual Report*, Mainliners themselves acknowledged the reasons why specialist HIV groups are so important. First, 'there is no reason why there should be a single model of service provision to suit all social groups'.[48] Often the only way in which truly accessible services can be provided for everyone affected by AIDS is by tailoring them to the needs of the various constituencies, as in the women-only sessions offered by most sexually transmitted disease clinics, the community language telephone lines of the National AIDS Helpline, or the support groups for heterosexual men provided by London Lighthouse. Quite contrary to the logical implications of the article's argument, specialization is the best way to ensure that appropriate services are available for everyone: indeed, Mainliners itself was established as an organization focusing on drugs and HIV because, as is the case with gay men's needs, 'the work needing to be done in this area remains largely neglected or approached tokenistically'.[49] Although the provision of needle exchanges has had a very substantial impact on the incidence of HIV infection among injecting drug users, targeted interventions for this high-risk group have also been neglected during the years of the 'Everybody is equally at risk' approach to the epidemic.

Resource allocation: biting the bullet

Responding to an article in the gay press written by me, the Socialist Workers Party's monthly magazine *Socialist Review* attacked moves to re-gay AIDS as 'a disastrous mistake' which 'plays into the hands of the bigots' and could cost lives. While accepting that gay health education had been appallingly neglected in recent years, it argued that 'the focus on category not behaviour' only encouraged generalized discrimination against *all* gay men by, for example, life assurance companies or surgeons; instead of arguing for a redistribution of prevention monies, activists should be calling for more money across the board.[50]

The attempts to avoid stigmatization by refusing to acknowledge the reality of the epidemic have been discussed earlier. It is clear that not only have those attempts failed, in as much as the likes of life assurance companies and surgeons have nevertheless discriminated against gay men *en masse*, as the article acknowledged; in fact, by leading to the deprioritization of HIV prevention initiatives for gay men – for fear of identifying them as being a high-risk group – the strategy has done real harm to gay men's interests.

However, the question remains whether safer sex educators should be criticizing the amount of money currently spent on campaigns targeting the general population, and lobbying to have the funds put towards initiatives targeting those most at risk. A rational approach to establishing priorities and determining the most appropriate local targeting of HIV prevention resources should take four factors into account.[51] First, it must assess current epidemiologically demonstrated risk. All data indicate that gay and bisexual men continue to be most immediately at risk from HIV infection in the United Kingdom today, constituting the majority of new HIV infections as well as of cumulative HIV and AIDS cases. It is also clear that gay and bisexual men, although most visible in urban settings, exist in all walks of life and in all parts of Britain.

Secondly, it should consider projected epidemiological risk, extrapolating from current trends to predict which groups are likely to be most seriously affected in the future. As discussed in Chapter 6, current data suggest that there may have been an increase in unsafe sex and in new HIV infections among gay and bisexual men in recent years. Studies have found that increasing numbers of men who previously tested negative are seroconverting; moreover, the proportion of men who had HIV-related symptoms when first tested has remained constant at around 50 per cent, indicating that the rising figures do not simply reflect men who became infected some years ago but delayed taking the test until recently. Furthermore, even a stable level of risk-taking among gay men would be likely to result in a growing incidence of new infections, as rising prevalence makes it increasingly probable that a given sexual partner will be infected with HIV. Although cases of HIV infection among heterosexuals are increasing, the absolute numbers remain low. By contrast, many hundreds of gay and bisexual men continue to test HIV-positive each year.

Thirdly, the allocation of prevention resources should be based on an assessment of which services already exist and which are lacking, in the overall profile of local and national initiatives to minimize HIV transmission. The results of the 1992 survey *HIV Prevention for Gay Men*, described earlier, suggest that such an assessment is likely to uncover a dearth of specific targeted prevention work for gay and bisexual men in both voluntary and statutory organizations.[52] Conversely, it would almost certainly discover that, in recent years, funded work has disproportionately targeted those at immeasurably lower risk than gay and bisexual men.

Finally, a rational method for establishing need should consider the cost and effectiveness of possible interventions. Such an analysis would inevitably conclude that virtually the only evidence of large-scale behaviour change in response to AIDS comes from the mass adoption of safer sex by gay and bisexual men in the early to mid-1980s. In other words, there is more reason to assume that the funding of HIV prevention initiatives among gay men can be efficient and effective than there is for any other social constituency. The apparent increases in unsafe sex and in new HIV infections among gay men in recent years have coincided with the widespread neglect of ongoing safer sex campaigns for gay men. The re-establishment and consolidation of safer sex as a social norm among gay men is likely to be much easier to achieve and much more cost-effective in terms of its impact on the epidemic than the task of creating such norms from scratch among heterosexuals.

While there are good reasons to campaign for all HIV prevention activities to be given increased funding, it must be recognized that this is unlikely to be forthcoming in the short term, if at all. It therefore does not seem unreasonable to suggest that available monies should be spent properly, in areas where there is real risk and a real chance of significant success, rather than on ill-conceived and ineffectual activities. In recent years some health authorities with substantial budgets to spend on promoting safer sex have been allocating those funds in ways that bear little or no relation to the actual need. For example, in 1990–91 Great Yarmouth and Waveney Health Authority Health Promotion Service targeted HIV/AIDS educational campaigns to no less than twelve defined population groups, including drug users, prostitutes and their clients, schoolchildren, church workers and the homeless.[53] Gay or bisexual men did not appear anywhere in the list. In circumstances such as these, it would be folly to give such bodies even more money to lavish on those who are at minimal risk from HIV, while gay men continue to be neglected. Gay men are much more at risk than most other people, because of the much higher prevalence of HIV in gay communities. This imbalance in the epidemiology should also be reflected in the weighting of resource allocation.[54]

The price of funding

Those who believe that the de-gaying of AIDS was the action of a 'homosexual lobby' have argued that it was largely a deliberate ploy to secure and expand funding for research and education on the disease. This theory implicitly acknowledges the role of homophobia in the early neglect of the epidemic, by accepting that the necessary resources would not have been made available if attention had been directed to the real epidemic which continues predominantly to affect gay men, rather than to an imagined or projected one in which everyone was at risk. A number of AIDS workers and gay activists have quietly expressed fears that the re-gaying of AIDS plays into the hands of those who view HIV disease as a self-inflicted condition which receives an inordinate amount of attention, and may thus lead to a reduction in resourcing that would ultimately damage gay men's interests.

This argument fails to take account of the fact that money gained under false pretences usually then has to be spent on those false pretences, and does not necessarily become available to help meet real needs. If the heterosexualization of the epidemic generated more money for AIDS education, the results of the survey of *HIV Prevention for Gay Men* show beyond any doubt that those resources have not reached those most at risk. The expansion of professional AIDS education services and parts of the voluntary sector in recent years has been secured on the basis of a perceived threat to 'low-risk' heterosexuals, and so those services have targeted heterosexuals at the expense of working where the risks are.

Re-gaying AIDS is therefore highly unlikely to result in the worsening of an already lamentable level of service provision for those genuinely at risk from HIV. Instead, it offers a real opportunity to ensure that the public monies that are available for promoting safer sex are allocated in accordance with a rational prioritization and targeting strategy.

Whose responsibility?

In this initial phase of activity, the prime objective in the re-gaying of AIDS has been to secure adequate funding for and institutional commitment to HIV prevention initiatives for gay and bisexual men. The focus of attention has therefore largely been on the statutory sector, who are responsible for the allocation of the vast majority of prevention resources. However, by targeting statutory institutions in this way, advocates of re-gaying AIDS run the risk of inadvertently consolidating the locus of control of gay men's health education within precisely those institutions which have proved so unresponsive to our needs in the past.

Moreover, this book has tried to stress the central importance of community ownership in the successful adoption of safer sex during the 1980s. Safer sex was a form of resistance to the epidemic and its attendant threats, which was created by gay men and disseminated and bolstered by the networks and structures of gay culture; it offered each individual the means to maintain the hard-won control over his sexual self-determination, while avoiding giving or getting HIV infection.

The next priority in the re-gaying of AIDS must therefore be to contest the supremacy of the professional statutory sector, and to support the development of new community-based responses to the ongoing prevention needs of gay and bisexual men. In this task, the reforms of the British National Health Service (NHS) since the late 1980s may provide a constructive framework. There has been a growing division of roles between 'purchasing' agencies, which commission and provide funds for the provision of health services, and 'providing' agencies, which actually undertake the work. The government's White Paper on the Health of the Nation has as a key theme the importance of building 'healthy alliances' in health service provision. These principles offer the prospect of fruitful collaborative approaches in which prevention work is funded by statutory agencies, but actually implemented and fronted by groups which are clearly identified with the gay population.

For this reason, it is crucial that the critique of the de-gaying of AIDS is accompanied by constructive measures to address the parallel de-AIDSing of lesbian and gay organizations. As discussed in Chapter 4, denial of the role of gay men within and in resistance to the epidemic has resulted in a polarization, in which AIDS organizations have failed to recognize their responsibilities to gay men, and gay organizations have refused to address the epidemic. Thus re-gaying requires simultaneous attention to the current shortcomings within the statutory sector, the voluntary sector *and* gay community institutions, if the needs of gay men during the AIDS crisis are to be properly addressed.

Conclusion

In countries throughout the world, gay men have led the fight against AIDS. After a period of uncertainty and adjustment, gay men gradually invented safer sex and spread the message through their social and sexual networks. Gay men founded AIDS organizations and laid on voluntary services to care for those who were sick. And when governments finally began to plan their responses, they were forced to recognize the expertise that gay men had developed.

During the late 1980s, however, the emphasis shifted as fears grew that the epidemic was enlarging and spreading significantly into the heterosexual population. But instead of developing new initiatives to co-exist alongside safer sex campaigns for gay men, gay men's ongoing needs were ignored, and funds were almost entirely diverted to heterosexual causes. Voluntary organizations heterosexualized themselves, gay organizations tried their best to ignore the epidemic, and AIDS became the professional responsibility of a statutory sector founded upon the philosophy that 'Everyone is equally at risk'. With hindsight, all these developments have been disastrous for gay men.

It has taken evidence of an increase in new HIV infections among gay men to draw attention to the problem. As gay men continue to constitute the majority of people newly testing HIV-positive, advocates of the re-gaying of AIDS aim to ensure that the needs of gay men are once again accorded the priority they deserve. The primary objective must be to re-establish a gay-community-based safer sex movement as effective as that in the early years of the epidemic. In recognition of those gay men whose endeavours revolutionized gay sexuality in the 1980s, in memory of those gay men for whom that revolution came too late, and in the interests of every sexually active gay man now and for the foreseeable future, we can aim for nothing less.

Notes

1. Peter Scott, 'Wake up! Fight back!', *Capital Gay*, 545, 22 May 1992.
2. Cindy Patton, 'Resistance and the erotic', *Radical America*, 20(6): 68–74 (1986), reprinted in *AIDS: Social Representations, Social Practices* (eds P. Aggleton, G. Hart and P. Davies), pp. 237–51. Falmer Press, London, 1989.
3. François Wasserfallen, *I European Conference on HIV and Homosexuality: Report*, Copenhagen, 17–18 February 1990.
4. Patton, *op. cit.*
5. *Ibid.*
6. Quoted in Simon Watney, 'The possibilities of permutation:

pleasure, proliferation, and the politics of gay identity in the age of AIDS', in *Fluid Exchanges* (ed. J. Miller), pp. 329–67. University of Toronto, Canada, 1992.

7.   Hans Moerkerk, 'AIDS prevention strategies in Europe: the gay response', speech at *I European Conference on HIV and Homosexuality*.

8.   Simon Watney, 'Re-gaying Aids', *Gay Times*, 138, p. 13, March 1990.

9.   Gay Men's Health Group, 'Some interesting facts', leaflet, Birmingham, 1991.

10. Peter Scott, *National AIDS Manual* (Spring 1993). NAM Publications, London, 1993.

11. Quoted in Neil McKenna, 'Too important for pussyfooting around', *Gay Times*, 161, p. 17, February 1992.

12. Edward King, Michael Rooney and Peter Scott, *HIV Prevention for Gay Men: A Survey of Initiatives in the UK*. North-West Thames Regional Health Authority, London, 1992.

13. Michael Rooney and Peter Scott, 'Working where the risks are', in *Working Where the Risks Are* (eds B. Evans, S. Sandberg and S. Watson). Health Education Authority, London, 1992.

14. King, Rooney and Scott, *op. cit.*, p. 10.

15. *Ibid.*, p. 23.

16. *Ibid.*, p. 23.

17. *Ibid.*, p. 13.

18. *Ibid.*, p. 24.

19. *Ibid.*, p. 25.

20. *Ibid.*, p. 14.

21. Advice and information on undertaking needs assessment for prevention work with gay or bisexual men are contained in Rooney and Scott, *op. cit.*; Peter Scott, 'Needs Assessment', in *HIV Prevention* (ed. P. Jones). North-West Thames Regional Health Authority HIV Project, London, 1992.

22. Health Education Authority, *Annual Report 1990/1*, p. 6. London, 1991.

23. Edward King, 'The seven deadly sins of the HEA', *The Pink Paper*, 230, 14th June 1992.

24. King, Rooney and Scott, *op. cit.*, p. 25.

25. *Ibid.*, p. 26.

26. Simon Watney, 'Gay Brits take back the fight', *NYQ*, 30 August 1992.

27. See Chapter 5.

28. Quoted in Simon Watney, 'The killing fields of Europe', *Outrage*, pp. 44–7, July 1992.

29. Gay Men Fighting AIDS, 'More information for gay men urged by new AIDS group', press release, 28 May 1992.

30. Keith Alcorn, 'InSIGHT: 10,364 and counting ...', *Capital Gay*, 545, 22 May 1992.

31. Quoted in Watney, 'Gay Brits take back the fight'.
32. Gerald M. Oppenheimer, 'Causes, cases and cohorts: the role of epidemiology in the historical construction of AIDS', in *AIDS: The Making of a Chronic Disease* (eds E. Fee and D. M. Fox), p. 62. University of California Press, Berkeley, CA, 1992.
33. *Ibid.*, p. 61.
34. *MMRW*, 4 March 1983.
35. *Ibid.*, p. 32.
36. See the criticisms of the term in: 'The re-gaying of AIDS', *Annual Report 1991*, p. 41. Brent HIV Centre, London, 1992.
37. Edward King, 'Safer sex revolutionaries', *The Pink Paper*, 205, 14 December 1991.
38. Watney, 'Gay Brits take back the fight'.
39. US Surgeon-General Everett Koop in *Everything You and Your Family Need to Know about AIDS*, Home Box Office, quoted in Michael Fumento, *The Myth of Heterosexual AIDS*, p. 152. Basic Books, New York, 1990.
40. Michael Callen, 'AIDS is a gay disease!', *People with AIDS Co-alition Newsline*, 42, March 1989.
41. Jonathan Mann *et al.* (eds), *AIDS in the World: A Global Report*, p. 15. Harvard University Press, Cambridge, MA, 1993.
42. 'Realism about Aids' (editorial), *The Independent*, p. 20, 2 December 1992.
43. Christopher Spence, letter, in: 'How Aids is spreading: the dangers of cynicism, apathy and myth', *The Independent*, p. 20, 4 December 1991.
44. Simon Watney, 'Hitting the target', *The Pink Paper*, **262**, 31 January 1993.
45. Personal communication, February 1993.
46. Nicola Field, 'Take-over bids and monopolies: HIV and the gay community', *Mainliners Ltd Newsletter*, 25/26, pp. 1–3, August–September 1992.
47. *Ibid.*, p. 3.
48. Mainliners, *Annual Report 1989–1990*. London, 1990.
49. *Ibid.*
50. Simon Ash, 'High risk of bigotry', *Socialist Review*, p. 25, May 1992.
51. This section is based heavily on the first draft of Peter Scott's 'A short paper on issues for purchasers in relation to HIV prevention for gay and bisexual men', an unpublished briefing paper to the Department of Health's Expert Advisory Group on AIDS, London, 1992.
52. King, Rooney and Scott, *op. cit.*
53. *Annual Report 1990–1991*, Great Yarmouth and Waveney Health Authority Health Promotion Service, Great Yarmouth, 1991.
54. See Edward King, 'Let's face facts' (letter), *Socialist Review*, p. 33, June 1992.

Index

C 2346 Y